DISCARDED

The Black Sociologists: The First Half Century

A Wadsworth Series:
Explorations in the Black Experience

General Editors

John H. Bracey, Jr., Northern Illinois University
August Meier, Kent State University
Elliott Rudwick, Kent State University

The anthologies in this series present significant scholarly work on particular aspects of the black experience in the United States. The volumes are of two types. Some have a "problems" orientation, presenting varying and conflicting interpretations of a controversial subject. Others are purely "thematic," simply presenting representative examples of the best scholarship on a topic. Together they provide guidelines into significant areas of research and writing in the field of Afro-American studies. The complete contents of all the books in the series are listed at the end of this volume.

The Black Sociologists: The First Half Century

Edited by

John H. Bracey, Jr.
Northern Illinois University

August Meier
Kent State University

Elliott Rudwick
Kent State University

Wadsworth Publishing Company, Inc.
Belmont, California

Acknowledgments

The authors wish to express their appreciation to Mrs. Barbara Hostetler, Mrs. Patricia Kufta, and Miss Eileen Petric at Kent State University for helping in the preparation of this manuscript, and to Miss Linda Burroughs and Mrs. Helen Peoples of the Kent State University Library. They are especially indebted to James G. Coke, former Director of the Kent State University Center for Urban Regionalism.

July 1970   *JHB*
AM
ER

ISBN–0–534–00018–5
L. C. Cat. Card No.: 72–154811
Printed in the United States of America

1 2 3 4 5 6 7 8 9 10—75 74 73 72 71

To St. Clair Drake
and to the memory of Horace
Cayton

JHB
AM
ER

Contents

The Black Sociologists: The First Half Century

Introduction

The half century from the appearance of W. E. B. Du Bois's *The Philadelphia Negro* in 1899 to the publication of St. Clair Drake and Horace Cayton's *Black Metropolis* in 1945 can appropriately be described as the golden age in the sociology of blacks in America. It included the pioneering work of W. E. B. Du Bois; the contributions of George Edmund Haynes, Bertram W. Doyle, Ira De A. Reid, Oliver Cromwell Cox,[1] and the social anthropologist Allison Davis; and the classic volumes by Charles S. Johnson, E. Franklin Frazier, St. Clair Drake, and Horace Cayton. Due to limitations of space, this volume will focus on the work of Du Bois and Haynes, pioneers of the sociology of the black experience; and on the contributions of five men — Johnson, Frazier, Doyle, Drake, and Cayton — who studied at the Department of Sociology of the University of Chicago, the training ground of nearly all of the eminent Negro sociologists in the era between the two world wars. From the work of these scholars came four sociological classics — Du Bois's *The Philadelphia Negro,* Johnson's *The Negro in Chicago,* Frazier's *The Negro Family in the United States,* and, most highly regarded of all, Drake and Cayton's *Black Metropolis.* Together with the others mentioned, these men produced a major corpus of scholarship.

The sociological study of black America was born in a climate of extreme racism — both in popular thought and among intellectuals and social scientists. As the nineteenth century drew to a close the Negro's position in American society was deteriorating steadily. Disfranchisement, lynchings, Jim Crow laws, farm tenancy, and peonage were the black man's lot in the South. Throughout the country, labor unions excluded him from the skilled trades. After 1900, race riots became commonplace in both North and South. It was the most oppressive era in the history of black Americans since the Civil War; historian Rayford Logan has appropriately called it "The Nadir." The movement for Oriental exclusion and the overseas imperialism against colored peoples in the Caribbean and the Pacific only reinforced this general racism of the period. Southern propagandists held that not only were blacks an innately inferior, immoral, and criminal race, but that in fact freedom caused a reversion to barbarism; many of them justified lynching on the basis of the black man's allegedly increasing tendency toward rape and believed that colonization of American blacks in Africa or the Caribbean was the only alternative to violent extermination. In the North weighty scholarly opinion in the biological sciences supported Southern racist doctrines, and eminent historians and political scientists reinterpreted Reconstruction and the triumph of white supremacy in a manner favorable to the white South. Almost alone among prominent social scientists, the anthropologist Franz Boas maintained that innate racial differences were inconsequential.

With the exception of W. I. Thomas, sociological theory prevalent before

World War I stressed the biological superiority of the white race and the "primitive-ness" of the "inferior" Negro's "racial temperament," which predisposed him to-ward "shiftlessness and sensuality," rendering him basically unassimilable. Thus, for example, articles in the *American Journal of Sociology* not only justified white supremacy doctrines but presented them as necessary fortifications for the preserva-tion of racial purity. As E. Franklin Frazier has described the situation, the "general point of view" of the first sociologists who directed their attention to the black man was that "the Negro was an inferior race because of either biological or social heredity or both; that the Negro because of his physical characteristics could not be assimilated; and that physical amalgamation was bad and therefore undesirable. These conclusions were generally supported by the marshalling of a vast amount of statistical data on the pathological aspects of Negro life." In short, as Frazier said, "The sociological theories which were implicit in the writings on the Negro problem were merely rationalizations of the existing racial situation."[2]

The early sociological study of race relations and the black community was part of a broader sociological concern with social problems and their amelioration. At the turn of the century the discipline of sociology was just emerging as an academic specialty out of a more generalized field of "social science" that included political economy, government, the study of social problems, and even history. The first formal department of sociology was organized in 1892 at the University of Chicago; the American Sociological Society was not founded until 1905 when sociologists separated from the American Economic Association. Thus in the 1890s sociology, economics, the study of social problems, and the field of social ethics were closely intertwined, and often not sharply distinguished. Impressed by the ability of the physical scientists to understand and manipulate man's environment for man's benefit, most of the early sociologists exhibited a strong interest in using their knowledge to uplift the lot of man by solving society's social problems. This interest was reformist rather than radical and was closely related to the developing field of social work.

W. E. B. Du Bois,[3] best known as the leading propagandist of the black protest during the first third of the twentieth century, was also the first black sociologist. Educated at Fisk, the University of Berlin, and Harvard — where he received a Ph.D. in history in 1895 — Du Bois was exposed to the best in social science training offered at the time, and, like his contemporaries, clearly combined the scientific and melioristic in his own work. As he later recalled:

I determined to put science into sociology through a study of the condition and problems of my own group. I was going to study the facts, any and all facts, concerning the American Negro and his plight, and by measurement and compari-son and research, work up to any valid generalization which I could.[4]

Du Bois's opportunity came in 1896 when municipal reformers in the Phila-delphia settlement house movement decided that a painstaking statistical study of

Philadelphia's blacks could serve as a guideline to improve their social conditions. For fifteen months Du Bois was a participant observer in a slum where one-fifth of the city's Negroes lived. Using a lengthy questionnaire, he personally interviewed hundreds of people and compiled voluminous data on such matters as family structure, income, occupations, and property holdings. The results added up to a vivid portrait of unemployment, poverty, and family breakdown. In *The Philadelphia Negro,* Du Bois criticized whites for offering "platitudes" and "sermons" rather than providing jobs without discrimination or giving extensive financial assistance. More important, he believed that whites must recognize Negro business and professional men as race leaders and grant them the status and power to solve the race's problems. Such a black "aristocracy" would administer social services like day nurseries and sewing schools; develop building and loan associations, newspapers, labor unions, and industrial enterprises; and would thus be in a position to uplift the masses by working to eliminate pauperism and crime within the race. Here Du Bois the social scientist became Du Bois the social reformer recommending solutions to the race problem. In short, foreshadowing his famous theory of leadership by the "Talented Tenth" of the race, Du Bois preached a philosophy of Negro self-help and solidarity, a program of racial self-elevation under the leadership of an educated black elite. The selection from Du Bois's *The Philadelphia Negro* reprinted here is a description of the organized community life of Philadelphia blacks at the turn of the century ("The Organized Life of Negroes").

Du Bois conceived of *The Philadelphia Negro* as the start of a larger research program. Speaking before the American Academy of Political and Social Science in the fall of 1897 he declared that "the first effective step toward the solving of the Negro question will be the endowment of a Negro college which . . . [will be] a centre of sociological research, in close connection and cooperation with Harvard, Columbia, Johns Hopkins, and the University of Pennsylvania."[5] White sociologists did not respond to this appeal; as E. Franklin Frazier remarked years later, "It appears that there was a feeling, perhaps unconscious and therefore all the more significant, that since the Negro occupied a low status and did not play an important role in American society, studies of the Negro were of less significance from the standpoint of social science."[6] Nevertheless, Du Bois, who had accepted a post at Atlanta University, embarked alone upon an ambitious plan to investigate the life of the black community. Considering that the University was a struggling and impoverished institution, it is a tribute to Du Bois's determination as both a social scientist and a social reformer that between 1897 and 1914 he actually supervised the preparation of sixteen Atlanta University sociological monographs on topics ranging from the black family through the Negro church and Negro education to black economic and business development.

Obliged to use only unpaid investigators on a part-time basis, it is not surprising that Du Bois's monographs were of uneven quality. They are notably lacking in sociological theorizing. Yet they represent a serious effort to introduce systematic induction into the field of race relations, when other sociologists were merely speculating about the Negro. The publications also carried the recommendations of an annual conference that brought educated blacks, and a sprinkling of sympathetic whites, to the campus for a discussion of the topic researched that year and its relevance to the future uplift of the race. Like *The Philadelphia Negro,* both the research and the annual conference resolutions dwelt upon the value of racial solidarity and self-help in advancing the black man's status in America.

Despite the seriousness of Du Bois's commitment to sociology, he was, in the main, overlooked by the profession. The *American Journal of Sociology,* founded at the University of Chicago in 1895, devoted many pages to social welfare problems. But it clearly considered Du Bois's work of minor importance. It ignored the monumental piece of research, *The Philadelphia Negro,* and during the sixteen years Du Bois was associated with the Atlanta publications, only two were reviewed in the *Journal.* On the other hand, the editors did publish glowing reviews of some frankly racist books, as well as articles with an avowedly Southern white view on slavery and race relations. Thus, ironically, Du Bois, who by training and research orientation toward both empiricism and reform, was part of the mainstream of American sociology as the discipline was emerging at the turn of the century, found himself relegated to the periphery of the profession. Except for reasons of racism it is difficult to account for his thus being shunted aside. Disillusioned, Du Bois turned from calm scholarship to overt protest and propaganda; in 1910 he left Atlanta University to take a full-time post as director of research for the NAACP and editor of its principal organ, *The Crisis.*

Thus it is not surprising that Du Bois's plea that the American Sociological Society and other learned organizations "put themselves on record as favoring a most thorough and unbiased scientific study of the race problem in America'" went unheeded. Nonetheless, a few careful studies, along the lines pioneered by Du Bois in his research on Philadelphia blacks, were made of the Negro communities in New York and Boston. These studies — by Mary White Ovington (*Half a Man: The Status of the Negro in New York,* 1911), George Edmund Haynes (*The Negro at Work in New York City: A Study in Economic Progress,* 1912), and John Daniels (*In Freedom's Birthplace: A Study of the Boston Negroes,* 1914) — were made by individuals directly involved in attempts to deal with the problems of Northern urban blacks. Of the three, one — Haynes — was a Negro. The first black man to earn a Ph.D. in sociology (he received his degree in 1912), he was educated at Columbia University. He became the first professor of sociology at Fisk University and at the same time held a post with the National Urban League, thus combining, as did Ovington and Daniels, careful research and social work. In addition to studying the economic life of blacks in New York, Haynes conducted early studies of black migration to the Northern cities prior to and during the First World War. In his career, the applied aspects of his interests soon overshadowed the scholarly. By the 1920s he had joined the staff of the Federal Council of Churches; he spent most of his career as a race relations expert for that organization. The article by Haynes reprinted here discusses the migration of rural blacks to the cities early in the twentieth century and the social conditions they faced in the emerging urban ghettos.

Like Haynes, Ira De Augustine Reid (who also earned his Ph.D. at Columbia University, and who served as vice president of the American Sociological Society and president of the Eastern Sociological Society) conducted a considerable amount of survey research on the condition of blacks in various parts of the country. From 1924 to 1934 he worked for the National Urban League. During this period he published *Negro Membership in American Labor Unions* (1930). His major works are *The Negro Immigrant* (1939), a study of West Indian migrants to New York; *In a Minor Key: Negro Youth in Story and Fact* (1940); and *Sharecroppers All* (1941), written in collaboration with the noted Southern white authority on farm tenancy, Arthur Raper.

Du Bois's plea for an objective study of American blacks and American race relations became the hallmark of the next stage in the history of the sociology of the black community — the monographs emanating from the famous Chicago school of American sociology. From the end of World War I until the middle 1930s, under the leadership of Robert E. Park and others, the University of Chicago's department of sociology dominated the field. One of Park's major interests was in race relations, and it was the University of Chicago that produced those five distinguished students of American blacks — Charles S. Johnson, E. Franklin Frazier, Bertram W. Doyle, St. Clair Drake, and Horace Cayton. All of these men, except Drake, were students of Park.

Park, after a decade in journalism, had pursued graduate training and taken his Ph.D. at Heidelberg in 1904. Soon afterwards he became secretary of the Congo Reform Association, which publicized and campaigned against the atrocities which the Belgians committed against blacks in the Congo. Meanwhile he came to know Booker T. Washington, principal of Tuskegee Institute in Alabama. At Washington's invitation, Park made his headquarters at Tuskegee, spending several years investigating the race problem in the South. In 1914, at the age of fifty, Park joined Albion Small and W. I. Thomas in the Department of Sociology at the University of Chicago. As a leading figure in the most influential sociology department in the nation, Park enjoyed an unusual opportunity to advance the sociological study of the black man in America. While sociologists like E. A. Ross of the University of Wisconsin were still upholding Anglo-Saxon purity and inveighing against blacks or Orientals, Park demanded that sociology cast off bias and emotional agitation and study race relations in varied societal contexts. In his cultivation of a spirit of objective inquiry, Park addressed not only the extreme racists but also students who were strong fighters for the black man's rights. To the latter group, Park reiterated his conviction that scientific knowledge could help to solve race problems, but that only detachment in research would produce scientific knowledge. Under his influence students attempted to analyze with as much objectivity as possible various forms of race prejudice, discrimination, and even interracial violence.

Given the rampant racism of the period and the prejudiced attitudes of most

American social scientists, Park's advocacy of detached scientific studies was very attractive to men like Johnson and Frazier. Probably no other person could have facilitated the transition of mainstream sociology's stance from racism to an attempt at objectivity in racial studies as easily as Robert E. Park. It should be made clear that he was no militant in the cause of racial equality. Indeed, as sociologist Ralph Turner points out, "For all of his concern with race relations, it is striking that the achievement of social and economic equality never emerges as a dominant goal in Park's thought."[8] This moderation, combined with Park's eminence in the field of sociology, served to legitimize the serious and scientific study of race relations among professional sociologists.

On the other hand, it should be pointed out that there was a practical and mildly reformist element in Park, who served as the first president of the Chicago Urban League. His research orientation included a strong interest in social problems. Much of the work of the Chicago school was directed toward studying the subject of urban social disorganization and urban pathology; and Park himself saw detached sociological knowledge as essential for the decisions of policy makers. According to Ernest W. Burgess, one of his colleagues at the University of Chicago, Park was drawn to the field of race relations precisely because he wanted "more than anything else to come to grips with a significant [practical] problem."[9]

If Park's emphasis upon urban studies and social problems is reflected in the work of his students who made race the focus of their interests, so also are his conceptual and methodological views. Park placed American race relations in a world-wide framework; he held that black-white relations in the United States, far from being a unique phenomenon, followed a sequential pattern that occurred whenever different races came into contact. In his methodology he stressed the anthropological techniques of participant observation and studying the total life of a community; he emphasized also the importance of understanding the relevant historical background of social institutions. He advocated the use of the case study approach of investigation, and was critical of quantified techniques. He believed it was the duty of the sociologist to ascertain the "natural history" of a phenomenon — to abstract from unique events the generalized patterns that characterized such things as the development of social institutions, the course of revolutions, or patterns in race relations. Specific conceptualizations of Park in the area of race that influenced the work of his students included the notions of racial conflict, competition, and accommodation. Park maintained that when large populations of diverse races came into contact, conflict and competition invariably resulted. Stabilization occurred when one race became dominant and the other accommodated to an inferior position. As part of the mechanism of accommodation there developed an "etiquette of race relations" which maintained "social distance" between the races, enabling them to coexist, although not on an egalitarian level. While competition and conflict produced prejudice and accommodation in the short run, the process of assimilation would inevitably occur. Park, studying the racial situation of his own time in the United States, dealt chiefly with the mechanisms of competi-

tion and accommodation, and never tried to explain how assimilation would ultimately be achieved.

The two leading black sociologists trained by Park were Charles S. Johnson
(1893–1956) and E. Franklin Frazier (1894–1962). Johnson, the son of a Baptist
minister in Bristol, Virginia, received his A.B. degree in 1916 from Virginia Union
University, at the time a leading liberal arts institution for Negro youth, and took
an undergraduate degree at the University of Chicago a year later. He worked
closely with Park for about four years (1917–1921). The 1919 race riot in Chicago
led to the creation of the Chicago Commission on Race Relations, to which Johnson
was appointed Associate Director. Under his supervision, the Commission published in 1922 the classic, *The Negro in Chicago: A Study of Race Relations and
a Race Riot.* From 1923 to 1929 he was editor of *Opportunity* magazine and research
director for the National Urban League; for two decades, 1928 to 1948, he was
chairman of the Department of Social Sciences at Fisk University, and most of his
major sociological works date from this period. In 1947, he was elected president
of Fisk University. Frazier, the son of a Baltimore bank messenger, attended Howard University on a scholarship. Receiving his A.B. in 1916, he taught at secondary
schools for three years; took an A.M. at Clark University in Massachusetts in 1920;
and in the fall of 1922 went to Atlanta as instructor in sociology at Morehouse
College and director of the Atlanta University School of Social Work. From 1927
to 1929 he pursued advanced work at the University of Chicago, receiving the Ph.D.
in 1931 with his *The Negro Family in Chicago* (published 1932). From 1929 to 1934
he worked under Charles S. Johnson at Fisk University, and then returned to
Howard University to head the Department of Sociology until 1959. Frazier remained in the department as a professor until his death in 1962.

Though the work of each man was quite distinctive, both owed much to Robert
E. Park. Frazier's books on the black family (*The Negro Family in Chicago,* 1932;
The Free Negro Family, 1932; and *The Negro Family in the United States,* 1939)
and on *Race and Culture Contacts in the Modern World,* (1957), and all of Johnson's
most important books (*The Negro in Chicago,* 1922; *Shadow of the Plantation,* 1934;
Growing up in the Black Belt, 1941; and *Patterns of Negro Segregation,* 1943) were
written in the spirit of scientific detachment urged by Park. Both Frazier and
Johnson continued, in the tradition pioneered by Du Bois, to make essentially
nonstatistical empirical studies; however, in contrast to Du Bois's works, the normative elements — the specific recommendations for social change — are virtually
absent. Johnson's work, *The Negro in Chicago,* though dealing with a highly emotional subject, appeared to contemporaries to demonstrate that race relations could
be studied objectively and scientifically, so dispassionate was its tone. The low-keyed
quality of Johnson's writing is so remarkable that, as one friend wrote, "All through
his studies he has kept his own detachment. . . . This 'scientific objectivity' sur-
prises people. His colored friends scold him for being a calm student rather than
a rabid reformer. White people get mad at his presumption in understanding them
and their customs better than they do themselves." Johnson's dispassionate style

is illustrated in the description of housing conditions reprinted here from *The Negro in Chicago* ("Black Housing in Chicago").[10]

Yet, like Du Bois, both Johnson and Frazier thought of their scholarship as a means for advancing the race; like Park, they had an abiding concern with social problems; and like Du Bois and Park, both thought of their scholarship as providing the basis for social action. And despite their unemotional tone, the first books of both Johnson and Frazier were informed by a deep concern for the problems of racial discrimination which they described. Johnson became profoundly interested in social problems when in college; to learn more about these problems he turned to social work in Richmond and then to graduate study at the University of Chicago. Frazier developed an ambition to study sociology because it appealed to him as the social science which best analyzed social problems and most nearly provided an explanation of race and class conflicts.

Subsequently, Frazier served for several years as director of the Atlanta University School of Social Work prior to pursuing his Ph.D. at the University of Chicago; in later years he continued on occasion to engage in applied research — most notably when he served as survey director for the Mayor's Committee on Harlem after the Harlem race riot of 1935, and as Chief of the Division of Applied Social Sciences of UNESCO (1951–1953). Johnson was even more involved in applied sociology. His longtime friend, Edwin R. Embree, has written of Johnson's University of Chicago period: "Before the end of his first year in Chicago he had started the research department of the new Urban League, created a fresh pattern in social study by an analysis of the Negro group in Milwaukee, and, under a Carnegie grant, launched a survey of the huge shifts in Negro population throughout the country."[11] Throughout his academic career, he performed important services to the United States government, including his report on Negro housing, which was prepared in connection with President Hoover's Conference on Home Building and Home Ownership and, most important, his 1937 report for President Roosevelt's Committee on Farm Tenancy. One of the finest examples of Johnson's concern for critical social problems is the slim volume he coauthored with Edwin Embree and Will Alexander, *The Collapse of Cotton Tenancy* (from which "The Plantation during the Depression" is reprinted here).

Although Johnson later branched out to investigate the rural South — a field in which Park had an interest of long standing — the early work of both Johnson and Frazier reflected Park's predominant concern with the urban setting. From Park both men undoubtedly received their attachment to the use of the case study. Both men made important community studies — Johnson's *The Negro in Chicago, Shadow of the Plantation,* and *Growing Up in the Black Belt;* and Frazier's *Negro Family in Chicago* and *Negro Youth at the Crossways.* In these books, Johnson and Frazier clearly showed the influence of the anthropological approach and the use of individual life histories as well as other kinds of personal documents advocated by Park and W. I. Thomas. Both Johnson and Frazier displayed an awareness of the relevance of history to an understanding of present-day race relations. Johnson evidenced this awareness most clearly in *The Negro in American Civilization* and *Shadow of the Plantation;* Frazier demonstrated it even more markedly in *The Negro Family in the United States, The Negro in the United States,* and *Black Bourgeoisie.*

Frazier probably displayed a greater tendency to use specific aspects of Park's theory than Johnson. His *Race and Culture Contacts in the Modern World* was an effort to do something Park had not himself done — test his model of a natural history of racial contacts by analysis of racial relationships throughout the modern world. His classic work *The Negro Family* is, as Burgess pointed out in his preface to the book, a specific application of the natural history of the family. G. Franklin Edwards, Frazier's longtime colleague at Howard University, observes that

the book analyzes the impact first of slavery and then of emancipation and urbanization upon the Negro family. These experiences produced in the Negro family variations from the dominant American family pattern — to wit, a more important role for the female; attachment of great significance to variations in skin color; and a higher incidence of illegitimacy, of common law relationships, and of other forms of family disorganization.[1f]

By explaining these phenomena in sociological terms, it offered an important corrective to contemporary explanations which accounted for deviations from white middle-class norms in terms of alleged racial characteristics. We reprint here the classic chapter on the black matriarchate.

Johnson's last major work, *Patterns of Negro Segregation,* also owed much to Park's concepts. Park had stressed segregation as part of the accommodative nature of the patterns of race adjustment which were dominant in his era; and Johnson's analysis applied Park's concepts of social distance and the etiquette of race relations — key aspects of the mechanism of accommodation which segregation represented. Park's ideas on racial etiquette had also been developed — and at greater length — in a book by Bertram Doyle, *The Etiquette of Race Relations in the South.* (In the article by Doyle included in this book, he summarizes his work.) Like Johnson and Frazier, Doyle, who received his Ph.D. at the University of Chicago, was not only a student of Park, but also taught at Fisk University. Subsequently he left the academic world to become a bishop in the Colored Methodist Episcopal Church.

In *Patterns of Negro Segregation,* as in other books, Johnson, like Frazier, clearly went beyond Park, and sought to show the impact of sociological forces upon the personality development of blacks. In *Shadow of the Plantation* and *Growing Up in the Black Belt,* he related the cultural influences of the plantation and the effects of racial status upon the personality of rural sharecroppers; in *Patterns of Negro Segregation,* he attempted to analyze the varying behavioral responses of different social classes in the black community to the system of racial separation and discrimination.

Both Frazier and Johnson went beyond Park most clearly in their interest in the black community's class structure and its impact on behavior and personality. Although social stratification was a relatively minor theme in Johnson's work, it had a major place in Frazier's writings. Frazier's long interest in Marxism, stemming from his student days at Howard University, when he was a member of the Intercollegiate Socialist Society, undoubtedly helped stimulate his abiding and critical interest in the class structure of the black community. His earliest analyses of the subject were written during the 1920s — his essay "Durham: Capital of the Black Middle Class," in Alain Locke's *The New Negro* (1925), and his "La Bourgeoisie Noire" (1929). His research on the subject culminated in his famous book *Black Bourgeoisie* (1957). He attacked the black middle and upper class for exploiting the black masses and hating the latter's way of life, for seeking to imitate white middle-class culture, and for covering up their inferiority complexes by an exaggerated emphasis upon their status and conspicuous consumption. The book contained many penetrating observations and suggestive hypotheses, but the basic thrust was impressionistic and polemical rather than scholarly. In this anthology we reprint Frazier's early essay "La Bourgeoisie Noire" and an article summarizing his later thinking on the subject, "The New Negro Middle Class."

Although both Frazier and Johnson admired and owed much to Park, each developed in his own way and made his own particular contribution. They were, in fact, markedly different men. As a scholar, Johnson was preeminently the fact finder, the describer. In his spirit of extreme detachment, in his gradualist solutions to racial problems, he was closer to Park than was Frazier. Frazier, on the other hand, was the more theoretical; he was also the more boldly critical — not only of the foibles of the black bourgeoisie, but of white racism as well. Thus in "The Pathology of Race Prejudice," an article published in 1925, he referred to the projective mechanisms operative in white women who accused black men of attempted rape; the resulting furor among Atlanta whites forced his precipitate departure from the city and the loss of his job there.

Frazier's and Johnson's work was received with respect and often acclaim by the sociological profession. Johnson served as a president of the Southern Sociological Society, Frazier of the Eastern Sociological Society; Johnson rose to the position of vice president of the American Sociological Society, and in 1948 Frazier became president of that organization. Park's professional stature was undoubtedly a factor in projecting these two men, with their solid record of accomplishment, into the hierarchy of the profession; but the recognition they received was also due in part to the changing racial attitudes of American social scientists. Among sociologists the transition was epitomized by the work of Howard W. Odum, who in 1910 had written a doctoral dissertation at Columbia University, "Social and Mental Traits of the Negro," that cloaked with scientific respectability the doctrine of inherent black inferiority; by the 1930s Odum had become both the leading Southern sociologist and a champion of racial equality. The work of both Johnson and Frazier had contributed to these changes in the attitudes of sociologists; Johnson in particular, through personal persuasion, was helpful in bringing his colleagues in the profession around to a more enlightened point of view. Both men (as well as Reid, Drake, and

Allison Davis) were on the staff that Gunnar Myrdal enlisted to help him in his research for the *American Dilemma* at the end of the 1930s; the publication of this opus in 1944, symbolizing the hegemony of the racial eqalitarian point of view among sociologists of race relations, in a sense marks the end of an era.

The last two sociologists represented in this anthology, St. Clair Drake and Horace Cayton, while products of the University of Chicago, were not in the Park tradition. Drake, in particular, was most directly influenced by W. Lloyd Warner, the anthropologist whose strong interest was social stratification. In addition to *Black Metropolis,* Warner stimulated other major studies, including *Deep South*[13] by Allison Davis, the black social scientist, and two white scholars, Mary and Burleigh Gardner. *Deep South,* a detailed study of race, class, and community in Natchez, Mississippi, preceded *Black Metropolis* by several years; though focusing on the Negro community rather than the entire town, the Drake and Cayton study was a complementary investigation of a larger Northern metropolis, Chicago.

The excerpt we have chosen from *Black Metropolis* exemplifies the Warner school's emphasis upon social stratification. Drake and Cayton, like Davis and the Gardners, adapted Warner's conceptualization of the white American class structure, modifying it to account for the differences in occupational distribution and wealth, and the divergent criteria of social stratification, in the white and black communities. Beyond this, *Black Metropolis* (like *Deep South*) is within the tradition of the holistic case studies of the black community, based upon participant observation, going back to Du Bois's *The Philadelphia Negro.* In fact it marks the culmination of this approach to the sociological study of American blacks.

Both Drake and Cayton had spent many years in the black community of Chicago. Cayton, grandson of Hiram R. Revels, one of the two black Reconstruction senators of Mississippi, had originally come to Chicago from his home in Seattle, where he had been trained at the University of Washington. Drake had studied at Hampton Institute in Virginia, where he first became acquainted with Professor Allison Davis. While studying at the University of Chicago, both Drake and Cayton became involved in a WPA research project investigating the general social conditions surrounding the problem of juvenile delinquency in Chicago's black belt. This research expanded in scope and out of it ultimately came *Black Metropolis.*

As a result of their long years of residence and research in the community, they were able to use the technique of participant observation quite effortlessly. The result was an unequalled masterpiece, written with verve and profound understanding, describing and analyzing the historical evolution of the Chicago black community, the discrimination which Negro citizens faced, and the ways in which they coped with it, family life, job exclusion, ghetto housing, politics, class structure, and protest movements. All are analyzed with extraordinary insight.

Although Drake and Cayton did not say so, like their predecessors they were writing in the spirit of using scientific study that would lead to knowledge and understanding of the black community and race relations, and hopefully would form the basis for reform and advancement of the black man's status in the United States.

All of the authors whose work is discussed here made it clear in their writings that blacks were human beings oppressed by a racist white society, though their tone ranged from the outright (though muted) criticism of Du Bois's *The Philadelphia Negro* through the detached descriptions of Charles S. Johnson and the analytical theorizing of Frazier to the slightly ironic spirit of *Black Metropolis.*

Their writing clearly showed the social pathology arising from white oppression and discrimination — the poverty, the family problems, and the psychological fantasies of the black bourgeoisie. At the same time, these authors also described the richness and diversity of black life and the inventiveness which Negroes displayed in creating institutions and life-styles that enabled them to cope and survive in a racist society. Finally, all of the writers hoped that their published works, by reaching an influential white audience, would promote social change.

Notes

[1] Some explanation is perhaps due for the omission of any selection from the work of Oliver Cromwell Cox. His major study, *Caste, Class and Race,* was published in 1948. Cox, an independent thinker, stood apart from the dominant tradition in the sociology of American race relations, and exerted little influence on later scholars.

[2] E. Franklin Frazier, "Race Contacts and the Social Structure," *American Sociological Review,* XIV (February 1949), p. 2; Frazier, "Sociological Theory and Race Relations," *American Sociological Review,* XII (June 1947), p. 268.

[3] For more detailed treatment of Du Bois as sociologist, see Elliott Rudwick, "Note on a Forgotten Black Sociologist: W. E. B. Du Bois and the Sociological Profession," *The American Sociologist,* IV (November 1969), pp. 303–306.

[4] W. E. B. Du Bois, *Dusk of Dawn* (New York, 1940), p. 51.

[5] W. E. B. Du Bois, "The Study of the Negro Problems," *Annals of the American Academy of Political and Social Science,* XI (January 1898), p. 22.

[6] E. Franklin Frazier, "Race Contacts and the Social Structure," p. 3.

[7] W. E. B. Du Bois, untitled remarks at "Symposium on Race Friction," *American Journal of Sociology,* XIII (May 1908), p. 836.

[8] Ralph H. Turner, ed., *Robert E. Park on Social Control and Collective Behavior* (Chicago, 1967), p. xvii.

[9] Ernest W. Burgess, "Social Planning and Race Relations," in Jitsuichi Masuoka and Preston Valien, eds., *Race Relations, Problems and Theory: Essays in Honor of Robert E. Park* (Chapel Hill, 1961), p. 15.

[10] In fact, in this volume, Johnson's work was limited to the descriptive sections, while the recommendations were the work of the members of the Chicago Commission on Race Relations appointed by the governor. In his latest scholarship, Johnson was more outspoken about the immoral nature of the country's race system, as the selection from *Patterns of Negro Segregation* included in this volume indicates. The quotation about Johnson is from Edwin R. Embree, *Thirteen Against the Odds* (New York, 1944), pp. 47–48.

[11] Ibid., p. 55.

[12] G. Franklin Edwards, "E. Franklin Frazier," *International Encyclopedia of the Social Sciences* (New York, 1968), V, p. 553.

[13] St. Clair Drake's contribution, both in the field work and in the preparation of the manuscript, was incalculable. See the Foreword of *Deep South* (Chicago, 1941), pp. vii–viii.

Early Pioneers

1

The Study of the Negro Problems

W. E. B. Du Bois

The present period in the development of sociological study is a trying one; it is the period of observation, research and comparison — work always wearisome, often aimless, without well-settled principles and guiding lines, and subject ever to the pertinent criticism: What, after all, has been accomplished? To this the one positive answer which years of research and speculation have been able to return is that the phenomena of society are worth the most careful and systematic study, and whether or not this study may eventually lead to a systematic body of knowledge deserving the name of science, it cannot in any case fail to give the world a mass of truth worth the knowing.

Being then in a period of observation and comparison, we must confess to ourselves that the sociologists of few nations have so good an opportunity for observing the growth and evolution of society as those of the United States. The rapid rise of a young country, the vast social changes, the wonderful economic development, the bold political experiments, and the contact of varying moral standards — all these make for American students crucial tests of social action, microcosmic reproductions of long centuries of world history, and rapid — even violent — repetitions of great social problems. Here is a field for the sociologist — a field rich, but little worked, and full of great possibilities. European scholars envy our opportunities and it must be said to our credit that great interest in the observation of social phenomena has been aroused in the last decade — an interest of which much is ephemeral and superficial, but which opens the way for broad scholarship and scientific effort.

In one field however, — and a field perhaps larger than any other single domain of social phenomena, there does not seem to have been awakened as yet a fitting realization of the opportunities for scientific inquiry. This is the group of social phenomena arising from the presence in this land of eight million persons of African descent.

It is my purpose in this paper to discuss certain considerations concerning the study of the social problems affecting American Negroes; first, as to the historical development of these problems; then as to the necessity for their careful systematic study at the present time; thirdly, as to the results of scientific study of the Negro

W. E. B. Du Bois, "The Study of the Negro Problems," *Annals of the American Academy of Political and Social Science,* XI (Jan. 1898), pp. 1–23.

up to this time; fourthly, as to the scope and method which future scientific inquiry should take, and, lastly, regarding the agencies by which this work can best be carried out.

I. Development of the Negro Problems

A social problem is the failure of an organized social group to realize its group ideals, through the inability to adapt a certain desired line of action to given conditions of life. If, for instance, a government founded on universal manhood suffrage has a portion of its population so ignorant as to be unable to vote intelligently, such ignorance becomes a menacing social problem. The impossibility of economic and social development in a community where a large per cent of the population refuse to abide by the social rules of order, makes a problem of crime and lawlessness. Prostitution becomes a social problem when the demands of luxurious home life conflict with marriage customs.

Thus a social problem is ever a relation between conditions and action, and as conditions and actions vary and change from group to group from time to time and from place to place, so social problems change, develop and grow. Consequently, though we ordinarily speak of the Negro problem as though it were one unchanged question, students must recognize the obvious facts that this problem, like others, has had a long historical development, has changed with the growth and evolution of the nation; moreover, that it is not *one* problem, but rather a plexus of social problems, some new, some old, some simple, some complex; and these problems have their one bond of unity in the act that they group themselves about those Africans whom two centuries of slave-trading brought into the land.

In the latter part of the seventeenth and early in the eighteenth centuries, the central and all-absorbing economic need of America was the creation of a proper labor supply to develop American wealth. This question had been answered in the West Indies by enslaving Indians and Negroes. In the colonies of the mainland it was answered by the importation of Negroes and indented servants. Immediately then there arose the question of the legal status of these slaves and servants; and dozens of enactments, from Massachusetts to Georgia, were made "for the proper regulation of slaves and servants." Such statutes sought to solve problems of labor and not of race or color. Two circumstances, however, soon began to differentiate in the problem of labor, problems which concerned slaves for life from those which concerned servants for limited periods; and these circumstances were the economic superiority of the slave system, and the fact that the slaves were neither of the same race, language nor religion as the servants and their masters. In laboring classes thus widely separated there naturally arose a difference in legal and social standing. Colonial statutes soon ceased to embrace the regulations applying to slaves and servants in one chapter, and laws were passed for servants on the one hand and for Negro slaves on the other.

As slave labor, under the peculiar conditions of colonial life, increased in value and efficiency, the importations of Africans increased, while those of indented servants decreased; this gave rise to new social problems, namely, those of protecting a feeble civilization against an influx of barbarism and heathenism. Between 1750 and 1800 an increasing number of laws began to form a peculiar and systematic slave code based on a distinct idea of social caste. Even as this slave code was developing, new social conditions changed the aspect of the problems. The laws hitherto had been made to fit a class distinguished by its condition more than by its race or color. There arose now, however, a class of English-speaking Negroes born on American soil, and members of Christian churches; there sprang from illicit intercourse and considerable intermarriage with indented servants, a number of persons of mixed blood; there was also created by emancipation and the birth of black sons of white women a new class of free Negroes: all these developments led to a distinct beginning of group life among Negroes. Repeated attempts at organized insurrection were made; wholesale running away, like that which established the exiles in Florida, was resorted to; and a class of black landholders and voters arose. Such social movements brought the colonists face to face with new and serious problems; which they sought at first to settle in curious ways, denying the rite of baptism, establishing the legal presumption that all Negroes and mulattoes were slaves, and finally changing the Slave Code into a Black Code, replacing a caste of condition by a caste of race, harshly stopping legal sexual intercourse, and seeking to prevent further complications by restricting and even suppressing the slave-trade.

This concerted and determined action again changed the character of the Negro problems, but they did not cease to be grave. The inability of the Negro to escape from a servile caste into political freedom turned the problems of the group into problems of family life. On the separated plantations and in households the Negro became a constituent member of the family, speaking its language, worshiping in its churches, sharing its traditions, bearing its name, and sometimes sharing its blood; the talented slaves found large freedom in the intimate intercourse with the family which they enjoyed; they lost many traditions of their fatherland, and their ideals blended with the ideals of their new country. Some men began to see in this development a physical, economic and moral danger to the land, and they busied themselves with questions as to how they might provide for the development of white and black without demoralizing the one or amalgamating with the other. The solution of these difficulties was sought in a widespread attempt to eliminate the Negro from the family as he had formerly been eliminated from the state, by a process of emancipation that made him and his sons not even half-free, with the indefinite notion of colonizing the anomalous serfs thus created. This policy was carried out until one-half the land and one-sixth of the Negroes were quasi-freemen (sic).

Just as the nation was on the point of realizing the futility of colonization, one of those strange incalculable world movements began to be felt throughout civilized states — a movement so vast that we call it the economic revolution of the nineteenth century. A world demand for crops peculiarly suited to the South, substituted in Europe the factory system for the house industry, and in America the large plantation slave system for the family patriarchy; slavery became an industrial system and not a training school for serfdom; the Black Codes underwent a sudden transformation which hardened the lot of the slave, facilitated the slave trade, hindered further emancipation and rendered the condition of the free Negro unbearable. The question of race and color in America assumed a new and peculiar importance when it thus lay at the basis of some of the world's greatest industries.

The change in industrial conditions, however, not only affected the demands of a world market, but so increased the efficiency of labor, that a labor system, which in 1750 was eminently successful, soon became under the altered conditions of 1850 not only an economic monstrosity, but a political menace, and so rapidly did the crisis develop that the whole evolution of the nation came to a standstill, and the settlement of our social problems had to be left to the clumsy method of brute force.

So far as the Negro race is concerned, the Civil War simply left us face to face with the same sort of problems of social condition and caste which were beginning to face the nation a century ago. It is these problems that we are to-day somewhat helplessly — not to say carelessly — facing, forgetful that they are living, growing social questions whose progeny will survive to curse the nation, unless we grapple with them manfully and intelligently.

2. The Present Negro Problems

Such are some of the changes of condition and social movement which have, since 1619, altered and broadened the social problems grouped about the American Negro. In this development of successive questions about one centre, there is nothing peculiar to American history. Given any fixed condition or fact — a river Nile, a range of Alps, an alien race, or a national idea — and problems of society will at every stage of advance group themselves about it. All social growth means a succession of social problems — they constitute growth, they denote that laborious and often baffling adjustment of action and condition which is the essence of progress, and while a particular fact or circumstance may serve in one country as a rallying point of many intricate questions of adjustment, the absence of that particular fact would not mean the absence of all social problems. Questions of labor, caste, ignorance and race were bound to arise in America; they were simply complicated here and intensified there by the presence of the Negro.

Turning now from this brief summary of the varied phases of these questions, let us inquire somewhat more carefully into the form under which the Negro problems present themselves to-day after 275 years of evolution. Their existence is plainly manifested by the fact that a definitely segregated mass of eight millions of Americans do not wholly share the national life of the people; are not an integral part of the social body. The points at which they fail to be incorporated into this group life constitute the particular Negro problems, which can be divided into two distinct but correlated parts, depending on two facts:

First — Negroes do not share the full national life because as a mass they have not reached a sufficiently high grade of culture.

Secondly — They do not share the full national life because there has always existed in America a conviction — varying in intensity, but always widespread — that people of Negro blood should not be admitted into the group life of the nation no matter what their condition might be.

Considering the problems arising from the backward development of Negroes, we may say that the mass of this race does not reach the social standards of the nation with respect to

(*a*) Economic condition.
(*b*) Mental training.
(*c*) Social efficiency.

Even if special legislation and organized relief intervene, freedmen always start life under an economic disadvantage which generations, perhaps centuries, cannot overcome. Again, of all the important constituent parts of our nation, the Negro is by far the most ignorant; nearly half of the race are absolutely illiterate, only a minority of the other half have thorough common school training, and but a remnant are liberally educated. The great deficiency of the Negro, however, is his small knowledge of the art of organized social life — that last expression of human culture. His development in group life was abruptly broken off by the slave ship, directed into abnormal channels and dwarfed by the Black Codes, and suddenly wrenched anew by the Emancipation Proclamation. He finds himself, therefore, peculiarly weak in that nice adaptation of individual life to the life of the group which is the essence of civilization. This is shown in the grosser forms of sexual immorality, disease and crime, and also in the difficulty of race organization for common ends in economic or in intellectual lines.

For these reasons the Negro would fall behind any average modern nation, and he is unusually handicapped in the midst of a nation which excels in its extraordinary economic development, its average of popular intelligence and in the boldness of its experiments in organized social life.

These problems of poverty, ignorance and social degradation differ from similar problems the world over in one important particular, and that is the fact that they are complicated by a peculiar environment. This constitutes the second class of Negro problems, and they rest, as has been said, on the widespread conviction among Americans that no persons of Negro descent should become constituent members of the social body. This feeling gives rise to economic problems, to educational problems, and nice questions of social morality; it makes it more difficult for black men to earn a living or spend their earnings as they will; it gives them poorer school facilities and restricted contact with cultured classes; and it becomes, throughout the land, a cause and excuse for discontent, lawlessness, laziness and injustice.

3. The Necessity of Carefully Studying These Problems

Such, barely stated, are the elements of the present Negro problems. It is to little purpose however to name the elements of a problem unless we can also say accurately to what extent each element enters into the final result: whether, for instance, the present difficulties arise more largely from ignorance than from prejudice, or *vice versa.* This we do not know, and here it is that every intelligent discussion of the American Negro comes to a standstill. Nearly a hundred years ago Thomas Jefferson complained that the nation had never studied the real condition of the slaves and that, therefore, all general conclusions about them were extremely hazardous. We of another age can scarcely say that we have made material progress in this study. Yet these problems, so vast and intricate, demanding trained research and expert analysis, touching questions that affect the very foundation of the republic and of human progress, increasing and multiplying year by year, would seem to urge the nation with increasing force to measure and trace and understand thoroughly the underlying elements of this example of human evolution.

Now first we should study the Negro problems in order to distinguish between the different and distinct problems affecting this race. Nothing makes intelligent discussion of the Negro's position so fruitless as the repeated failure to discriminate between the different questions that concern him. If a Negro discusses the question, he is apt to discuss simply the problem of race prejudice; if a Southern white man writes on the subject he is apt to discuss problems of ignorance, crime and social degradation; and yet each calls the problem he discusses *the* Negro problem, leaving in the dark background the really crucial question as to the relative importance of the many problems involved. Before we can begin to study the Negro intelligently, we must realize definitely that not only is he affected by all the varying social forces that act on any nation at his stage of advancement, but that in addition to these there is reacting upon him the mighty power of a peculiar and unusual social environment which affects to some extent every other social force.

In the second place we should seek to know and measure carefully all the forces and conditions that go to make up these different problems, to trace the historical development of these conditions, and discover as far as possible the probable trend of further development. Without doubt this would be difficult work, and it can with much truth be objected that we cannot ascertain, by the methods of sociological research known to us, all such facts thoroughly and accurately. To this objection it is only necessary to answer that however difficult it may be to know all about the Negro, it is certain that we can know vastly more than we do, and that we can have our knowledge in more systematic and intelligible form. As things are, our opinions upon the Negro are more matters of faith than of knowledge Every school-boy is ready to discuss the matter, and there are few men that have not settled convictions. Such a situation is dangerous. Whenever any nation allows impulse, whim or hasty conjecture to usurp the place of conscious, normative, intelligent action, it is in grave danger. The sole aim of any society is to settle its problems in accordance with its highest ideals, and the only rational method of accomplishing this is to study those problems in the light of the best scientific research.

Finally, the American Negro deserves study for the great end of advancing the cause of science in general. No such opportunity to watch and measure the history and development of a great race of men ever presented itself to the scholars of a modern nation. If they miss this opportunity — if they do the work in a slip-shod, unsystematic manner — if they dally with the truth to humor the whims of the day, they do far more than hurt the good name of the American people; they hurt the cause of scientific truth the world over, they voluntarily decrease human knowledge of a universe of which we are ignorant enough, and they degrade the high end of truth-seeking in a day when they need more and more to dwell upon its sanctity.

4. The Work Already Accomplished

It may be said that it is not altogether correct to assert that few attempts have been made to study these problems or to put the nation in possession of a body of truth in accordance with which it might act intelligently. It is far from my purpose to disparage in any way the work already done by students of these questions; much valuable effort has without doubt been put upon the field, and yet a careful survey of the field seems but to emphasize the fact that the work done bears but small proportion to the work still to be done.[1]

Moreover the studies made hitherto can as a whole be justly criticised in three particulars: (1) They have not been based on a thorough knowledge of details; (2) they have been unsystematical; (3) they have been uncritical.

In few subjects have historians been more content to go on indefinitely repeating current traditions and uninvestigated facts. We are still gravely told that the slave trade ceased in 1808, that the docility of Africans made slave insurrections almost unknown, and that the Negro never developed in this country a self-conscious group life before 1860. In the hasty endeavor to cover a broad subject when the details were unknown, much superficial work has been current, like that, for instance, of a newspaper reporter who spent "the odd intervals of leisure in active newspaper work" for "nearly eighteen months," in the District of Columbia, and forthwith published a study of 80,000 Negroes, with observations on their institutions and development.

Again, the work done has been lamentably unsystematic and fragmentary. Scientific work must be subdivided, but conclusions which affect the whole subject must be based on a study of the whole. One cannot study the Negro in freedom and come to general conclusions about his destiny without knowing his history in slavery. A vast set of problems having a common centre must, too, be studied according to some general plan, if the work of different students is to be compared or to go toward building a unified body of knowledge. A plan once begun must be carried out, and not like that of our erratic census reports, after allowing us to follow the size of farms in the South for three decades, suddenly leave us wondering as to the relation of farms and farm families. Students of black codes should not stop suddenly with 1863, and travelers and observers whose testimony would be of great value if arranged with some system and reasonably limited in time and space, must not ramble on without definite plan or purpose and render their whole work of doubtful value.

Most unfortunate of all, however, is the fact that so much of the work done on the Negro question is notoriously uncritical; uncritical from lack of discrimination in the selection and weighing of evidence; uncritical in choosing the proper point of view from which to study these problems, and, finally, uncritical from the distinct bias in the minds of so many writers. To illustrate, the layman who does not pretend to first hand knowledge of the subject and who would learn of students is to-day woefully puzzled by absolutely contradictory evidence. One student declares that Negroes are advancing in knowledge and ability; that they are working, establishing homes, and going into business, and that the problem will soon be one of the past. Another student of equal learning declares that the Negro is degenerating — sinking into crime and social immorality, receiving little help from education, still in the main a menial servant, and destined in a short time to settle the problem by dying entirely out. Such and many other contradictory conclusions arise from the uncritical use of material. A visitor to a great Negro school in the South catches the inspiration of youth, studies the work of graduates, and imbibes the hopes of teachers and immediately infers from the situation of a few hundred the general condition of a population numbering twice that of Holland. A college graduate sees the slums of a Southern city, looks at the plantation field hands, and has some experience with Negro servants, and from the laziness, crime and disease which he finds, draws conclusions as to eight millions of people, stretched from Maine to Texas and from Florida to Washington. We continually judge the whole from the part we are familiar with; we continually assume the material we have at hand to be typical; we reverently receive a column of figures without asking who collected them, how they were arranged, how far they are valid and what chances of error they contain; we receive the testimony of men without asking whether they were trained or ignorant, careful or careless, truthful or given to exaggeration, and, above all, whether they are giving facts or opinions. It is so easy for a man who has already formed his conclusions to receive any and all testimony in their favor without carefully weighing and testing it, that we sometimes find in serious scientific studies very curious proof of broad conclusions. To cite an extreme case, in a recently published study of the Negro, a part of the argument as to the physical condition of all these millions, is made to rest on the measurement of fifteen black boys in a New York reformatory.

The widespread habit of studying the Negro from one point of view only, that of his influence on the white inhabitants, is also responsible for much uncritical work. The slaves are generally treated as one inert changeless mass, and most studies of slavery apparently have no conception of a social evolution and development among them. The slave code of a state is given, the progress of anti-slavery sentiment, the economic results of the system and the general influence of man on master are studied, but of the slave himself, of his group life and social institutions, of remaining traces of his African tribal life, of his amusements, his conversion to Christianity, his acquiring of the English tongue — in fine, of his whole reaction against his environment, of all this we hear little or nothing, and would apparently be expected to believe that the Negro arose from the dead in 1863. Yet all the testimony of law and custom, of tradition and present social condition, shows us that the Negro at the time of emancipation had passed through a social evolution which far separated him from his savage ancestors.

The most baneful cause of uncritical study of the Negro is the manifest and far-reaching bias of writers. Americans are born in many cases with deep, fierce convictions on the Negro question, and in other cases imbibe them from their environment. When such men come to write on the subject, without technical training, without breadth of view, and in some cases without a deep sense of the sanctity of scientific truth, their testimony, however interesting as opinion, must of necessity be worthless as science. Thus too often the testimony of Negroes and their friends has to be thrown out of court on account of the manifest prejudice of the writers; on the other hand, the testimony of many other writers in the North and especially in the South has to be received with reserve on account of too evident bias.

Such facts make the path of students and foreign observers peculiarly thorny. The foreigner's views, if he be not exceptionally astute, will depend largely on his letters of introduction; the home student's views, on his birthplace and parentage. All students are apt to fail to recognize the magnitude and importance of these problems, and to succumb to the vulgar temptation of basing on any little contribution they make to the study of these problems, general conclusions as to the origin and destiny of the Negro people in time and eternity. Thus we possess endless final judgments as to the American Negro emanating from men of influence and learning, in the very face of the fact known to every accurate student, that there exists to-day no sufficient material of proven reliability, upon which any scientist can base definite and final conclusions as to the present condition and tendencies of the eight million American Negroes; and that any person or publication purporting to give such conclusions simply makes statements which go beyond the reasonably proven evidence.

5. A Program of Future Study

If we admit the deep importance of the Negro problems, the necessity of studying them, and certain shortcomings in work done up to this time, it would seem to be the clear duty of the American people, in the interests of scientific knowledge and social reform, to begin a broad and systematic study of the history and condition of the American Negroes. The scope and method of this study, however, needs to be generally agreed upon beforehand in its main outlines, not to hinder the freedom of individual students, but to systematize and unify effort so as to cover the wide field of investigation.

The scope of any social study is first of all limited by the general attitude of public opinion toward truth and truth-seeking. If in regard to any social problem there is for any reason a persistent refusal on the part of the people to allow the truth to be known, then manifestly that problem cannot be studied. Undoubtedly much of the unsatisfactory work already done with regard to the Negro is due to this cause; the intense feeling that preceded and followed the war made a calm balanced research next to impossible. Even to-day there are certain phases of this question which we cannot hope to be allowed to study dispassionately and thoroughly, and these phases, too, are naturally those uppermost in the public mind. For instance, it is extremely doubtful if any satisfactory study of Negro crime and lynching can be made for a generation or more, in the present condition of the public mind, which renders it almost impossible to get at the facts and real conditions. On the other hand, public opinion has in the last decade become sufficiently liberal to open a broad field of investigation to students, and here lies the chance for effective work

The right to enter this field undisturbed and untrammeled will depend largely on the attitude of science itself. Students must be careful to insist that science as such — be it physics, chemistry, psychology, or sociology — has but one simple aim: the discovery of truth. Its results lie open for the use of all men — merchants, physicians, men of letters, and philanthropists, but the aim of science itself is simple truth. Any attempt to give it a double aim, to make social reform the immediate instead of the mediate object of a search for truth, will inevitably tend to defeat both objects. The frequent alliance of sociological research with various panaceas

and particular schemes of reform, has resulted in closely connecting social investigation with a good deal of groundless assumption and humbug in the popular mind.
There will be at first some difficulty in bringing the Southern people, both black
and white, to conceive of an earnest, careful study of the Negro problem which has
not back of it some scheme of race amalgamation, political jobbery, or deportation
to Africa. The new study of the American Negro must avoid such misapprehensions
from the outset, by insisting that historical and statistical research has but one
object, the ascertainment of the facts as to the social forces and conditions of
one-eighth of the inhabitants of the land. Only by such rigid adherence to the true
object of the scholar, can statesmen and philanthropists of all shades of belief be
put into possession of a reliable body of truth which may guide their efforts to the
best and largest success.

In the next place, a study of the Negro, like the study of any subject, must
start out with certain generally admitted postulates. We must admit, for instance,
that the field of study is large and varying, and that what is true of the Negro in
Massachusetts is not necessarily true of the Negro in Louisiana; that what was true
of the Negro in 1850 was not necessarily true in 1750; and that there are many
distinct social problems affecting the Negro. Finally, if we would rally to this
common ground of scientific inquiry all partisans and advocates, we must explicitly
admit what all implicitly postulate — namely, that the Negro is a member of the
human race, and as one who, in the light of history and experience, is capable to
a degree of improvement and culture, is entitled to have his interests considered
according to his numbers in all conclusions as to the common weal.

With these preliminary considerations we may say that the study of the Negro
falls naturally into two categories, which though difficult to separate in practice,
must for the sake of logical clearness, be kept distinct. They are (a) the study of
the Negro as a social group, (b) the study of his peculiar social environment.

The study of the Negro as a social group may be, for convenience, divided into
four not exactly logical but seemingly most practicable divisions, viz:

1. Historical study,
2. Statistical investigation,
3. Anthropological measurement,
4. Sociological interpretation.

The material at hand for historical research is rich and abundant; there are
the colonial statutes and records, the partially accessible archives of Great Britain,
France and Spain, the collections of historical societies, the vast number of executive
and congressional reports and documents, the state statutes, reports and publica
tions, the reports of institutions and societies, the personal narratives and opinions
of various observers and the periodical press covering nearly three centuries. From
these sources can be gathered much new information upon the economic and social

development of the Negro, upon the rise and decline of the slave-trade, the character, distribution and state of culture of the Africans, the evolution of the slave codes as expressing the life of the South, the rise of such peculiar expressions of Negro social history, as the Negro church, the economics of plantation life, the possession of private property by slaves, and the history of the oft-forgotten class of free Negroes. Such historical research must be subdivided in space and limited in time by the nature of the subject, the history of the different colonies and groups being followed and compared, the different periods of development receiving special study, and the whole subject being reviewed from different aspects.

The collection of statistics should be carried on with increased care and thoroughness. It is no credit to a great modern nation that so much well-grounded doubt can be thrown on our present knowledge of the simple matters of number, age, sex and conjugal condition in regard to our Negro population. General statistical investigations should avoid seeking to tabulate more intricate social conditions than the ones indicated. The concrete social status of the Negro can only be ascertained by intensive studies carried on in definitely limited localities, by competent investigators, in accordance with one general plan. Statistical study by groups is apt to be more accurately done and more easily accomplished, and able to secure more competent and responsible agents than any general census. General averages in so complicated a subject are apt to be dangerously misleading. This study should seek to ascertain by the most approved methods of social measurement the size and condition of families, the occupations and wages, the illiteracy of adults and education of children, the standard of living, the character of the dwellings, the property owned and rents paid, and the character of the organized group life. Such investigations should be extended until they cover the typical group life of Negroes in all sections of the land and should be so repeated from time to time in the same localities and with the same methods, as to be a measure of social development.

The third division of study is anthropological measurement, and it includes a scientific study of the Negro body. The most obvious peculiarity of the Negro — a peculiarity which is a large element in many of the problems affecting him — is his physical unlikeness to the people with whom he has been brought into contact. This difference is so striking that it has become the basis of a mass of theory, assumption and suggestion which is deep-rooted and yet rests on the flimsiest basis of scientific fact. That there are differences between the white and black races is certain, but just what those differences are is known to none with an approach to accuracy. Yet here in America is the most remarkable opportunity ever offered of studying these differences, of noting influences of climate and physical environment, and particularly of studying the effect of amalgamating two of the most diverse races in the world — another subject which rests under a cloud of ignorance.

The fourth division of this investigation is sociological interpretation; it should include the arrangement and interpretation of historical and statistical matter in the light of the experience of other nations and other ages; it should aim to study those finer manifestations of social life which history can but mention and which statistics can not count, such as the expression of Negro life as found in their hundred newspapers, their considerable literature, their music and folklore and their germ of esthetic life — in fine, in all the movements and customs among them that manifest the existence of a distinct social mind.

The second category of studies of the Negro has to do with his peculiar social environment. It will be difficult, as has been intimated, to separate a study of the group from a study of the environment, and yet the group action and the reaction of the surroundings must be kept clearly distinct if we expect to comprehend the Negro problems. The study of the environment may be carried on at the same time with a study of the group, only the two sets of forces must receive distinct measurement.

In such a field of inquiry it will be found difficult to do more than subdivide inquiry in time and space. The attempt should be made to isolate and study the tangible phenomena of Negro prejudice in all possible cases; its effect on the Negro's physical development, on his mental acquisitiveness, on his moral and social condition, as manifested in economic life, in legal sanctions and in crime and lawlessness. So, too, the influence of that same prejudice on American life and character would explain the otherwise inexplicable changes through which Negro prejudice has passed.

The plan of study thus sketched is, without doubt, long, difficult and costly, and yet is not more than commensurable with the size and importance of the subject with which it is to deal. It will take years and decades to carry out such a plan, with the barest measure of success, and yet there can be no doubt but that this plan or something similar to it, points to the quickest path toward the ultimate solution of the present difficulties.

6. The Proper Agents for This Work

In conclusion it will not be out of place to suggest the agencies which seem best fitted to carry out a work of this magnitude. There will, without doubt, always be room for the individual working alone as he wills; if, however, we wish to cover the field systematically, and in reasonable time, only organized and concerted efforts will avail; and the requisite means, skill and preparation for such work can be furnished by two agencies alone: the government and the university.

For simple, definite inquiries carried out periodically on a broad scale we should depend on the national and state governments. The decennial census properly organized under civil service rules should be the greatest single agency for collecting general information as to the Negro. If, however, the present Congress cannot be induced to organize a census bureau under proper Civil Service rules, and in accordance with the best expert advice, we must continue for many years more to depend on clumsy and ignorant methods of measurement in matters demanding accuracy and trained technique. It is possible also for the different national bureaus and for the state governments to study certain aspects of the Negro question over wide areas. A conspicuous example of this is the valuable educational statistics collected by Commissioner Harris, and the series of economic studies just instituted by the Bureau of Labor.

On the whole it may be laid down as axiomatic that government activity in the study of this problem should confine itself mainly to the ascertainment of simple facts covering a broad field. For the study of these social problems in their more complicated aspects, where the desideratum is intensive study, by trained minds, according to the best methods, the only competent agency is the university. Indeed, in no better way could the American university repay the unusual munificence of its benefactors than by placing before the nation a body of scientific truth in the light of which they could solve some of their most vexing social problems.

It is to the credit of the University of Pennsylvania that she has been the first to recognize her duty in this respect, and in so far as restricted means and opportunity allowed, has attempted to study the Negro problems in a single definite locality. This work needs to be extended to other groups, and carried out with larger system; and here it would seem is the opportunity of the Southern Negro college. We hear much of higher Negro education, and yet all candid people know there does not exist to-day in the centre of Negro population a single first-class fully equipped institution devoted to the higher education of Negroes; not more than three Negro institutions in the South deserve the name of *college* at all; and yet what is a Negro college but a vast college settlement for the study of a particular set of peculiarly baffling problems? What more effective or suitable agency could be found in which to focus the scientific efforts of the great universities of the North and East, than an institution situated in the very heart of these social problems, and made the centre of careful historical and statistical research? Without doubt the first effective step toward the solving of the Negro question will be the endowment of a Negro college which is not merely a teaching body, but a centre of sociological research, in close connection and co-operation with Harvard, Columbia, Johns Hopkins and the University of Pennsylvania.

In this direction the Negro conferences of Tuskegee and Hampton are tending; and there is already inaugurated an actual beginning of work at Atlanta University. In 1896 this university brought into correspondence about one hundred Southern college-bred men and laid before them a plan of systematic investigation into certain problems of Negro city life, as, for instance, family conditions, dwellings, rents, ownership of homes, occupations, earnings, disease and death-rates. Each investigator took one or more small groups to study, and in this way fifty-nine groups, aggregating 5000 people in various parts of the country, were studied, and the results have been published by the United States Bureau of Labor. Such purely scientific work, done with an eye single to ascertaining true conditions, marks an era in our conception of the place of the Negro college, and it is certainly to be desired that

Atlanta University may be enabled to continue this work as she proposes to do.

Finally the necessity must again be emphasized of keeping clearly before students the object of all science, amid the turmoil and intense feeling that clouds the discussion of a burning social question. We live in a day when in spite of the brilliant accomplishments of a remarkable century, there is current much flippant criticism of scientific work; when the truth-seeker is too often pictured as devoid of human sympathy, and careless of human ideals. We are still prone in spite of all our culture to sneer at the heroism of the laboratory while we cheer the swagger of the street broil. At such a time true lovers of humanity can only hold higher the pure ideals of science, and continue to insist that if we would solve a problem we must study it, and that there is but one coward on earth, and that is the coward that dare not know.

Note

[1] A bibliography of the American Negro is a much needed undertaking. The existing literature may be summarized briefly as follows: In the line of historical research there are such general studies of the Negro as Williams' "History of the Negro Race in America," Wilson's, Goodell's, Blake's, Copley's, Greeley's and Cobb's studies of slavery, and the treatment of the subject in the general histories of Bancroft, Von Holst and others. We have, too, brief special histories of the institution of slavery in Massachusetts, Connecticut, New York, New Jersey, Pennsylvania, the District of Columbia, Maryland and North Carolina. The slave trade has been studied by Clarkson, Buxton, Benezet, Carey and others; Miss McDougall has written a monograph on fugitive slaves; the Slave Codes have been digested by Hurd, Stroud, Wheeler, Goodell and Cobb; the economic aspects of the slave system were brilliantly outlined by Cairues, and a great amount of material is available, showing the development of anti-slavery opinion. Of statistical and sociological material the United States Government has collected much in its census and bureau reports; and congressional investigations, and state governments and societies have added something to this. Moreover, we have the statistical studies of DeBow, Helper, Gannett and Hoffman, the observations of Olmsted and Kemble, and the studies and interpretations by Chambers, Otken, Bruce, Cable, Fortune, Brackett, Ingle and Tourgée; foreign students, from De Tocqueville and Martineau to Halle and Bryce, have studied the subject; something has been done in collecting folklore and music, and in studying dialect, and some anthropological material has been collected. Beside this, there is a mass of periodical literature, of all degrees of value, teeming with opinions, observations, personal experiences and discussions.

The Organized
Life of Negroes

W. E. B. Du Bois

History of the Negro Church in Philadelphia

We have already followed the history of the rise of the Free African Society, which was the beginning of the Negro Church in the North. We often forget that the rise of a church organization among Negroes was a curious phenomenon. The church really represented all that was left of African tribal life, and was the sole expression of the organized efforts of the slaves. It was natural that any movement among freedmen should centre about their religious life, the sole remaining element of their former tribal system. Consequently when, led by two strong men, they left the white Methodist Church, they were naturally unable to form any democratic moral reform association; they must be led and guided, and this guidance must have the religious sanction that tribal government always has. Consequently Jones and Allen, the leaders of the Free African Society, as early as 1791 began regular religious exercises, and at the close of the eighteenth century there were three Negro churches in the city, two of which were independent.[1]

St. Thomas' Church has had a most interesting history. It early declared its purpose "of advancing our friends in a true knowledge of God, of true religion, and of the ways and means to restore our long lost race to the dignity of men and Christians."[2] The church offered itself to the Protestant Episcopal Church and was accepted on condition that they take no part in the government of the general church. Their leader, Absalom Jones, was ordained deacon and priest, and took charge of the church. In 1804 the church established a day school which lasted until 1816.[3] In 1849 St. Thomas' began a series of attempts to gain full recognition in the Church by a demand for delegates to the Church gatherings. The Assembly first declared that it was not expedient to allow Negroes to take part. To this the vestry returned a dignified answer, asserting that "expediency is no plea against the violation of the great principles of charity, mercy, justice and truth." Not until 1864 was the Negro body received into full fellowship with the Church. In the century and more of its existence St. Thomas' has always represented a high grade of

From W. E. B. Du Bois, *The Philadelphia Negro: A Social Study,* University of Pennsylvania, 1899.

intelligence, and to-day it still represents the most cultured and wealthiest of the Negro population and the Philadelphia born residents. Its membership has consequently always been small, being 246 in 1794, 427 in 1795, 105 in 1860, and 391 in 1897.[4]

The growth of Bethel Church, founded by Richard Allen, on South Sixth Street, has been so phenomenal that it belongs to the history of the nation rather than to any one city. From a weekly gathering which met in Allen's blacksmith shop on Sixth near Lombard, grew a large church edifice; other churches were formed under the same general plan, and Allen, as overseer of them, finally took the title of bishop and ordained other bishops. The Church, under the name of African Methodist Episcopal, grew and spread until in 1890 the organization had 452,725 members, 2481 churches and $6,468,280 worth of property.[5]

By 1813[6] there were in Philadelphia six Negro churches with the following membership:[7]

St. Thomas', P. E.	560
Bethel, A. M. E.	1272
Zoar, M. E.	80
Union, A. M. E.	74
Baptist, Race and Vine Streets	80
Presbyterian	300
	2366

The Presbyterian Church had been founded by two Negro missionaries, father and son, named Gloucester, in 1807.[8] The Baptist Church was founded in 1809. The inquiry of 1838 gives these statistics of churches:

Denomination	Number of Churches	Members	Annual Expenses	Value of Property	Incumbrance
Episcopalian	1	100	$1,000	$36,000	
Lutheran	1	10	120	3,000	$1,000
Methodist	8	2,860	2,100	50,800	5,100
Presbyterian	2	325	1,500	20,000	1,000
Baptist	4	700	1,300	4,200	
Total	16	3,995	$6,020	$114,000	$7,100

Three more churches were added in the next ten years, and then a reaction followed.[9] By 1867 there were in all probability nearly twenty churches, of which we have statistics of seventeen: see table on p. 31.[10]

Since the war the growth of Negro churches has been by bounds, there being twenty-five churches and missions in 1880, and fifty-five in 1897.

So phenomenal a growth as this here outlined means more than the establishment of many places of worship. The Negro is, to be sure, a religious creature — most primitive folk are — but his rapid and even extraordinary founding of churches is not due to this fact alone, but is rather a measure of his developement,

Statistics of Negro Churches, 1867

Name	Founded	Number of Members	Value of Property	Pastor's Salary
P. E.				
St. Thomas'	1792			
Methodist				
Bethel	1794	1,100	$50,000	$600
Union	1827	467	40,000	850
Wesley	1817	464	21,000	700
Zoar	1794	400	12,000	
John Wesley	1844	42	3,000	No regular salary
Little Wesley	1821	310	11,000	500
Pisgah	1831	116	4,600	430
Zion City Mission	1858	90	4,500	
Little Union	1837	200		
Baptist				
First Baptist	1809	360	5,000	
Union Baptist		400	7,000	600
Shiloh	1842	405	16,000	600
Oak Street	1827	137		
Presbyterian				
First Presbyterian	1807	200	8,000	
Second Presbyterian	1824			
Central Presbyterian	1844	240	16,000	

an indication of the increasing intricacy of his social life and the consequent multi-plication of the organ which is the function of his group life — the church. To understand this let us inquire into the function of the Negro church.

The Function of the Negro Church

The Negro church is the peculiar and characteristic product of the transplanted African, and deserves especial study. As a social group the Negro church may be said to have antedated the Negro family on American soil; as such it has preserved, on the one hand, many functions of tribal organization, and on the other hand, many of the family functions. Its tribal functions are shown in its religious activity, its social authority and general guiding and co-ordinating work; its family functions are shown by the fact that the church is a centre of social life and intercourse; acts as newspaper and intelligence bureau, is the centre of amusements — indeed, is the world in which the Negro moves and acts. So far reaching are these functions of the church that its organization is almost political. In Bethel Church, for instance, the mother African Methodist Episcopal Church of America, we have officials and organizations as shown in the table on p. 32.

Or to put it differently, here we have a mayor, appointed from without, with great administrative and legislative powers, although well limited by long and zealously cherished custom; he acts conjointly with a select council, the trustees, a board of finance, composed of stewards and stewardesses, a common council of

The Bishop of the District	⎫
The Presiding Elder	⎬ Executive
The Pastor	⎭
The Board of Trustees	Executive Council
General Church Meeting	Legislative
The Board of Stewards	⎫
The Board of Stewardesses	⎬ Financial Board
The Junior Stewardesses	⎭
The Sunday School Organization	Educational System
Ladies' Auxiliary, Volunteer Guild, etc.	Tax Collectors
Ushers' Association	Police
Class Leaders	⎫
Local Preachers	⎬ Sheriffs and Magistrates
Choir	Music and Amusement
Allen Guards	Militia
Missionary Societies	Social Reformers
Beneficial and Semi-Secret Societies, etc.	Corporations

committees and, occasionally, of all church members. The various functions of the church are carried out by societies and organizations. The form of government varies, but is generally some form of democracy closely guarded by custom and tempered by possible and not infrequent secession.

The functions of such churches in order of present emphasis are:

1. The raising of the annual budget.

2. The maintenance of membership.

3. Social intercourse and amusements.

4. The setting of moral standards.

5. Promotion of general intelligence.

6. Efforts for social betterment

1. The annual budget is of first importance, because the life of the organization depends upon it. The amount of expenditure is not very accurately determined beforehand, although its main items do not vary much. There is the pastor's salary, the maintenance of the building, light and heat, the wages of a janitor, contributions to various church objects, and the like, to which must be usually added the interest on some debt. The sum thus required varies in Philadelphia from $200 to $5000. A small part of this is raised by a direct tax on each member. Besides this, voluntary contributions by members roughly gauged according to ability, are expected, and a strong public opinion usually compels payment. Another large source of revenue is the collection after the sermons on Sunday, when, amid the reading of notices and a subdued hum of social intercourse, a stream of givers walk to the pulpit and place in the hands of the trustee or steward in charge a contribution, varying from a cent to a dollar or more. To this must be added the steady revenue from entertainments, suppers, socials, fairs, and the like. In this way the Negro churches of Philadelphia raise nearly $100,000 a year. They hold in real estate $900,000 worth of property, and are thus no insignificant element in the economics of the city.

2. Extraordinary methods are used and efforts made to maintain and increase the membership of the various churches. To be a popular church with large membership means ample revenues, large social influence and a leadership among the colored people unequaled in power and effectiveness. Consequently people are attracted to the church by sermons, by music and by entertainments; finally, every year a revival is held, at which considerable numbers of young people are converted. All this is done in perfect sincerity and without much thought of merely increasing membership, and yet every small church strives to be large by these means and every large church to maintain itself or grow larger. The churches thus vary from a dozen to a thousand members.

3. Without wholly conscious effort the Negro church has become a centre of social intercourse to a degree unknown in white churches even in the country. The various churches, too, represent social classes. At St. Thomas' one looks for the well-to-do Philadelphians, largely descendants of favorite mulatto house-servants, and consequently well-bred and educated, but rather cold and reserved to strangers or newcomers; at Central Presbyterian one sees the older, simpler set of respectable Philadelphians with distinctly Quaker characteristics — pleasant but conservative; at Bethel may be seen the best of the great laboring class — steady, honest people, well dressed and well fed, with church and family traditions; at Wesley will be found the new arrivals, the sight-seers and the strangers to the city — hearty and easy-going people, who welcome all comers and ask few questions; at Union Baptist one may look for the Virginia servant girls and their young men; and so on throughout the city. Each church forms its own social circle, and not many stray beyond its bounds. Introductions into that circle come through the church, and thus the stranger becomes known. All sorts of entertainments and amusements are furnished by the churches: concerts, suppers, socials, fairs, literary exercises and debates, cantatas, plays, excursions, picnics, surprise parties, celebrations. Every holiday is the occasion of some special entertainment by some club, society or committee of the church; Thursday afternoons and evenings, when the servant girls are free, are always sure to have some sort of entertainment. Sometimes these exercises are free, sometimes an admission fee is charged, sometimes refreshments or articles are on sale. The favorite entertainment is a concert with solo singing, instrumental music, reciting, and the like. Many performers make a living by appearing at these entertainments in various cities, and often they are persons of training and ability, although not always. So frequent are these and other church exercises that there are few Negro churches which are not open four to seven nights in a week and sometimes one or two afternoons in addition.

Perhaps the pleasantest and most interesting social intercourse takes place on Sunday; the weary week's work is done, the people have slept late and had a good breakfast, and sally forth to church well dressed and complacent. The usual hour of the morning service is eleven, but people stream in until after twelve. The sermon is usually short and stirring, but in the larger churches elicits little response other than an "Amen" or two. After the sermon the social features begin; notices on the various meetings of the week are read, people talk with each other in subdued tones, take their contributions to the altar, and linger in the aisles and corridors long after dismission to laugh and chat until one or two o'clock. Then they go home to good dinners. Sometimes there is some special three o'clock service, but usually nothing save Sunday-school, until night. Then comes the chief meeting of the day; probably ten thousand Negroes gather every Sunday night in their churches. There is much music, much preaching, some short addresses; many strangers are there to be looked at; many beaus bring out their belles, and those who do not gather in crowds at the church door and escort the young women home. The crowds are usually well behaved and respectable, though rather more jolly than comports with a puritan idea of church services.

In this way the social life of the Negro centres in his church — baptism, wedding and burial, gossip and courtship, friendship and intrigue — all lie in these walls. What wonder that this central club house tends to become more and more luxuriously furnished, costly in appointment and easy of access!

4. It must not be inferred from all this that the Negro is hypocritical or irreligious. His church is, to be sure, a social institution first, and religious after-wards, but nevertheless, its religious activity is wide and sincere. In direct moral teaching and in setting moral standards for the people, however, the church is timid, and naturally so, for its constitution is democracy tempered by custom. Negro preachers are often condemned for poor leadership and empty sermons, and it is said that men with so much power and influence could make striking moral reforms. This is but partially true. The congregation does not follow the moral precepts of the preacher, but rather the preacher follows the standard of his flock, and only exceptional men dare seek to change this. And here it must be remembered that the Negro preacher is primarily an executive officer, rather than a spiritual guide. If one goes into any great Negro church and hears the sermon and views the audience, one would say: either the sermon is far below the calibre of the audience, or the people are less sensible than they look; the former explanation is usually true. The preacher is sure to be a man of executive ability, a leader of men, a shrewd and affable president of a large and intricate corporation. In addition to this he may be, and usually is, a striking elocutionist; he may also be a man of integrity, learning, and deep spiritual earnestness; but these last three are sometimes all lacking, and the last two in many cases. Some signs of advance are here manifest: no minister of notoriously immoral life, or even of bad reputation, could hold a large church in Philadelphia without eventual revolt. Most of the present pastors are decent, respectable men; there are perhaps one or two exceptions to this, but the exceptions are doubtful, rather than notorious. On the whole then, the average Negro preacher in this city is a shrewd manager, a respectable man, a good talker, a pleasant companion, but neither learned nor spiritual, nor a reformer.

The moral standards are therefore set by the congregations, and vary from church to church in some degree. There has been a slow working toward a literal obeying of the puritan and ascetic standard of morals which Methodism imposed on the freedmen; but condition and temperament have modified these. The grosser forms of immorality, together with theatre-going and dancing, are specifically denounced; nevertheless, the precepts against specific amusements are often violated by church members. The cleft between denominations is still wide, especially between Methodists and Baptists. The sermons are usually kept within the safe ground of a mild Calvinism, with much insistence on Salvation, Grace, Fallen Humanity and the like.

The chief function of these churches in morals is to conserve old standards and create about them a public opinion which shall deter the offender. And in this the Negro churches are peculiarly successful, although naturally the standards conserved are not as high as they should be.

5. The Negro churches were the birthplaces of Negro schools and of all agencies which seek to promote the intelligence of the masses; and even to-day no agency serves to disseminate news or information so quickly and effectively among Negroes as the church. The lyceum and lecture here still maintain a feeble but persistent existence, and church newspapers and books are circulated widely. Night schools and kindergartens are still held in connection with churches, and all Negro celebrities, from a bishop to a poet like Dunbar, are introduced to Negro audiences from the pulpits.

6. Consequently all movements for social betterment are apt to centre in the churches. Beneficial societies in endless number are formed here; secret societies keep in touch; co-operative and building associations have lately sprung up; the minister often acts as an employment agent; considerable charitable and relief work is done and special meetings held to aid special projects.[11] The race problem in all its phases is continually being discussed, and, indeed, from this forum many a youth goes forth inspired to work.

Such are some of the functions of the Negro church, and a study of them indicates how largely this organization has come to be an expression of the organized life of Negroes in a great city.

The Present Condition of the Churches

The 2441 families of the Seventh Ward were distributed among the various denominations, in 1896, as shown in the table on p. 36.

Probably half of the "unconnected and unknown" habitually attend church.

In the city at large the Methodists have a decided majority, followed by the Baptists, and further behind, the Episcopalians. Starting with the Methodists, we find three bodies: the African Methodist Episcopal, founded by Allen, the A. M.

Families

Methodists	842
Baptists	577
Episcopalians	156
Presbyterians	74
Catholic	69
Shakers	2
Unconnected and unknown	721
	2441

E. Zion, which sprung from a secession of Negroes from white churches in New York in the eighteenth century; and the M. E. Church, consisting of colored churches belonging to the white Methodist Church, like Zoar.

The A. M. E. Church is the largest body and had, in 1897, fourteen churches and missions in the city, with a total membership of 3210, and thirteen church edifices, seating 6117 persons. These churches collected during the year, $27,074.13. Their property is valued at $202,229 on which there is a mortgage indebtedness of $30,000 to $50,000. Detailed statistics are given in the table on the next page.

These churches are pretty well organized, and are conducted with vim and enthusiasm. This arises largely from their system. Their bishops have been in some instances men of piety and ability like the late Daniel A. Payne. In other cases they have fallen far below this standard; but they have always been men of great influence, and had a genius for leadership — else they would not have been bishops. They have large powers of appointment and removal in the case of pastors, and thus each pastor, working under the eye of an inspiring chief, strains every nerve to make his church a successful organization. The bishop is aided by several presiding elders, who are traveling inspectors and preachers, and give advice as to appointments. This system results in great unity and power; the purely spiritual aims of the church, to be sure, suffer somewhat, but after all this peculiar organism is more than a church, it is a government of men.

The headquarters of the A. M. E. Church are in Philadelphia. Their publishing house, at Seventh and Pine, publishes a weekly paper, and a quarterly review, besides some books, such as hymnals, church disciplines, short treatises, leaflets and the like. The receipts of this establishment in 1897 were $16,058.26, and its expenditures $14,119.15. Its total outfit and property is valued at $45,513.64, with an indebtedness of $14,513.64.

An episcopal residence for the bishop of the district has recently been purchased on Belmont avenue. The Philadelphia Conference disbursed from the general church funds in 1897, $985 to superannuated ministers, and $375 to widows of ministers. Two or three women missionaries visited the sick during the year and some committees of the Ladies' Mission Society worked to secure orphans' homes.[12] Thus throughout the work of this church there is much evidence of enthusiasm and persistent progress.[13]

A. M. E. Churches in Philadelphia, 1897

Name of Church	Number of Members	No. of Societies Mission-ary	No. of Societies Church Auxiliary	Parsonage	Seating Capacity	General Church Support	Local Church Expenses	Pastor's Salary	Missionary and Educational	Charity	Total Income	Value of Church Property	Indebtedness
Bethel	1,104	1	21	1	1,500	$ 924.00	$ 1,560(?)	$1,500.00	$137.45	$ 435.87	$ 4,557.32	$ 94,000.00	(?)
Murray Chapel	70	2	3		350	233.00	697.94	700.00	23.97	50.00	1,704.91	5,000.00	$ 137.00
Zion Mission	28	1	1		350	139.00	481.97	653.49	35.54	50.00	1,360.92	7,000.00	1,093.25
Germantown	19	2	2	1	450	156.87	1,685.26	1,000.00	39.83	41.18	2,913.14	14,500.00	7,400.00
Frankford	127	2	3	1	400	142.50	500(?)	600.00	39.50	15.00	1,297.00	15,000.00	1,869.46
Darby	44	1	1		300	86.65	300.07	270.00	3.12	2.26	677.00	3,329.00	203.95
Allen Chapel	578	1	4		550	312.82	750(?)	964.75	53.25	132.60	2,213.42	15,000.00	3,651.00
Disney	22	1	4		200	35.75	129.36	122.05	3.75	3.00	300.91	2,400.00	904.00
York	48	1	2		317	106.50	524.20	600.00	55.40	12.00	1,790.60	6,000.00	2,700.00
Tioga						10.33	182.42	286.05			478.80		
Payne	25		1		200	20.13	583.68	47.62	1.25	8.38	661.46	3,000.00	2,454.00
Union	674	1	5	1	1,000	502.88	2,471.81	1,400.00	53.20	135.00	4,602.89		
Mt. Pisgah	315	2	5	1	500	391.85	793.38	1,000.00	79.00	465.67	3,749.90	25,000.00	8,038.62
Morris Brown	46		2			74.75	287.58	265.62	8.93	8.88	645.86	12,000.00	7,162.00
Total	3,210	15	54	5	6,117	$3,137.03	$14,665.47	$9,398.58	$554.19	$1,358.81	$27,074.13	$202,229.00	$35,613.28

There are three churches in the city representing the A. M. E. Zion connection. They are:

Wesley	Fifteenth and Lombard Sts.
Mount Zion	Fifty-fifth above Market St.
Union	Ninth St. and Girard Ave.

No detailed statistics of these churches are available; the last two are small, the first is one of the largest and most popular in the city; the pastor receives $1500 a year and the total income of the church is between $4000 and $5000. It does considerable charitable work among its aged members, and supports a large sick and death benefit society. Its property is worth at least $25,000.

Two other Methodist churches of different denominations are: Grace U. A. M. E., Lombard street, above Fifteenth; St. Matthew Methodist Protestant, Fifty-eighth and Vine streets. Both these churches are small, although the first has a valuable piece of property.

The Methodist Episcopal Church has six organizations in the city among the Negroes; they own church property valued at $53,700, have a total membership of 1202, and an income of $16,394 in 1897. Of this total income, $1235, or 7½ per cent, was given for benevolent enterprises. These churches are quiet and well conducted, and although not among the most popular churches, have nevertheless a membership of old and respected citizens.

There were in 1896 seventeen Baptist churches in Philadelphia, holding property valued at more than $300,000, having six thousand members, and an annual income of, probably, $30,000 to $35,000. One of the largest churches has in the last five years raised between $17,000 and $18,000.

The Baptists are strong in Philadelphia, and own many large and attractive churches, such as, for instance, the Union Baptist Church, on Twelfth street; Zion Baptist, in the northern part of the city; Monumental, in West Philadelphia, and the staid and respectable Cherry Street Church. These churches as a rule have large membership. They are, however, quite different in spirit and methods from the Methodists; they lack organization, and are not so well managed as business institutions. Consequently statistics of their work are very hard to obtain, and indeed in many cases do not even exist for individual churches. On the other hand, the Baptists are peculiarly clannish and loyal to their organization, keep their pastors a long time, and thus each church gains an individuality not noticed in Methodist churches. If the pastor is a strong, upright character, his influence for good is marked. At the same time, the Baptists have in their ranks a larger percentage of illiteracy than probably any other church, and it is often possible for an inferior man to hold a large church for years and allow it to stagnate and retrograde. The Baptist policy is extreme democracy applied to church affairs, and no wonder that this often results in a pernicious dictatorship. While many of the Baptist pastors of Philadelphia are men of ability and education, the general average is below that

Colored M. E. Churches in Philadelphia, 1897

Church	Members	Salary, etc, of Pastor	Contributions to Presiding Elders and Bishops	Value of Church	Value of Parsonage	Building and Improvements during Year	Paid on Indebtedness	Present Indebtedness	Current Expenses	Benevolent Collections
Bainbridge Street	354	$1312	$151	$20,000		$190	$601	$4,433	$1274	$326
Frankford	72	720	35	1,500		15	146	130	155	87
Germantown	165	828	72	4,000			400	1,000	270	177
Haven	72	440	39	3,400		24		3,836	277	25
Waterloo Street	31	221	27	800		450	50	90	22	37
Zoar	508	1270	220	20,000	$4000	3522	2171	5,800	257	583
Total	1202	$4791	544	$49,700	$4000	$4201	$3368	$15,289	$2255	$1235

Colored Baptist Churches of Philadelphia, 1896

Church	Member-ship	Value of Property	Expended in Missions, Local and Foreign	Annual Income
Monumental	435	$ 30,000	$ 7.00	
Cherry Street	800	50,000		
Union	1,020	50,000	58.10	
St. Paul	422	25,000	1.00	
Ebenezer	189	12,000	3.36	
Macedonia	76	1,000	3.00	
Bethsaida	78			
Haddington	50			
Germantown	305	24,800		
Grace	57	2,000	5.50	
Shiloh	1,000	50,000		$3,600
Holy Trinity	287	10,000	3.00	
Second, Nicetown	164	2,000	9.73	
Zion	700	40,000		
Providence				
Cherry Street Mission				
Tabernacle				
Total	5,583	$296,800		

of the other churches — a fact due principally to the ease with which one can enter the Baptist ministry.[14] These churches support a small publishing house in the city, which issues a weekly paper. They do some charitable work, but not much.[15]

There are three Presbyterian churches in the city:

Name	Members	Value of Property	Annual Income	
Berean	98	$75,000	$1,135	Parsonage
Central	430	50,000	1,800	Parsonage
First African	105	25,000	1,538	

Central Church is the oldest of these churches and has an interesting history. It represents a withdrawal from the First African Presbyterian Church in 1844. The congregation first worshiped at Eighth and Carpenter streets, and in 1845 purchased a lot at Ninth and Lombard, where they still meet in a quiet and respectable house of worship. Their 430 members include some of the oldest and most respectable Negro families of the city. Probably if the white Presbyterians had given more encouragement to Negroes, this denomination would have absorbed the best elements of the colored population; they seem, however, to have shown some desire to be rid of the blacks, or at least not to increase their Negro membership in Philadelphia to any great extent. Central Church is more nearly a simple religious organization than most churches; it listens to able sermons, but does little outside its own doors.[16]

Berean Church is the work of one man and is an institutional church. It was formerly a mission of Central Church and now owns a fine piece of property bought by donations contributed by whites and Negroes, but chiefly by the former. The conception of the work and its carrying out, however, is due to Negroes. This church conducts a successful Building and Loan Association, a kindergarten, a medical dispensary and a seaside home, beside the numerous church societies. Probably no church in the city, except the Episcopal Church of the Crucifixion, is doing so much for the social betterment of the Negro.[17] The First African is the oldest colored church of this denomination in the city.

The Episcopal Church has, for Negro congregations, two independent churches, two churches dependent on white parishes, and four missions and Sunday-schools. Statistics of three of these are given in the table on page 42.

The Episcopal churches receive more outside help than others and also do more general mission and rescue work. They hold $150,000 worth of property, have 900–1000 members and an annual income of $7000 to $8000. They represent all grades of the colored population. The oldest of the churches is St. Thomas'. Next comes the Church of the Crucifixion, over fifty years old and perhaps the most effective church organization in the city for benevolent and rescue work. It has been built up virtually by one Negro, a man of sincerity and culture, and of peculiar energy. This church carries on regular church work at Bainbridge and Eighth and at two branch missions; it helps in the Fresh Air Fund, has an ice mission, a vacation school of thirty-five children, and a parish visitor. It makes an especial feature of good music with its vested choir. One or two courses of University Extension lectures are held here each year, and there is a large beneficial and insurance society in active operation, and a Home for the Homeless on Lombard street. This church especially reaches after a class of neglected poor whom the other colored churches shun or forget and for whom there is little fellowship in white churches. The rector says of this work:

As I look back over nearly twenty years of labor in one parish, I see a great deal to be devoutly thankful for. Here are people struggling from the beginning of one year to another, without ever having what can be called the necessaries of life. God alone knows what a real struggle life is to them. Many of them must always be "moving on," because they cannot pay the rent or meet other obligations.

I have just visited a family of four, mother and three children. The mother is too sick to work. The eldest girl will work when she can find something to do. But the rent is due, and there is not a cent in the house. This is but a sample. How can such people support a church of their own? To many such, religion often becomes doubly comforting. They seize eagerly on the promises of a life where these earthly distresses will be forever absent.

If the other half only knew how this half is living — how hard and dreary, and often hopeless, life is — the members of the more favored half would gladly help to do all they could to have the gospel freely preached to those whose lives are so devoid of earthly comforts.

Twenty or thirty thousand dollars (and that is not much), safely invested, would enable the parish to do a work that ought to be done and yet is not being

Colored Protestant Episcopal Churches in Philadelphia,* 1897

	Church	Members	Rectors and Assistants	Church Societies	Offerings of Church		Total Income	Expenditures							Value Real and Personal Estate	Encumbrances	Endowment
					For Parish	Purposes outside of Parish		Salary of Rector	Current Expense	Poor	Total Parochial Expenses	Diocesan	General Missions, etc.	Total Expense			
Independent	Crucifixion and One Mission	310	2	9	$437.58	$879.40	$2995.93	$1200	$2477.98	$73	$2632.98	$35.00	$101.37	$2769.35	$45,000		$11,000
	St. Thomas	391	1	9	1457.90	10.00	2347.53	760	2008.00	70	2475.81			2582.98	60,000	$5388.73	
	St. Michael and All Angels	90	1	9	227.08	6.67	1270.79	760	1381.89	70	1411.89	6.50		1420.56	25,000	1200.00	

* Besides these, there are the following churches, from which statistics were not obtained: St. Mark's, Zion Sunday-school, St. Faith's Mission, and St. Simon's Chapel. The first is supported mainly by a white parish, and has a new building; the second and third are small Missions; the fourth is a promising out-growth of the Church of the Crucifixion.

done at present. The poor could then have the gospel preached to them in a way that it is not now being preached.

The Catholic church has in the last decade made great progress in its work among Negroes and is determined to do much in the future. Its chief hold upon the colored people is its comparative lack of discrimination. There is one Catholic church in the city designed especially for Negro work — St. Peter Clavers at Twelfth and Lombard — formerly a Presbyterian church; recently a parish house has been added. The priest in charge estimates that 400 or 500 Negroes regularly attend Catholic churches in various parts of the city. The Mary Drexel Home for Colored Orphans is a Catholic institution near the city which is doing much work. The Catholic church can do more than any other agency in humanizing the intense prejudice of many of the working-class against the Negro, and signs of this influence are manifest in some quarters.

We have thus somewhat in detail reviewed the work of the chief churches. There are beside these continually springing up and dying a host of little noisy missions which represent the older and more demonstrative worship. A description of one applies to nearly all; take for instance one in the slums of the Fifth Ward:

The tablet in the gable of this little church bears the date 1837. For sixty years it has stood and done its work in the narrow lane. What its history has been all this time it is difficult to find out, for no records are on hand, and no one is here to tell the tale.

The few last months of the old order was something like this: It was in the hands of a Negro congregation. Several visits were paid to the church, and generally a dozen people were found there. After a discourse by a very illiterate preacher, hymns were sung, having many repetitions of senseless sentiment and exciting cadences. It took about an hour to work up the congregation to a fervor aimed at. When this was reached a remarkable scene presented itself. The whole congregation pressed forward to an open space before the pulpit, and formed a ring. The most excitable of their number entered the ring, and with clapping of hands and contortions led the devotions. Those forming the ring joined in the clapping of hands and wild and loud singing, frequently springing into the air, and shouting loudly. As the devotions proceeded, most of the worshipers took off their coats and vests and hung them on pegs on the wall. This continued for hours, until all were completely exhausted, and some had fainted and been stowed away on benches or the pulpit platform. This was the order of things at the close of sixty years' history. . . . When this congregation vacated the church, they did so stealthily, under cover of darkness, removed furniture not their own, including the pulpit, and left bills unpaid.[18]

There are dozens of such little missions in various parts of Philadelphia, led by wandering preachers. They are survivals of the methods of worship in Africa and the West Indies. In some of the larger churches noise and excitement attend the services, especially at the time of revival or in prayer meetings. For the most part, however, these customs are dying away.

To recapitulate, we have in Philadelphia fifty-five Negro churches with 12,845 members owning $907,729 worth of property with an annual income of at least $94,968. And these represent the organized efforts of the race better than any other organizations. Second to them however come the secret and benevolent societies, which we now consider.

Secret and Beneficial Societies, and Co-operative Business

The art of organization is the one hardest for the freedman to learn, and the Negro shows his greatest deficiency here; whatever success he has had has been shown most conspicuously in his church organizations, where the religious bond greatly facilitated union. In other organizations where the bond was weaker his success has been less. From early times the precarious economic condition of the free Negroes led to many mutual aid organizations. They were very simple in form: an initiation fee of small amount was required, and small regular payments; in case of sickness, a weekly stipend was paid, and in case of death the members were assessed to pay for the funeral and help the widow. Confined to a few members, all personally known to each other, such societies were successful from the beginning. We hear of them in the eighteenth century, and by 1838 there were 100 such small groups, with 7448 members, in the city. They paid in $18,851, gave $14,172 in benefits and had $10,023 on hand. Ten years later about eight thousand members belonged to 106 such societies. Seventy-six of these had a total membership of 5187. They contributed usually 25 cents to 37½ cents a month; the sick received $1.50 to $3.00 a week, and death benefits of $10.00 to $20.00 were allowed. The income of these seventy-six societies was $16,814.23; 681 families were assisted.[19]

These societies have since been superseded to some extent by other organizations; they are still so numerous, however, that it is impractical to catalogue all of them; there are probably several hundred of various kinds in the city.

To these were early added the secret societies, which naturally had great attraction for Negroes. A Boston lodge of black Masons received a charter direct from England, and independednt orders of Odd Fellows, Knights of Pythias, etc., grew up. During the time that Negroes were shut out of the public libraries there were many literary associations with libraries. These have now disappeared. Outside the churches the most important organizations among Negroes to-day are: Secret societies, beneficial societies, insurance societies, cemeteries, building and loan associations, labor unions, homes of various sorts and political clubs. The most powerful and flourishing secret order is that of the Odd Fellows, which has two hundred thousand members among American Negroes. In Philadelphia there are 19 lodges with a total membership of 1188, and $46,000 worth of property. Detailed statistics are in the next table.[20]

This order owns two halls in the city worth perhaps $40,000. One is occupied by the officers of the Grand Lodge, which employs several salaried officials and clerks. The order conducts a newspaper called the *Odd Fellows' Journal*.

There are 19 lodges of Masons in the city, 6 chapters, 5 commanderies, 3 of the Scottish Rite, and 1 drill corp. The Masons are not so well organized and conducted as the Odd Fellows, and detailed statistics of their lodges are not available. They own two halls worth at least $50,000, and probably distribute not less than $3000 to $4000 annually in benefits.

Besides these chief secret orders there are numerous others, such as the American Protestant Association, which has many members, the Knights of Pythias, the Galilean Fisherman, the various female orders attached to these, and a number of others. It is almost impossible to get accurate statistics of all these orders, and any estimate of their economic activity is liable to considerable error. However, from general observation and the available figures, it seems fairly certain that at least four thousand Negroes belong to secret orders, and that these orders annually collect at least $25,000, part of which is paid out in sick and death benefits, and part invested. The real estate, personal property and funds of these orders amount to no less that $125,000.

The function of the secret society is partly social intercourse and partly insurance. They furnish pastime from the monotony of work, a field for ambition and intrigue, a chance for parade, and insurance against misfortune. Next to the church they are the most popular organizations among Negroes.

Of the beneficial societies we have already spoken in general. A detailed account of a few of the larger and more typical organizations will now suffice. The Quaker City Association is a sick and death benefit society, seven years old, which confines its membership to native Philadelphians. It has 280 members and distributes $1400 to $1500 annually. The Sons and Daughters of Delaware is over fifty years old. It has 106 members, and owns $3000 worth of real estate. The Fraternal Association was founded in 1861; it has 86 members, and distributes about $300 a year. It "was formed for the purpose of relieving the wants and distresses of each other in time of affliction and death, and for the furtherance of such benevolent views and objects as would tend to establish and maintain a permanent and friendly intercourse among them in their social relations in life." The Sons of St. Thomas was founded in 1823 and was originally confined to members of St. Thomas Church. It was formerly a large organization, but now has 80 members, and paid out in 1896, $416 in relief. It has $1500 invested in government bonds. In addition to these there is the Old Men's Association, the Female Cox Association, the Sons and Daughters of Moses, and a large number of other small societies.

There is arising also a considerable number of insurance societies, differing from the beneficial in being conducted by directors. The best of these are the

Colored Odd Fellows' Lodges in Philadelphia, 1896

Name	Organized	Members	Sick Benefit to Members	Death Benefit	Widows Relieved	Widows Buried	Orphans Buried	Amount Paid for Sick	Amount Paid for Funerals	Amount Paid Widows	Amount Paid in Charity	Whole Amount Paid Out	Amount Invested	Value of Property	Balance in Fund	Total Property, Funds, etc.
Unity	1844	121	3		2			$ 291.85	$ 25.00	$ 6.80	$ 10.00	$ 627.07	$ 763.75	$ 660.00	$ 42.97	$ 2547.61
Good Samaritan	1864	80	3	1				104.00	85.00			307.96	712.99	113.85	18.66	845.50
Fraternal	1864	88	7					84.00			28.36	249.42	452.50	250.00	820.84	1,522.34
Phoenix	1846	98	5					98.50	121.00			419.65	1420.30	100.00	163.11	1,620.30
Covenant	1847	77						214.00	160.00	7.50	5.00	547.50	450.00	550.00	86.00	1,036.50
Friendship	1847	24		1				43.50			6.00	98.93		200.00	5.00	205.00
Carthagenian	1848	113	15					272.00	70.00	5.00		798.19	2362.50	583.65	2281.25	5,227.40
Mt. Olive	1848	70	7	1				109.00			16.00	383.51	62.50	600.00	587.39	1,633.40
Good Hope	1855	46	4	1	1			36.00	10.00	15.00	12.00	348.44	248.00	1,500.00	60.72	1,809.82
Mt. Lebanon	1857	36	3	1	1	3	2	22.20	149.50	10.00		245.32	50.00	50.00	50.00	150.00
Equity	1867	173	6		1		1	134.55	175.00	25.00		415.99	200.00	20,000.00	100.00	28,300.00
St. Albans	1875	31	1					6.20	30.00			78.95		2,500.00	25.00	275.00
Keystone	1873	15	2						20.00						4.00	4.00
Gideon	1875	17	2	1	1			56.00	40.00	4.00	10.00	144.00		50.00	10.00	60.00
Beth Eden	1876	31	5	1	1			54.00	13.00	8.00	3.50	133.05		75.00	20.00	95.00
Philadelphia	1886	36	2		1			32.00	40.00	10.00		181.06		350.00	5.24	355.24
Pennsylvania	1889															
John Rhodes	1891	15									10.00	15.00	10.00	33.00	40.00	40.00
Quaker City	1892	96	10					220.18	20.00	5.00		417.00			67.00	100.00
Total		1167	75	7	8	3	3	$1777.98	$958.50	$96.30	$100.86	$5381.04	$6732.54	$27,615.50	$4387.18	$45,827.11

Crucifixion, connected with the Church of the Crucifixion, and the Avery, connected with Wesley A. M. E. Z. Church; both have a large membership and are well conducted. Nearly every church is beginning to organize one or more such societies, some of which in times past have met disaster by bad management. The True Reformers of Virginia, the most remarkable Negro beneficial organization yet started, has several branches here. Beside these there are numberless minor societies, as the Alpha Relief, Knights and Ladies of St. Paul, the National Co-operative Society, Colored Women's Protective Association, Loyal Beneficial, etc. Some of these are honest efforts and some are swindling imitations of the pernicious white petty insurance societies.

There are three building and loan associations conducted by Negroes. Some of the directors in one are white, all the others are colored. The oldest association is the Century, established October 26, 1886. Its board of directors is composed of teachers, upholsterers, clerks, restaurant keepers and undertakers, and it has had marked success. Its income for 1897 was about $7000. It has $25,000 in loans outstanding.

The Berean Building and Loan Association was established in 1888 in connection with Berean Presbyterian Church; 13 of the 19 officers and directors are colored. Its income for 1896 was nearly $30,000, and it had $60,000 in loans; 43 homes have been bought through this association.[21]

The Pioneer Association is composed entirely of Negroes, the directors being caterers, merchants and upholsterers. It was founded in 1888 and has an office on Pine street. Its receipts in 1897 were $9000, and it had about $20,000 in loans. Nine homes are at present being bought in this association.

There are arising some loan associations to replace the pawn-shops and usurers to some extent. The Small Loan Association, for instance, was founded in 1891, and has the following report for 1898:

Shares sold	$1144.00
Assessments on shares	114.40
Repaid loans	4537.50
Interest	417.06
Cash in treasury	275.54
Dividends paid	222.67
Loans made	4626.75
Expenses	82.02

The Conservative is a similar organization, consisting of ten members.

This account has attempted to touch only the chief and characteristic organizations, and makes no pretensions to completeness. It shows, however, how intimately bound together the Negroes of Philadelphia are. These associations are largely experiments, and as such, are continually reaching out to new fields. The latest ventures are toward labor unions, co-operative stores and newspapers. There are the following labor unions, among others: The Caterers' Club, the Private Waiters' Association, the Coachmen's Association, the Hotel Brotherhood (of waiters), the

Cigar-makers' Union (white and colored), the Hod-Carriers' Union, the Barbers' Union, etc.

Of the Caterers' Club we have already heard.[22] The Private Waiters' Association is an old beneficial order with well-to-do members. The private waiter is really a skilled workman of high order, and used to be well paid. Next to the guild of caterers he ranked as high as any class of Negro workmen before the war — indeed the caterer was but a private waiter further developed. Consequently this labor union is still jealous and exclusive and contains some members long retired from active work. The Coachmen's Association is a similar society; both these organizations have a considerable membership, and make sick and death benefits and social gatherings a feature. The Hotel Brotherhood is a new society of hotel waiters and is conducted by young men on the lines of the regular trades unions, with which it is more or less affiliated in many cities. It has some relief features and considerable social life. It strives to open and keep open work for colored waiters and often arranges to divide territory with whites, or to prevent one set from supplanting the other. The Cigar-makers' Union is a regular trades union with both white and Negro members. It is the only union in Philadelphia where Negroes are largely represented. No friction is apparent. The Hod-Carriers' Union is large and of considerable age but does not seem to be very active. A League of Colored Mechanics was formed in 1897 but did not accomplish anything. There was before the war a league of this sort which flourished, and there undoubtedly will be attempts of this sort in the future until a union is effected.[23]

The two co-operative grocery stores, and the caterers' supply store have been mentioned.[24] There was a dubious attempt in 1896 to organize a co-operative tinware store which has not yet been successful.[25]

With all this effort and movement it is natural that the Negroes should want some means of communication. This they have in the following periodicals conducted wholly by Negroes:

A. M. E. Church *Review,* quarterly, 8vo, about ninety-five pages.
Christian Recorder, eight page weekly newspaper. (Both these are organs of the A. M. E. Church.)
Baptist *Christian Banner,* four page weekly newspaper. (Organ of the Baptists.)
Odd Fellows' *Journal,* eight page weekly newspaper. (Organ of Odd Fellows.)
Weekly *Tribune,* eight page weekly newspaper, seventeen years established.
The *Astonisher,* eight page weekly newspaper (Germantown).
The *Standard-Echo,* four page weekly newspaper (since suspended).

The *Tribune* is the chief news sheet and is filled generally with social notes of all kinds, and news of movements among Negroes over the country. Its editorials are usually of little value chiefly because it does not employ a responsible editor. It is in many ways however an interesting paper and represents pluck and perseverance on the part of its publisher. The *Astonisher* and *Standard Echo* are news sheets.

The first is bright but crude. The *Recorder, Banner* and *Journal* are chiefly filled with columns of heavy church and lodge news. The *Review* has had an interesting history and is probably the best Negro periodical of the sort published; it is often weighted down by the requirements of church politics, and compelled to publish some trash written by aspiring candidates for office; but with all this it has much solid matter and indicates the trend of thought among Negroes to some extent. It has greatly improved in the last few years. Many Negro newspapers from other cities circulate here and widen the feeling of the community among the colored people of the city.

One other kind of organization has not yet been mentioned, the political clubs, of which there are probably fifty in the city. They will be considered in another chapter.

Institutions

The chief Negro institutions of the city are: The Home for Aged and Infirmed Colored Persons, the Douglass Hospital and Training School, the Woman's Exchange and Girls' Home, three cemetery companies, the Home for the Homeless, the special schools, as the Institute for Colored Youth, the House of Industry, Raspberry street schools and Jones' school for girls, the Y. M. C. A., and University Extension Centre.

The Home for the Aged, situated at the corner of Girard and Belmont avenues, was founded by a Negro lumber merchant, Steven Smith, and is conducted by whites and Negroes. It is one of the best institutions of the kind; its property is valued at $400,000, and it has an annual income of $20,000. It has sheltered 558 old people since its foundation in 1864.

The Douglass Memorial Hospital and Training School is a curious example of the difficult position of Negroes: for years nearly every hospital in Philadelphia has sought to exclude Negro women from the course in nurse-training, and no Negro physician could have the advantage of hospital practice. This led to a movement for a Negro hospital; such a movement however was condemned by the whites as an unnecessary addition to a bewildering number of charitable institutions; by many of the best Negroes as a concession to prejudice and a drawing of the color line. Nevertheless the promoters insisted that colored nurses were efficient and needed training, that colored physicians needed a hospital, and that colored patients wished one. Consequently the Douglass Hospital has been established and its success seems to warrant the effort.[26]

The total income for the year 1895–96 was $4,656.31; sixty-one patients were treated during the year, and thirty-two operations performed; 987 out-patients were treated. The first class of nurses was graduated in 1897.

The Woman's Exchange and Girls' Home is conducted by the principal of the Institute for Colored Youth at 756 South Twelfth street. The exchange is open at stated times during the week, and various articles are on sale. Cheap lodging and board is furnished for a few school girls and working girls. So far the work of the exchange has been limited but it is slowly growing, and is certainly a most deserving venture.[27]

The exclusion of Negroes from cemeteries has, as before mentioned, led to the organization of three cemetery companies, two of which are nearly fifty years old. The Olive holds eight acres of property in the Twenty-fourth Ward, claimed to be worth $100,000. It has 900 lot owners; the Lebanon holds land in the Thirty-sixth Ward, worth at least $75,000. The Merion is a new company which owns twenty-one acres in Montgomery County, worth perhaps $30,000. These companies are in the main well-conducted, although the affairs of one are just now somewhat entangled.

The Home for the Homeless is a refuge and home for the aged connected with the Church of the Crucifixion. It is supported largely by whites but not entirely. It has an income of about $500. During 1896, 1108 lodgings were furnished to ninety women, 8384 meals given to inmates, 2705 to temporary lodgers, 2078 to transients, and 812 to invalids.

The schools have all been mentioned before. The Young Men's Christian Association has had a checkered history, chiefly as it would seem from the wrong policy pursued; there is in the city a grave and dangerous lack of proper places of amusement and recreation for young men. To fill this need a properly conducted Young Men's Christian Association, with books and newspapers, baths, bowling alleys and billiard tables, conversation rooms and short interesting religious services is demanded; it would cost far less than it now costs the courts to punish the petty misdemeanors of young men who do not know how to amuse themselves. Instead of such an institution however the Colored Y. M. C. A. has been virtually an attempt to add another church to the numberless colored churches of the city, with endless prayer-meetings and loud gospel hymns, in dingy and uninviting quarters. Consequently the institution is now temporarily suspended. It had accomplished some good work by its night schools, and social meetings.

Since the organization of the Bainbridge Street University Extension Centre, May 10, 1895, lectures have been delivered at the Church of the Crucifixion, Eighth and Bainbridge streets, by Rev. W. Hudson Shaw, on English History; by Thomas Whitney Surette, on the Development of Music; by Henry W. Elson, on American History, and by Hilaire Belloc, on Napoleon. Each of these lecturers, except Mr. Belloc, has given a course of six lectures on the subject stated, and classes have been held in connection with each course. The attendance has been above the average as compared with other Centres in the city.

Beside these efforts there are various embryonic institutions: A day nursery in the Seventh Ward by the Woman's Missionary Society, a large organization which does much charitable work; an industrial school near the city, etc. There are, too, many institutions conducted by whites for the benefit of Negroes, which will be mentioned in another place.

Much of the need for separate Negro institutions has in the last decade disappeared, by reason of the opening of the doors of the public institutions to colored people. There are many Negroes who on this account strongly oppose efforts which they fear will tend to delay further progress in these lines. On the other hand, thoughtful men see that invaluable training and discipline is coming to the race through these institutions and organizations, and they encourage the formation of them.

The Experiment of Organization

Looking back over the field which we have thus reviewed — the churches, societies, unions, attempts at business co-operation, institutions and newspapers — it is apparent that the largest hope for the ultimate rise of the Negro lies in this mastery of the art of social organized life. To be sure, compared with his neighbors, he has as yet advanced but a short distance; we are apt to condemn this lack of unity, the absence of carefully planned and laboriously executed effort among these people, as a voluntary omission — a bit of carelessness. It is far more than this, it is lack of social education, of group training, and the lack can only be supplied by a long, slow process of growth. And the chief value of the organizations studied is that they are evidences of growth. Of actual accomplishment they have, to be sure, something to show, but nothing to boast of inordinately. The churches are far from ideal associations for fostering the higher life — rather they combine too often intrigue, extravagance and show, with all their work, saving and charity; their secret societies are often diverted from their better ends by scheming and dishonest officers, and by the temptation of tinsel and braggadocio; their beneficial associations, along with all their good work, have an unenviable record of business inefficiency and internal dissension. And yet all these and the other agencies have accomplished much, and their greatest accomplishment is stimulation of effort to further and more effective organization among a disorganized and headless host. All this world of co-operation and subordination into which the white child is in most cases born is, we must not forget, new to the slave's sons. They have been compelled to organize before they knew the meaning of organization; to co-operate with those of their fellows to whom co-operation was an unknown term; to fix and fasten ideas of leadership and authority among those who had always looked to others for guidance and command. For these reasons the present efforts of Negroes in working together along various lines are peculiarly promising for the future of both races.

Notes

[1] St. Thomas, Bethel and Zoar. The history of Zoar is of interest. It "extends over a period of one hundred years, being as it is an offspring of St. George's Church, Fourth and Vine streets, the first Methodist Episcopal church to be established in this country, and in whose edifice the first American Conference of that denomination was held. Zoar Church had its origin in 1794, when members of St. George's Church established a mission in what was then known as Campingtown, now known as Fourth and Brown streets, at which place its first chapel was built. There it remained until 1883, when economic and sociological causes made necessary the selection of a new site. The city had grown, and industries of a character in which the Negroes were not interested had developed in the neighborhood, and, as the colored people were rapidly moving to a different section of the city, it was decided that the church should follow, and the old building was sold. Through the liberality of Colonel Joseph M. Bennett a brick building was erected on Melon street, above Twelfth.

"Since then the congregation has steadily increased in numbers, until in August of this year it was found necessary to enlarge the edifice. The corner stone of the new front was laid two months ago. The present membership of the church is about 550." — *Public Ledger,* November 15, 1897.

[2] See Douglass' "Annals of St. Thomas'."

[3] It was then turned into a private school and supported largely by an English educational fund.

[4] St. Thomas' has suffered often among Negroes from the opprobrium of being "aristocratic," and is to-day by no means a popular church among the masses. Perhaps there is some justice in this charge, but the church has nevertheless always been foremost in good work and has many public spirited Negroes on its rolls.

[5] Cf. U.S. Census, Statistics of Churches, 1890.

[6] In 1809 the leading Negro churches formed a "Society for Suppressing Vice and Immorality," which received the endorsement of Chief Justice Tilghman, Benjamin Franklin, Jacob Rush, and others.

[7] "Condition of Negroes, 1838," pp. 39–40.

[8] Cf. Robert Jones' "Fifty Years in Central Church." John Gloucester began preaching in 1807 at Seventh and Bainbridge.

[9] In 1847 there were 19 churches; 12 of these had 3974 members; 11 of the edifices cost $67,000. "Statistical Inquiry," 1848, pp. 29, 30.

In 1854 there were 19 churches reported and 1677 Sunday-school scholars. Bacon, 1856.

[10] See Inquiry of 1867.

[11] Cf. Publications of Atlanta University No. 3, "Efforts of American Negroes for Social Betterment."

[12] An account of the present state of the A. M. E. Church from its own lips is interesting, in spite of its somewhat turgid rhetoric. The following is taken from the minutes of Philadelphia Conference, 1897:

Report on State of the Church
"To the Bishop and Conference: We your Committee on State of the Church beg leave to submit the following:

"Every truly devoted African Methodist is intensely interested in the condition of the church that was handed down to us as a precious heirloom from the hands of a God-fearing, self-sacrificing ancestry; the church that Allen planted in Philadelphia, a little over a century ago has enjoyed a marvelous development. Its grand march through the procession of a hundred years has been characterized by a series of brilliant successes, completely refuting the foul calumnies cast against it and overcoming every obstacle that endeavored to impede its onward march, giving the strongest evidence that God was in the midst of her; she should not be moved.

"From the humble beginnings in the little blacksmith shop, at Sixth and Lombard streets, Philadelphia, the Connection has grown until we have now fifty-five annual conferences, beside mission fields, with over four thousand churches, the same number of itinerant preachers, near six hundred thousand communicants, one and a half million adherents, with six regularly organized and well-manned departments, each doing a magnificent work along special lines, the whole under the immediate supervision of eleven bishops, each with a marked individuality and all laboring together for the further development and perpetuity of the church. In this the Mother Conference of the Connection, we have every reason to be grateful to Almighty God for the signal blessings He has so graciously poured out upon us. The spiritual benedictions have been many. In response to earnest effort and faithful prayers by both pastors and congregations, nearly two thousand persons have professed faith in Christ, during this conference year. Five thousand dollars have been given by the membership and friends of the Connectional interests to carry on the machinery of the church, besides liberal contributions for the cause of missions, education, the Sunday-school Union and Church Extension Departments, and beside all this, the presiding elder and pastors have been made to feel that the people are perfectly willing to do what they can to maintain the preaching of the word, that tends to elevate mankind and glorify God.

"The local interests have not been neglected; new churches have been built, parsonages erected, church mortgages have been reduced, auxiliary societies to give everybody in the church a chance to work for God and humanity, have been more extensively organized than ever before.

"The danger signal that we see here and there cropping out, which is calculated to bring discredit upon the Church of Christ, is the unholy ambition for place and power. The means ofttimes used to bring about the desired results, cause the blush of shame to tinge the brow of Christian manhood. God always has and always will select those He designs to use as the leaders of his Church.

"Political methods that are in too many instances resorted to, are contrary to the teaching and spirit of the Gospel of Christ. Fitness and sobriety will always be found in the lead.

"Through mistaken sympathy we find that several incompetent men have found their way into the ministerial ranks; men who can neither manage the financial nor spiritual interests of any church or bring success along any line, who are continuously on the wing from one conference to the other. The time has come when the strictest scrutiny must be exercised as to purpose and fitness of candidates, and if admitted and found to be continuous failures, Christian charity demands that they be given an opportunity to seek a calling where they can make more success than in the ministry. These danger signals that flash up now and then must be observed and everything contrary to the teachings of God's word and the spirit of the discipline weeded out. The church owes a debt of gratitude to the fathers who have always remained loyal and true; who labored persistently and well for the upbuilding of the connection, that they can never repay.

"Particular care should be taken that no honorable aged minister of our great Church should be allowed to suffer for the necessaries of life. We especially commend to the consideration of every minister the Ministers' Aid Association, which is now almost ready to be organized, the object of which is to help assuage the grief and dry the tears of those who have been left widowed and fatherless.

"Our Publication Department is making heroic efforts for the larger circulation of our denominational papers and literature generally. These efforts ought to be, and must needs be heartily seconded by the Church. Lord Bacon says: 'Talking makes a ready man, writing an exact man, but reading makes a full man.' We want our people at large to be brim-ful of information relative to the growth of the church, the progress of the race, the upbuilding of humanity and the glory of God.

"Our missionary work must not be allowed to retrograde. The banner that Allen raised must not be allowed to trail, but must go forward until the swarthy sons of Ham everywhere shall gaze with a longing and loving look upon the escutcheon that has emblazoned on it, as its motto: 'The Fatherhood of God and the Brotherhood of man,' and the glorious truth flashing over the whole world that Jesus Christ died to redeem the universal family of mankind. Disasters and misfortunes may come to us, but strong men never quail before adversities. The clouds of to-day may be succeeded by the sunshine of to-morrow."

[13] Cf., *e. g.*, the account of the founding of new missions in the minutes of the Philadelphia Conference, 1896.

[14] Baptists themselves recognize this. One of the speakers in a recent association meeting, as reported by the press, "deprecated the spirit shown by some churches in spreading their differences to their detriment as church members, and in the eyes of their white brethren; and he recommended that unworthy brethren from other States, who sought an asylum of rest here, be not admitted to local pulpits except in cases where the ministers so applying are personally known or vouched for by a resident pastor. The custom of recognizing as preachers men incapable of doing good work in the pulpit, who were ordained in the South after they had failed in the North, was also condemned, and the President declared that the times demand a ministry that is able to preach. The practice of licensing incapable brethren for the ministry, simply to please them, was also looked upon with disfavor, and it was recommended that applicants for ordination be required to show at least ability to read intelligently the Word of God or a hymn."

[15] One movement deserves notice — the Woman's Auxiliary Society. It consists of five circles, representing a like number of colored Baptist churches in this city, viz., the Cherry Street, Holy Trinity, Union, Nicetown and Germantown, and does general missionary work.

[16] See Jones' "Fifty Years in Central Street Church," etc. The system and order in this church is remarkable. Each year a careful printed report of receipts and expenditures is made. The following is an abstract of the report for 1891:

Receipts

Finance Committee	$ 977.39
Pew Rents	709.75
Legacy	760.77
Other Receipts	329.54
	$2777.45

Expenditures

Pastor's Salary	$1000.00
Other Salaries	476.00
Repayment of Loan	409.00
Interest on Mortgage	60.96
Donations to General Church	31.57
General Expenses, etc.	759.23
	$2736.76
Balance	$ 40.69

[17] For history and detailed account of this work see Anderson's "Presbyterianism and the Negro," Phila., 1897.

[18] Rev. Charles Daniel, in the *Nazarene*. The writer hardly does justice to the weird witchery of those hymns sung thus rudely.

[19] Cf. report of inquiries in above years.

[20] From Report of Fourth Annual Meeting of the District Grand Lodge of Pennsylvania, G. U. of O. F., 1896.

[21] This association has issued a valuable little pamphlet called "Helpful Hints on Home," which it distributes. This explains the object and methods of building and loan associations.

[22] See *supra*, p. 119 ff.

[23] The College Settlement was interested in this organization, but the movement was evidently premature.

[24] See *supra*, p. 117 and p. 119.

[25] An interesting advertisement of this venture is appended; it is a curious mixture of business, exhortation and simplicity. The present state of the enterprise is not known:

"NOTICE TO ALL.
"WE CALL YOUR ATTENTION
"TO THIS WORK.
"THE UNION TIN-WARE MANUFACTURING CO.

"Is now at work, chartered under the laws of the States of New Jersey and Pennsylvania.

"The purpose of said Company is to manufacture everything in the TIN-WARE LINE that the law allows, and to sell stock all over the United States of America; and put in members enough in every city to open a Union Tin-Ware Store, and if the promoter finds that he has not enough members in a city to open a Tin-Ware Store, then he shall open it with money from the factory. SHARES are $10.00, they can be paid on installment plan; and you do not have any monthly dues to pay, but on the 20th of every December or whenever the Stockholders appoint the time, the dividend shall be declared.

"We will make this one of the grandest organizations ever witnessed by the Race, if you lend us your aid. This Store will contain Groceries, Dry Goods and Tin-Ware, and you can do your dealing at your own store. This factory will give you work, and learn you a trade."

[26] Since the opening of the hospital colored nurses have had less trouble in white institutions, and one colored physician has been appointed intern in a large hospital. Dr. N. F. Mossell was chiefly instrumental in founding the Douglass Hospital.

[27] In connection with this work, Bethel Church often holds small receptions for servant girls on their days off, when refreshments are served and a pleasant time is spent. The following is a note of similar enterprise at another church: "The members of the Berean Union have opened a 'Y' parlor, where young colored girls employed as domestics can spend their Thursday afternoon both pleasantly and profitably. The parlor is open from 4 until 10 p.m., every Thursday, and members of the Union are present to welcome them. A light supper is served for ten cents. The evening is spent in literary exercises and social talk. The parlor is in the Berean Church, South College avenue, near Twentieth street."

Conditions among Negroes in the Cities

George E. Haynes

Fifty years after four millions of Negro slaves were made freedmen, there is still the responsibility upon the nation to make that seeming freedom really free. So many other national problems thrust themselves upon the attention of the people today that there is danger lest the nation grow forgetful of the tremendous portent of this special responsibility left it from the past. The present generation is doubtless just as loyal to the principles of liberty and just as faithful to the ideals of democracy as were the fathers of the republic, but the principles and ideals of the American people are meeting the challenge of latter day problems, and the people may become unmindful of unfinished tasks. Thus the condition of the Negro may receive less attention from the nation; his economic and social difficulties may be less generally known; his migrations and concentration in cities, North and South, are given less attention. The increasing segregated settlements and life of Negroes within the cities may excite less concern. The resulting intensified industrial, housing, health and other maladjustments and the Negro's heroic struggles to overcome these maladjustments are in these days likely to be little considered. These conditions demand thought.

1. The Urban Movement

But social changes do not frequently keep time with social thought, for they are usually the result of unconscious social forces. Many of the changes among Negroes, especially the change from country to city, have been of such a character.

The past half century has seen an acceleration of the urban migration of the entire population. The Negro has been in that population stream. At times and in

George E. Haynes, "Conditions among Negroes in the Cities," *Annals of the American Academy of Political and Social Science,* XLIX, 1913, pp. 105–119. Reprinted by permission of the publisher.

places his movement cityward has been affected by special influences, but where influences have been similar his movement has been similar.

The Emancipation Proclamation not only abolished the ownership of the slave, but it also released him from the soil. With this breaking down of the economic system based upon slavery, many of the landless freedmen fell victims to the *wanderlust* which has usually affected the masses in times of sudden social upheaval. Thousands of Negroes flocked to the Union Army posts, located in towns and cities. The Ku-Klux terrorism and the mistaken notion of federal paternalistic care added their power to the other forces which operated, during and immediately after the war, to thrust the Negro into the towns. In fourteen Southern cities between 1860 and 1870 the white population increased 16.7 per cent, and the Negro 90.7 per cent; in eight Northern cities (counting all the boroughs of New York City as now constituted as one) the Negro population increased 51 per cent.

But with the removal of exceptional influences, the Negro immigration was reduced. Figures for white and Negro population in principal Southern cities are obtainable from 1870 to 1910, as follows:

```
1870 to 1880 the whites increased 20.3 per cent, Negroes 25.5 per cent
1880 to 1890 the whites increased 35.7 per cent, Negroes 38.7 per cent
1890 to 1900 the whites increased 20.8 per cent, Negroes 20.6 per cent
1900 to 1910 the whites increased 27.7 per cent, Negroes 20.6 per cent
```

Just how far the increase of whites and Negroes in Southern cities has been proportionately affected by the drift to Northern cities from Southern territory cannot be ascertained, as the numbers of Southern whites who migrate North are unknown. Surmises may be made from the per cent increase of Negroes in eight Northern cities, which was as follows:

```
1870 to 1880                      36.4 per cent
1880 to 1890                      32.3 per cent
1890 to 1900                      59.2 per cent
```

The increase of the urban population, both white and Negro was greater than the rural increase between 1890 and 1900 (the best periods for which we have figures for good comparisons) for both the Continental United States and for the Southern States. In 242 Southern towns and cities which had at least 2500 inhabitants in 1890, the Negroes increased, 1890 to 1900, nearly one-third faster than Negroes in the rural districts. "In the country districts of the South the Negroes increased (1809 to 1900) about two-thirds as fast as the whites; in the cities they increased nearly seven-eighths as fast." Figures for the white and Negro increase in both city and country districts follow:

Per Cent Increase, 1890 to 1900

	Cities		Country Districts	
	White	Negro	White	Negro
Continental United States	35.7	35.2	12.4	13.7
South Atlantic and South Central Divisions	36.7	31.8	22.9	14.6

The trend of all these figures shows that where the influences and conditions are similar the movements of the two races have been similar.

The causes, besides the breaking down of the slave regime, that have operated to draw the Negro to urban centers have been those fundamental economic, social and individual causes which have affected the general population. Chief among these has been the growth of industrial and commercial activities in urban centers. From 1880 to 1900 Southern cities (according to the showing of the census figures of manufactures, which are only approximately exact) have increased 143.3 per cent in total value of manufactured products, and 60.9 per cent in the average number of wage-earners, exclusive of proprietors, salaried officers and clerks, in manufacturing enterprises.

Railroad building, total tonnage and gross earnings show the development of commerce. In thirteen Southern states from 1860 to 1900, railway mileage increased 461.9 per cent. Total tonnage for most of this territory increased 90.5 per cent in the years from 1890 to 1900, while the total freight, passenger, express and mail earnings increased 48.4 per cent in the same decade.

All the facts available show that the Negro shares the influence of these developments. That he is a main factor in the labor of the South is evident. In a number of Southern cities the white and Negro increases in selected gainful occupations were as follows, between 1890 and 1900: in domestic and personal service, male whites increased 42.3 per cent, Negroes 31.1 per cent; in trade and transportation occupations, male whites increased 25.2 per cent, Negroes 39.1 per cent; in manufacturing and mechanical pursuits, male whites 16.3 per cent, Negroes 11.6 per cent.

The divorce of the Negro from the soil after emancipation, and the growth of the industrial and commercial centers are causes which are supplemented by the effect of higher wages paid weekly or monthly in the city on the economic motives of workers; by the trend of legislation, especially labor laws, which favor the city and which, in practical effect in some parts of the South, make harder the uninviting lot of the land tenant; by improved educational and amusement facilities, and by the contact with the moving crowds; while the paved and lighted streets, the greater comforts of the houses and other conveniences which the rustic imagines he can easily get and the dazzling glare of the unknown great world are viewed in decided contrast to the hard, humdrum conditions and poor accommodations on plantation and farm.

The available facts and figures bear out the conclusion that along with the white population the Negroes, under the influence of causes likely to operate for an indefinite period, will continue to migrate to the towns and cities, and that they will come in comparatively large numbers to stay.

Already the Negro urban population has grown to considerable proportions. In 1860 it is estimated that about 4.2 per cent of all the Negroes in the United States were urban dwellers (places of 4,000 or more). By 1890 it had risen to 19.8 per cent (places of 2,500 or more; the figures for 1890 and since are not, therefore, comparable with those for censuses preceding); in 1900 it was 22.7 per cent, and in 1910, 27.4 per cent, or more than one-fourth of the total Negro population. In 1910 thirty-nine cities had 10,000 or more Negroes, and the following twelve cities had more than 40,000 Negroes each:

Atlanta, Ga.	51,902
Baltimore, Md.	84,749
Birmingham, Ala.	52,305
Chicago, Ill.	44,103
Louisville, Ky.	40,622
Memphis, Tenn.	52,441
New Orleans, La.	89,262
New York, N.Y.	91,709
Philadelphia, Pa.	84,459
Richmond, Va.	46,733
St. Louis, Mo.	43,960
Washington, D.C.	94,446

Negroes constituted one-fourth or more of the total population of twenty-seven principal cities (25,000 or more total population), and in four of these cities — viz., Montgomery, Ala., Jacksonville, Fla., Savannah, Ga. and Charleston, S.C. — the Negro population was something more than one-half.

2. Segregation Within the City

Migration to the city is being followed by segregation into districts and neighborhoods within the city. In Northern cities years ago Negro residents, for the most part, lived where their purses allowed. With the influx of thousands of immigrants from the South and the West Indies, both native Negro and newcomer have been lumped together into distinct neighborhoods. In Southern cities domestic servants usually still live upon the premises of their employers or near by. But the growing Negro business and professional classes and those engaged in other than domestic and personal service find separate sections in which to dwell. Thus the Negro ghetto is growing up. New York has its "San Juan Hill" in the West Sixties, and its Harlem district of over 35,000 within about eighteen city blocks; Philadelphia has its Seventh Ward; Chicago has its State Street; Washington its North West neighborhood, and Baltimore its Druid Hill Avenue. Louisville has its Chestnut Street and its "Smoketown"; Atlanta its West End and Auburn Avenue. These are examples taken at random which are typical of cities, large and small, North and South.

This segregation within the city is caused by strong forces at work both within and without the body of the Negroes themselves. Naturally, Negroes desire to be together. The consciousness of kind in racial, family and friendly ties binds them closer to one another than to their white fellow-citizens. But as Negroes develop in intelligence, in their standard of living and economic power, they desire better houses, better public facilities and other conveniences not usually obtainable in the sections allotted to their less fortunate black brothers. To obtain these advantages they seek other neighborhoods, just as the European immigrants who are crowded into segregated sections of our cities seek better surroundings when they are economically able to secure them.

But a prejudiced opposition from his prospective white neighbors confronts the Negro, which does not meet the immigrant who has shuffled off the coil of his Continental condition. Intelligence and culture do not often discount color of skin. Professions of democratic justice in the North, and deeds of individual kindness in the South, have not yet secured to Negroes the unmolested residence in blocks with white fellow-citizens. In Northern cities where larger liberty in some avenues obtains, the home life, the church life and much of the business and community life of Negroes are carried on separately and apart from the common life of the whole people. In Southern communities, with separate streetcar laws, separate places of amusement and recreation, separate hospitals and separate cemeteries, there is sharp cleavage between whites and Negroes, living and dead. With separation in neighborhoods, in work, in churches, in homes and in almost every phase of their life, there is growing up in the cities of America a distinct Negro world, isolated from many of the impulses of the common life and little known and understood by the white world about it.

3. The Sequel of Segregation

In the midst of this migration and segregation, the Negro is trying to make a three-fold adjustment, each phase of which requires heroic struggle. First, there is the adjustment that all rural populations have to make in learning to live in town. Adjustment to conditions of housing, employment, amusement, etc., is necessary for all who make the change from country to city. The Negro must make a second adjustment from the status of a chattel to that of free contract, from servitude to citizenship. He has to realize in his own consciousness the self-confidence of a free man. Finally, the Negro must adjust himself to the white population in the cities, and it is no exaggeration of the facts to say that generally today the attitude of this white population is either indifferent or prejudiced or both.

Now, the outcome of segregation in such a serious situation is first of all to create an attitude of suspicion and hostility between the best elements of the two races. Too much of the Negro's knowledge of the white world comes through demagogues, commercial sharks, yellow journalism and those "citizens" who compose the mobs, while too much of the white man's knowledge of the Negro people is derived from similar sources, from domestic servants and from superficial observation of the loafers about the streets. The best elements of both races, thus entirely removed from friendly contact, except for the chance meeting of individuals in the market place, know hardly anything of their common life and tend to become more suspicious and hostile toward each other than toward strangers from a far country.

The white community is thus frequently led to unjust judgments of Negroes and Negro neighborhoods, as seen in the soubriquets of "little Africa," "black bottom," "Niggertown," "Smoketown," "Buzzard's Alley," "Chinch row," and as indicated by the fact that the individuals and families who live in these neighborhoods are all lumped by popular opinion into one class. Only here and there does a white person come to know that "there are Negroes and Negroes just as there are white folks and white folks." The most serious side of this attitude and opinion is, that the Negro is handicapped by them in securing the very things that would help him in working out his own salvation.

1. The Sequel in Housing Conditions

In the matter of the housing conditions under which he must live, reliable investigations have shown that in several cities the "red-light" districts of white people are either in the midst of, or border closely upon Negro neighborhoods. Also respectable Negroes often find it impossible to free themselves from disreputable and vicious neighbors of their own race, because the localities in which both may live are limited. And on top of this, Negroes often pay higher rentals for accommodations similar to those of white tenants, and, frequently, improved houses are secured only when white people who occupied them have moved on to something better. In Southern cities, many of the abler classes of Negroes have escaped the environment of the vicious element by creating decent neighborhoods through home ownership, and by eternal vigilance, excluding saloons, gambling places or other degrading agencies. For the poorer and less thrifty element, in a number of towns and cities, loose building regulations allow greedy landlords to profit by "gun-barrel" shanties and cottages, by "arks," of which the typical pigeon-house would be a construction model, and by small houses crowded upon the same lot, often facing front street, side street and the alley, with lack of sewerage and with other sanitary neglect, which an inspector of one Southern city described as "a crying disgrace to any civilized people."

Yet, in the face of these handicaps, thousands of homes that would do credit to any people on earth are springing up in these cities. In the absence or with the indifference of sanitary authorities, intelligent Negroes are not only struggling to free themselves from disease-breeding surroundings, but they are teaching the unintelligent throng. In spite of spontaneous schemes of real estate owners and agents to keep them out of desirable neighborhoods, in spite of the deliberate designs of city segregation ordinances such as have been passed in several cities and attempted in others, in spite of intimidation, the abler Negroes in some cities are buying homes and creating decent neighborhoods in which to live. However, the larger proportion are rent payers and not owners, hence they need intelligent leadership and influential support in their efforts for improved housing and neighborhood conditions.

2. The Economic Sequel

Three facts should be placed in the foreground in looking at the economic conditions of the segregated Negro in the city. First, the masses of those who have migrated to town are unprepared to meet the exacting requirements of organized industry, and the keen competition of more efficient laborers. Second, organized facilities for training these inefficient, groping seekers for something better are next to nothing in practically all the cities to which they are flocking. They, therefore, drift hit or miss into any occupations which are held out to their unskilled hands and untutored brains. Natural aptitude enables many to "pick up" some skill, and these succeed in gaining a stable place. But the thousands work from day to day with that weak tenure and frequent change of place from which all unskilled, unorganized laborers suffer under modern industry and trade.

The third fact of prime importance is the prejudice of the white industrial world, which the Negro must enter to earn his food, shelter and raiment. This prejudice, when displayed by employers, is partly due to the inefficiency indicated above and the failure to discriminate between the efficient individual and this untrained throng. When exhibited by fellow wage-earners, it is partly due to fear of probable successful competitors and to the belief that the Negro has "his place" fixed by a previous condition of servitude. But in the cases of many employers and employees, as shown in numbers of instances carefully investigated, the opposition to the Negro in industrial pursuits is due to a whimsical dislike of any workman who is not white and especially of one who is black!

The general result of this inefficiency, of this lack of facilities and guidance for occupational training which would overcome the defect, and of this dwarfing prejudice is far-reaching. In both Northern and Southern cities the result is a serious limitation of the occupational field for Negroes, thus robbing them of better income and depriving the community of a large supply of valuable potential labor. Examination of occupational statistics for Northern cities shows that from about three-fourths to about nine-tenths of Negro males engaged in gainful occupations are employed in domestic and personal service. Workmen in industries requiring skill are so well organized in the North that Negroes in any numbers must enter the trades through union portals. Only in late years, and frequently at the time of strikes, as in the building trades' strike of 1900, the stockyards' strike of 1904, and the teamsters' strike of 1905 in Chicago, has the Negro been recognized as a fellow-workman whose interests are common with the cause of organized labor. A large assortment of testimony lately gathered by Atlanta University from artisans and union officials in all parts of the country gives firm ground for the conclusion that, except in some occupations, largely the building and mining trades, white union men are yet a long distance from heartily receiving Negro workmen on equal terms.

In Southern cities Negro labor is the main dependence and manual labor is slow to lose the badge of servitude. But for selected occupations in Southern cities between 1890 and 1900 the rate of increase in domestic and personal service occupations among Negroes was greater than those in manufacturing and mechanical pursuits, and than those in trade and transportation, if draymen, hackmen, and teamsters are omitted from the last classification. The occupations of barbering, whitewashing, laundering etc., are being absorbed by white men. The white firemen of the Georgia Railroad and Queen and Crescent Railway struck because these companies insisted upon giving Negro firemen employment on desirable trains. These are indications of a possible condition when the desire of white men for places held by Negroes becomes a matter of keen competition. An able writer on the Negro problem has asserted that in the South the Negroes can get any work "under the sun." But since an increasing proportion of modern industry is conducted in the shade, the Southern city Negro of tomorrow may find it as difficult to wedge his way into the better paid occupations as does his black brother in the North now.

When it comes to the question of business experience and opportunity, the sea is still thicker with reefs and shoals. A Negro who wants training and experience in some line of business that he may begin some enterprise of his own, finds, except in very rare cases, the avenues to positions in white establishments which would give him this experience closed. The deadline of his desire is a messenger's place or a porter's job. How can a porter learn to run a mercantile establishment or a messenger understand how to manage a bank? His only alternative, inexperienced as he may be, is to risk his meager savings in venturing upon an unsounded sea. Shipwreck is necessarily the rule, and successful voyage the exception.

The successes, however, in both industry and trade are multiplying, and with substantial encouragement may change the rule to exception in the teeth of excessive handicaps. There was an increase between 1890 and 1900 of 11.6 per cent of Negroes engaged in selected skilled and semi-skilled occupations in Southern cities. In 1910 the executive council of the American Federation of Labor unanimously passed a resolution inviting Negroes, along with other races, into its ranks. Some of its affiliated bodies have shown active sympathy with this sentiment, and have taken steps in different cities to bring in Negro workmen. All of eleven Negro inventors of 1911 were city dwellers. The "Freedmen's Bank," which had branches in about thirty-five cities and towns, failed in 1873. During its existence it held deposits of over $50,000,000 of savings of the freedmen. Although the confidence of the freedmen was shaken to its foundation, they have rallied and in 1911 there were 64 private Negro banks in the towns and cities of the country. Many of these are thriving institutions. There is no means of knowing the number and importance of other Negro business enterprises. But judging from studies of Negro business enterprises made in Philadelphia and in New York City, and from the widespread attendance upon the annual meetings of the National Negro Business League, substantial progress is triumphing over unusual obstacles.

3. The Sequel in Health and Morals

Crowded into segregated districts; living in poor houses for the most part, for which they pay high rentals; often untaught and without teachers in the requirements of town life; walled in by inefficiency, lack of training and the chance to get the training; usually restricted from well-paid occupations by the prejudice of fellow-employees and frequently by the prejudice of employers; with a small income and the resulting low standard of living, the wonder is not that Negroes have a uniformly higher death-rate than whites in the cities and towns, but that the mortality is as small as it is and shows signs of decrease. Forced by municipal indifferences or design in many cities to live in districts contaminated by houses and persons of ill-fame; unable often to drive from their residential districts saloons and dens of vice; feeling the pressure of the less moral elements of both races, and feeling that weight of police and courts which the poor and the oppressed undoubtedly experience, the marvel is not that the criminal records outrun other elements of our urban population, but that impartial observers both North and South testify to the large law-abiding Negro citizenship, and to the thousands of pure individuals, Christian homes and communities.[1]

In speaking of the Negro death-rate in Southern cities, Frederick L. Hoffman, who cannot be charged with favorable bias, said in 1906, "without exception, the death-rates are materially in excess of the corresponding death-rates of the white population, but there has also been in this case a persistent decline in the general death-rate from 38.1 per 1,000 in 1871 to 32.9 in 1886 and 28.1 in 1904." Data from other investigations for five Southern cities (three cities not included in Mr. Hoffman's studies) show results similar to his. Figures for the death-rate of Negroes in Northern cities are not available.

Infant mortality, tuberculosis and pneumonia are chief causes of the excessive death-rate. Negroes in cities have an excessive number of female breadwinners, and a large proportion of these are married women. The neglect of the child, while the mother is "working out" during the long hours of domestic service, and ignorance of child nurture are the ingredients of the soothing-syrup which lulls thousands of small children into the sleep of death. Undernourishment due to low pay, bad housing, poor sanitation, ignorant fear of "night air" and lack of understanding of the dangers of infection make Negroes the prey of diseases now clearly proven preventable. With an aroused public conscience for sanitation and adequate leadership in education on matters of health these conditions are gradually removable.

The mental and moral conditions of a people cannot be shown by case counting. Tables of criminal statistics are quite as much a commentary on the culture conditions of the whole community as upon the accused Negro. The best study of crime in cities showed that down to 1903 there was a general tendency toward a decrease among Negroes. Available testimony for Southern cities from the days of the Freedmen's Bureau superintendence down to the present time is decidedly in favor of the Negro, even under an archaic penal system. Personal observation for fifteen years during residence in and repeated visits to a score of the larger cities and a number of the smaller ones, leave the writer with a firm conviction of decided advancement. The intelligence and character demanded of ministers, teachers, doctors, lawyers and other professional classes, the drawing of social lines based upon individual worth, the improved type of amusement and recreation frequently in evidence and similar manifestations are a part of the barometer which clearly shows progress.

4. The Sequel in Miscellaneous Conditions

To make the view of urban situation among Negroes full and clear, a number of conditions which exist in some cities but are absent in others should be included in the list. In many cities the sequel of segregation means less effective police patrol and inadequate fire protection: in others it means unpaved streets, the absence of proper sewerage and lack of other sanitary supervision and requirements.

The provision which people have for the play life of their children and themselves is nearly as important as the conditions of labor. Facilities for amusement and recreation, then, are of great importance to the Negro. Wholesome amusement for all the people is just beginning to receive deserved attention. But the Negro is in danger of being left out of account in the movement. Playgrounds in Negro neighborhoods are so rare as to excite curiosity, and organized play is just being heard of in the Negro world. There is hardly a city where unhindered access to theatres and moving picture shows exists. In a few Southern cities "Negro parks" of fair attractiveness are being provided because exclusion from public parks used by whites has been the custom. Here and there enterprising Negroes are starting playhouses for their own people.

In the provision for education, the opportunity of the city Negro is much greater than that of his rural brother. Yet, while one rejoices over this fact, candor compels consideration of the relative educational chances of the black boy and the white one. Some of the Northern cities which have no official or actual separation in public schools may be passed without scrutiny. In others and in some border cities like St. Louis, Washington and Louisville, where there are separate schools, the standards and equipment for the Negro schools compare favorably. Also a large need of praise is due Southern communities for the great advance which has been made in public opinion and financial support for Negro education. Yet, in many cities, although local pride may apply names and give glowing descriptions, those who have seen the public school systems at close range know that they are poor compared with white schools in the same places. The bona-fide Negro public high schools in the cities of the South can be counted on the fingers of the two hands. Public schools all over the land have been tardy to the call of the educational needs of the masses of the people. The "dead hand" of past aims, content and methods of education still clasps many communities in its icy grip. It is well-nigh impossible to tell in a generalized statement the significance of this condition as applied to the city Negro. The hopeful sign of the situation is the awakening of the South to the need.

4. Suggestions for Solution

The recital of the foregoing facts and conclusions would be of little consequence unless it led somewhere. The summary of the discussion presents a clear case of a large nation-wide Negro migration to towns and cities, such as is taking place among the entire people; a segregation within the city of Negroes into distinct neighborhoods with a decreasing contact with the larger community and its impulses; accompanying housing, economic, health, moral, educational and other conditions which are more critical and are receiving less attention than similar problems among the white people. With such a problem before us, what should be done?

1. There should be an organized effort to acquaint the Negro in the country with the desirability of his remaining where he is unless by education and training he is prepared to meet the exactions of adjustments to city life. The roseate picture of city existence should be corrected. Simultaneously with the agricultural and other improvements of country life calculated to make its economic and social conditions more attractive should go an effort to minimize the activities of labor agents, employment agency sharks and the other influences that lure the rustics from home.

2. Recognizing that already more than two score cities and towns have large Negro populations in the first stages of adjustment, organized effort should be made to help the Negro to learn to live in town. The thoughtful white and colored people in each community will have to break the bonds of this increasing segregation and come into some form of organized community cooperation. The danger most to be feared is antagonism between the better element of both races, because they may not know and understand each other. The meeting on the high levels of mutual

sympathy and cooperation will work wonders with prejudices and conventional barriers.

3. The cooperative movement of the white and colored citizens of each locality should work out a community program for the neighborhood, housing, economic, educational, religious and other improvement of the Negro. The time is at hand when we should not let this matter longer drift.

4. Such a movement should sooner or later become conscious of the national character of the problem and the towns and cities should unite for the exchange of plans, methods and experience and for general cooperation and for developing needed enthusiasm.

5. The Negro must have more and better trained leadership in these local situations. Slowly but surely we are listening to the lesson of group psychology and common sense and are beginning to use the most direct way of influencing the customs and habits of a people by giving them teachers and exemplars of their own kind. If the Negro is to be lifted to the full stature of American civilization, he must have leaders — wise, well-trained leaders — who are learned in the American ways of thinking and of doing things. And it should never be forgotten that the Negro himself has valuable contributions to make to American life.

6. The final suggestion is that the white people of each locality can best foster mutual confidence and cooperation of Negroes by according them impartial community justice. This means "a square deal" in industry, in education and in other parts of the common life. It means equality of opportunity.

These conditions among Negroes in the cities arise as much from the many changes which are taking place in the life of the Negro as from the changes taking place in the life of the nation. The Negro is awakening to a race consciousness and to the consciousness of American citizenship. His migration is a part of his groping efforts to better his condition; he is trying to engage in industry and commerce and is accumulating wealth. Above the ruins of the slave cabin he is building homes. Upon the ash-cleared hearth of the chattel he is developing the sacredness of family relationships. Where once he toiled that the children of others might have leisure and learning, he is trying to erect schools and colleges for the education of his own. In lieu of the superstition and ignorance which savagery and serfdom had made his daily portion, the Negro is trying to cultivate an ethical and religious life beautiful in holiness and achieving in service. In these efforts for self-realization in the city the Negro needs the fair dealing, the sympathy and the cooperation of his white brother. For the problem of his adjustment is only a part of the great human problem of justice for the handicapped in democratic America.

Note

---

[1] The writer has had to condense into a few clauses here the conclusions from a large amount of testimony and facts.

In the Robert E. Park Tradition

2

Black Housing in Chicago

Charles S. Johnson

A. A Study of Negro Families

Consideration of the housing problem as a continuing factor in the experience of Negro families led to an effort to study it from a new angle of approach — through histories of typical families in the Negro community.

The data thus gathered afford an opportunity to present an interpretative account of Negro family life, setting forth the intimate problems confronting Negroes in Chicago, their daily social difficulties, the reflection in their home life of their struggle for existence, just how they live, how they participate in the activities of the Negro community and the community at large, their own opinions concerning civic problems, their housing experience, how much they earn and how much they save, how much they spend and what value they receive from these expenditures, how they spend their spare time, and how they seek to improve their condition in the community.

A selection was made of 274 Negro families living in all sections of Chicago. Three Negro women, well equipped to deal intelligently and sympathetically with these families, gathered this information. These 274 families lived in 238 blocks, the distribution being such that no type of neighborhood or division of the Negro population was overlooked. The questionnaire employed contained five pages of questions and required an interview of about two hours. Special effort was made to secure purely social information without the aid of leading questions.

1. General Living Conditions

For the most part the physical surroundings of the Negro family, as indicated by these family histories, are poor. The majority of these houses fall within the classifications noted as Types "C" and "D" in the discussion of the physical condition of housing.

On the South Side, where most of the Negro population lives, the low quality

Charles S. Johnson, "The Negro Housing Problem," *The Negro In Chicago: A Study of Race Relations and a Race Riot,* 1922, pp. 152–186.

of housing is widespread, although there are some houses of a better grade which are greatly in demand.

The ordinary conveniences, considered necessities by the average white citizen, are often lacking. Bathrooms are often missing. Gas lighting is common, and electric lighting is a rarity. Heating is commonly done by wood or coal stoves, and furnaces are rather exceptional; when furnaces are present, they are sometimes out of commission.

Under the heading of "Housing Conditions" such notations as these are often found:

No gas, bath, or toilet. Plumbing very bad; toilet leaks; bowl broken; leak in kitchen sink; water stands in kitchen; leak in bath makes ceiling soggy and wet all the time. Plastering off in front room. General appearance very bad inside and out. Had to get city behind owner to put in windows, clean, and repair plumbing. Heat poor; house damp. Plumbing bad; leaks. Hot-water heater out of order. Needs repairing done to roof and floors. In bad repair; toilet in yard used by two families. Toilet off from dining-room; fixtures for gas; no gas; just turned off; no bath; doors out of order; won't fasten. Sanitary conditions poor; dilapidated condition; toilet won't flush; carries water to bathtub. Plumbing bad; roof leaks; plastering off; no bath or gas; general repairs needed; very dirty. Plumbing bad; plastering off in toilet; window panes broken and out; no bath or gas. Plastering off from water that leaks from flat above; toilet leaks; does not flush; washbowl and bath leak very badly; repairs needed on back porch; rooms need calcimining. No water in hydrant in hall; no toilet, bath, or gas; general repair needed. Water not turned on for sink in kitchen; water for drinking and cooking purposes must be carried in; toilet used by four families; asked landlord to turn on water in kitchen; told them to move; roof leaks; stairs and back porch in bad order. Sewer gas escapes from basement pipes; water stands in basement. House dirty; flues in bad condition; gas pipes leak; porch shaky. No heat and no hot water; no repairing done; no screens; gas leaks all over house; stationary tubs leak. Water pipes rotted out; gas pipes leak. Toilet leaks; plastering off; windowpanes out. Plastering off; large rat holes all over; paper hanging from ceiling.

This is the common situation of the dweller in the districts mentioned. The variations are in degree rather than kind. To dwellings a little better in sanitation and repair than those just described, the adjective "fair" was given.

Occasionally a Negro family manages to escape from this wretched type of dwelling in the "Black Belt." Some who were financially able purchased homes in Woodlawn, for example, where they live much as white residents do, supplied with the comforts and conveniences of life and in fairly clean, wholesome surroundings. There, as a rule, the physical equipment of their dwellings is good and is kept in repair. In some instances they have hot-water heating, electric lighting, and gas for cooking purposes. They ordinarily redecorate once a year, take proper care of their garbage, keep the lawns cut and the premises clean; and otherwise reveal a natural and normal pride of ownership.

In this respect the Negro residents of Woodlawn are far more fortunate than many of their race brothers who have purchased dwellings in the "Black Belt." Many of these purchases have been made by migrants on long-time payments, and large expenditure would be required to put the houses in repair and keep them so. Purchases made by Negroes in Woodlawn have been chiefly of substantial dwellings, not necessarily new but in good condition and needing only ordinary repairs from time to time.

2. Why Negroes Move

Except where the property is owned by Negroes there is frequent moving. The records obtained of these movements give a great variety of reasons. A strong desire to improve living conditions appears with sufficient frequency to indicate that it is the leading motive. Buying a home is one of the ways of escape from intolerable living conditions, but removal to other houses or flats is more often tried. For example, a man who now owns his home near Fifty-first Street and South Wabash Avenue — living there with his two brothers and five lodgers — has moved six times, "to live in a better house and a better neighborhood." A family now living near Thirty-first Street and Prairie Avenue, resident in Chicago since 1893, has moved four times, three times to obtain better houses in better neighborhoods and once to get nearer to work. A man and wife living near Fifty-third and South Dearborn streets have moved four times since coming to Chicago in 1908. A family living on East Forty-fifth Street and paying $60 a month rent for six rooms has moved twice since 1900 to "better and cleaner houses." Another family paying $65 a month for eight rooms on East Bowen Avenue has moved twice since 1905 into better houses and neighborhoods. "Better house" and "better neighborhood" were the most frequently given reasons.

Of kindred nature are these: leaky roof; house cold; dirty; inconvenient; did not like living in rear flat; to better conditions; better houses away from questionable places; landlord would not clean; first floor not healthy; small and undesirable; not desirable flat; poor plumbing; didn't like neighborhood; moved to better quarters; landlord would not repair; house too damp; no windows; owner would not fix water pipes; more room wanted; better environment for children; better street; no yard for children; better people; house in bad condition; more conveniences for roomers. . . .

The lodger problem   The prevalence of lodgers is one of the most conspicuous problems in the Negro housing situation. It is largely a social question. The difficulty of finding a home adequate for a family of four or five persons at a reasonable rent has forced many Negroes to take over large buildings in better localities and in better physical condition but with much higher rents. To meet these rents they have taken lodgers. It was seldom possible to investigate the character of the lodgers. The arrangement of these large houses, originally intended for single-family use, prevents family privacy when lodgers are added, making a difficult situation for families with children. Again, the migration brought to the city many unattached men and women who could find no other place to live except in families. Thus it happens that in Negro families the lodger problem is probably more pressing than in any other group of the community. Not only do lodgers constitute a social problem for the family, but, having little or no interest in the appearance and condition of the property, they are in many instances careless and irresponsible and contribute to the rapid deterioration of the buildings.

As previously explained, the term "lodgers," in this report, includes relations as well as other adults unrelated to the family. It was apparent in the study that there was a large number of relative-lodgers in Negro families. The recent migration from the South had a distinct bearing on this situation. Many Negroes came to Chicago at the solicitation of relatives and remained in their households until they could secure homes for themselves. The migration further accounts for the accentuation of the lodger problem during the period immediately following it. The 274 family histories include 1,319 persons, of whom 485, or 35 per cent, were lodgers, living in 62 per cent of the households. The greatest number of households with lodgers were those living in five room dwellings. There were thirty-eight such households. Living in six- and seven-room dwellings were thirty-four families with lodgers. Families with only one lodger were most numerous. There were fifty-five such families as compared with thirty-nine having two lodgers, twenty-five with three lodgers, twenty-three with four lodgers, thirteen with six lodgers, eight with five lodgers, and seven with more than six lodgers.

Naturally the lodger evil was found in its worst form in the congested parts of the South Side. In the district from Thirty-first to Thirty-ninth Streets seventy-two of the ninety-nine families had lodgers. In twenty-two families there was but one, however, as against twelve with three and four, eleven with two, and six with five and six lodgers. Two families had ten each, and one had thirteen. This last case was that of a widow who rented nine sleeping-rooms in her ten-room house, in addition to catering at odd moments. It was a typical rooming-house as distinguished from a family taking lodgers. One family that had ten lodgers consisted of a man, his wife, and a son twenty-five years old; they had eight bedrooms, seven opening into a hall. The other family that had ten lodgers consisted of the parents and two children, a boy of eight and a girl of seven, and had a ten-room house. The lodgers were two men and three women, with five children. Five of the ten rooms were used as sleeping rooms.

In the district north of Thirty-first Street an increased number of lodgers appeared in only one family, that of a man and his wife, without children. They lived in a ten-room house, using eight of the rooms for sleeping purposes and accommodating seven male and five female lodgers.

In the district from Thirty-ninth to Sixtieth Street was one instance of seven male lodgers in a seven-room house with the man who owned the property. Two of the lodgers were his brothers. There was no heat and no bathroom. The house had been reported to the health department.

In the Lake Park district one, two, or three lodgers were the rule, only five of the twenty-eight families with lodgers in that district being outside of those three classes. Eight lodgers were found in an eight-room dwelling. The family consisted of man and wife, and the only female lodger was their niece. Five rooms were used for sleeping purposes.

In the other district no instances of excessive overcrowding due to lodgers were found.

Complaint has often been made of the numerical preponderance of lodgers over children among Chicago Negroes, and comment has been made on the economic significance. It has been suggested, for example, that economic pressure had lowered the birth-rate among Negroes and increased the infant-mortality rate. As indicated by the 274 family histories, the number of lodgers among the Negro population exceeds the number of children, that is, the number of boys less than twenty-one years and girls less than eighteen. The School of Civics and Philanthropy, in its housing studies, counted as children those less than twelve years of age. On this basis it found in its study of the Negroes of the South and West sides that there were less than half as many children as lodgers on the South Side, but a more normal situation in the West Side. Even extending the ages of children, as has been done in the present report, the situation does not appear in a much better light.

The proportion of lodgers and of children in the districts covered by the Commission is shown in Table 1.

Table 1

District	Percentage of Lodgers	Percentage of Children
South Side:		
Thirty-first to Thirty-ninth	45.9	15.4
Twenty-second to Thirty-first	37.8	20.4
Thirty-ninth to Sixtieth	30.1	21.4
West Side	21.8	32.0
Lake Park	42.1	16.9
North Side	15.2	25.0
Woodlawn	26.9	30.0
Ogden Park	12.3	45.0
Total of 274 families	35.0	22.7

By way of comparison similar figures from other housing studies of the Chicago School of Civics might be mentioned, the children in each instance being less than twelve years old.

Among the Slovaks of the Twentieth Ward, 13 per cent were lodgers and 32 per cent children; in South Chicago, 27.3 per cent lodgers and 25.7 per cent children; among the Greeks and Italians near Hull-House, 13 per cent lodgers and 30 per cent children; among the Lithuanians of the Fourth Ward, 28 per cent lodgers and 27 per cent children.

As far as the South Side is concerned, the situation with regard to the balance between lodgers and children has become aggravated since the earliest School of Civics report was issued, whereas the situation on the West Side has improved somewhat.

Where there were children and lodgers together, a considerable number of instances were found which suggest probable injury to health or morals, and some-times both. Even where lodgers are relatives, impairment of health and morals is threatened in certain circumstances, especially if the overcrowding is flagrant. For example, a household on South Dearborn Street near Thirty-fourth Street consisted of a father, mother, a son of nineteen years, and a baby girl of four months, with three lodgers, two men and one woman — seven persons living in seven rooms and sleeping in all parts of the house. One of the lodgers was a sister-in-law, another a nephew by marriage, and the third, a stranger, had a bedroom to himself. In a ten-room house in East Thirty-second Street parents having a boy of eight years and a girl of seven years were found to have taken in ten lodgers, two of whom were men. In another instance five children, four of them boys of eight, five, four, and two years and a girl of eleven, lived with their parents and two lodgers in a six-room house.

In Ogden Park, a district which shows a high percentage of children, lodgers sometimes are added to the family. In one house of five rooms, for example, there were found living twelve persons — father, mother, two sons, sixteen and seventeen years of age, four daughters, thirty-three, twenty-four, twenty-two, and thirteen years of age, and four lodgers — a daughter, her husband, and their two infants. There were only two bedrooms for the twelve persons. Another instance was that of a family of father, mother, four sons, nine, five, three, and two years, and two daughters, seven years and three weeks, with a sister of one of the parents for a lodger. The nine persons lived in five rooms. There were only two beds in the house, and one of the bedrooms was not in use.

On the South Side near Thirty-first Street there was a case where a man lodger occupied one bedroom, the other being used by the parents and their eight-year-old daughter — four persons in a four room flat. On South Park Avenue near Twenty-ninth Street two lodgers, a son-in-law and a nephew, occupied two of the six rooms, while the husband and wife, a son of twenty-three years, and a daughter of twenty-one years lived in the other four rooms, which included the kitchen and dining-room. A similar instance was found, on Indiana Avenue near Thirtieth Street, where two male lodgers lived with a family consisting of the parents, a son of twenty, and a daughter of eighteen, all in six rooms, two of which were not sleeping-rooms. On Lake Park Avenue near Fifty-sixth Street a family, including father, mother, and daughter of twenty, slept in the kitchen in order that three lodgers, one male and two female, might be accommodated in the five-room flat. In a five-room flat on Kenwood Avenue near Fifty-third Street the two male lodgers occupied both bedrooms, while the mother and her boy of nine and girl of seven years lived in the kitchen and dining-room. Seven persons were found living in a six-room house on East Fortieth Street; they were father, mother, a son of five years, a daughter of seven years, and an infant, with a male and a female lodger, friends of the parents. Virtually the whole house was used for sleeping purposes.

These are examples of the arrangements that sometimes occur when children and lodgers are found in the same dwelling. The fact that in the main Chicago Negroes live in more rooms per dwelling than immigrants, whose standard of living has not yet risen, does not necessarily mean that the Negroes have a greater appreciation of a house with more rooms. The explanation in many cases is that the Negroes take whatever living quarters happen to be available, which often are large residences abandoned by well-to-do whites, and then adapt their mode of living to the circumstances. Lodgers are one of the sources of revenue that aid in paying the rent. Negro families often expressed a desire to live by themselves if they could find a dwelling of suitable size for reasonable rent. They sometimes complained of lodgers and declared that they would prefer not to take them at all, especially women lodgers. The objection to married couples and unattached men was not so pronounced.

Smaller houses thus would seem to be a factor in the solution of the lodger problem. A Negro real estate dealer was asked if the Negro was as contented or as much disposed to live in a cottage as white people, or whether he wanted to live in spacious quarters where he could draw a revenue from roomers. The reply was that the Negro would rather live by himself. This is evidenced by the fact that many Negroes would rather live in an apartment and rent two or three rooms than take a large house and have it full of roomers.

Lodgers are often found in the smaller dwellings occupied by Negroes. Rent is often the determining factor in the selection of the smaller dwelling. When it is so high that it forms too large a proportion of income, economic necessity often drives the Negro family to admit one or more lodgers at the expense of overcrowding and its attendant harmfulness. This was noted in certain districts where the dwellings as a rule were small.

Rents and lodgers   An effort was made to determine the economic necessity for lodgers as expressed by the relation of the wages of heads of families to the amounts of rent paid. It is assumed that in a normal family budget rent should not exceed one-fifth of the income of the head of the family. Wide variations from that proportion were revealed.

Facts as to both rent and wages were difficult to secure, owing to the variable earnings of various members of the family, variable sums received from lodgers, and other factors. For example, seventeen occupants owned their houses. In seventy-eight other cases information obtained by the investigators was not adequate or could not, for various reasons, be used in calculations.

The remaining 179 cases out of the 274 provided data from which the following facts are presented: In three instances the rent exceeded the income of the head of the family; in thirty-one instances the rent equaled one-half the income of the head of the family, and in an equal number it amounted to one-third. In one case the rent was equal to three-fourths of the income, and in twenty-three cases the rent equaled one-fourth. Thus eighty-nine instances were disclosed in which the rent was in excess of one-fifth of the income of the head of the family. In most of these cases, particularly the extreme ones, the income of the head of the family was greatly supplemented by money received from lodgers or from earnings of other members of the family.

The remaining ninety families in which the rent amounted to one-fifth or less of the income of the head of the family were divided as follows: Twenty-four fell in the one-fifth column, twenty-seven in the one-sixth column, fourteen in the one-seventh column, eleven in the one-eighth column, while fourteen were in the "low" column. The last named included those ranging from one-ninth to one-twenty-third.

On the South Side, in the district from Thirty-first to Thirty-ninth Street, rents exceeded the one-fifth proportion in one-half of the sixty-two families studied, two of them paying rent in excess of income, eight paying one-half of income for rent, fourteen paying one-third, and seven paying one-fourth. Of the remaining thirty-one families in that district, seven fell in the one-fifth column, twelve in the one-sixth column, six in the one-seventh column, four in the one-eighth column and two in the "low," being one-ninth and one-eleventh.

Rents were high also in the Lake Park district, where twenty-five families of a total of thirty-six were paying in excess of the one-fifth proportion. Fourteen of these paid one-half of the income for rent, five paid one-fourth, four paid one-third, one paid three-quarters, and in one instance rent exceeded income. In only five instances was the normal one-fifth paid, two paid one-sixth, two paid one-seventh, while two paid one-ninth and one-eleventh respectively.

In the district north of Thirty-first Street, eighteen out of a total of thirty-eight families paid in excess of the one-fifth proportion: four paid one-half, nine paid one-third, and five paid one-fourth. Six families paid the normal one-fifth, five paid one-sixth, two paid one-seventh, one one-eighth, and six less than that, running as low as one-twenty-third.

The Ogden Park area was found to be a district of low rents. None of the eight families studied paid as much as the normal one-fifth. Two paid one-sixth, one paid one-seventh, three one-eighth, one one-ninth, and one one-twelfth.

The other districts did not show much variation from the normal proportion.

Examination was made of all the factors in instances where the rent equaled one-half or more of the income of the head of the family or amounted to one-third. With regard to the former it was assumed, for the purpose of the study, that it compelled renting rooms to lodgers. With regard to the one-third column, lodgers were assumed to be an economic necessity when they offered the only source of income in addition to that of the head of the family. On these bases it was found that in forty-six families supplementary income afforded by lodgers was necessary, that in three instances they were the sole source of the income, while one instance was presented of a widow whose children partly supported her, but insufficiently for their common needs.

While in most instances of high rents and low income on the part of the head of the family good reason appeared for taking lodgers, in not a few instances further analysis revealed other sources of income which might indicate that there was no economic necessity for lodgers. There was one instance on Forest Avenue, for example, where the relation of the rent to the father's income was one-third, but where his sons earned more than double his income. In another family on South State Street near Thirtieth Street, the father earned $125 a month and paid $50 a month rent, but additional income was derived from the wife, son and daughter, in addition to that obtained from lodgers. There was likewise the case of a waiter living on Lake Park Avenue whose rent was $30 a month as against wages of $10 a week. In addition to the tips he doubtless received in his work, his wife earned $18 a week, and $6 a week was derived from lodgers. In one instance a man living near Fifty-sixth Street and Wabash Avenue paid rent equal to one-third of his wages, but had considerable income from investments.

Such instances tend to explain why only forty-eight families were found in which lodgers seemed to be an economic necessity in aiding to pay rents, when eighty-nine cases were revealed in which the rent was in excess of one-fifth of the wages of the head of the family. The family histories also showed that various means besides lodgers supplemented the insufficient income of a family head. In some cases the wife or children worked, and not infrequently their incomes exceeded those of the father. . . .

B. Physical Aspects of Negro Housing

The purpose of this section of the report is to describe by a selection of types the physical condition of houses occupied as residences by Negroes. This description includes the structure, age, repair, upkeep, and other factors directly affecting the appearance, sanitation, and comfort of dwellings available for Negro use.

In 1909 the Chicago School of Civics and Philanthropy included Negro housing in a series of general housing studies. This study was confined to the two largest areas of Negro residence, those on the South and West sides. Both of these were studied generally, and in each a selected area, of four blocks in one case and three blocks in the other, was studied intensively.

The South Side area included parts of the Second, Third, and Thirteenth wards between Fifteenth and Fifty-fifth streets, with State Street as the main thoroughfare. The four blocks bounded by Dearborn Street, Twenty-seventh Street, Armour Avenue, and Thirty-second Street were intensively studied. It was found that within these four blocks 94 per cent of the heads of families were Negroes. The buildings were one- and two-story, with a considerable amount of vacant space in the lots. Half the lots had less than 50 per cent of their space covered. The houses were for the most part intended for single families but had been converted into two-flat buildings. Rooms were poorly lighted and ventilated, the sanitation bad, and the alley and grounds about the houses covered with rubbish and refuse.

Comparisons with other districts studied showed the following: Of houses in a Polish district, 71 per cent were in good repair; in a Bohemian district, 57 per cent; Stock Yards district, 54 per cent; Jewish and South Chicago districts, 28 per cent; and in the Negro district, 26 per cent. A study made three years later by the School of Civics covering the same area showed a decrease of 16 per cent of buildings in good repair. Five buildings had been closed by the Department of Health as no longer fit for habitation. There were leaks in the roofs, sinks, and windows of five-sixths of the dwellings. In describing a typical house in this area, the report said:

There was no gutter and the roof leaked in two places, the sink drain in the basement leaked, keeping it continually damp, the opening of the chimney let the rain come down there, the windowpane in front rattled from lack of putty. The conditions in these houses are typical; almost every tenant tells of rain coming in through roof, chimney or windows, and cases of fallen plaster and windows without putty were too common to be noted. One aspect of the situation that should not be overlooked is the impossibility of putting these old houses in good condition. Leaks may be repaired, plaster may be replaced, windows may be made tight, and these things would certainly improve most of the houses, but when all were done it would not alter the fact that these are old houses, poorly built, through which the wind can blow at will.

Lack of repairs to the houses in the "Black Belt" is accounted for by the fact that owners do not regard the buildings as worth repairing, and that tenants can always be found, even though it is necessary to reduce rents somewhat. This reduction is indeed notable. The School of Civics found that while in 1909 50 per cent of the houses examined on the South Side rented for as much as $16 a month, in 1917 only 13 per cent could command as high a rental as that; that in 1909 the prevailing rents were $15 and $16 as against $10 and $12 in 1917.

On the West Side the area studied generally was that bounded by Lake Street, Ashland, Austin, and Western avenues. Here the situation was little better. One-third of the families visited in the three selected blocks bounded by Fulton and Paulina streets, Carroll Avenue and Robey Street were Negroes. The remaining two-thirds, represented sixteen nationalities. It was reported that the white residents could get advantages and improvements for their houses that a Negro could not. While 35 per cent of the houses were reported in good repair, 31 per cent were described as "absolutely dilapidated" and in a worse state of repair than those in any other districts studied except the Jewish district. The report said:

> Broken-down doors, unsteady flooring, and general dilapidation were met by the investigators at every side. Windowpanes were out, doors hanging on single hinges or entirely fallen off, and roofs rotting and leaking. Colored tenants reported that they found it impossible to persuade their landlords either to make the necessary repairs or to release them from their contracts; and that it was so hard to find better places in which to live that they were forced either to make the repairs themselves, which they could rarely afford to do, or to endure the conditions as best they might. Several tenants ascribed cases of severe and prolonged illness to the unhealthful conditions of the houses in which they were living.

That there was a continuing demand even for the shacks and shanties of the "Black Belt" is evidenced in a report made by the Urban League of Chicago in 1917 that only one out of every thirteen Negro applicants for houses to rent could be supplied. At the height of the demand applications for houses were coming in at the rate of 460 to 600 a day, and only ninety-nine were available for renting purposes. This was due, of course, to the growing stream of Negroes arriving daily from the South.

Covering the same area on the South Side as that studied by the School of Civics in 1917 a canvass was also made in 1917 by Caswell W. Crews, a student at the University of Chicago. He found that tenants had remained in these dwellings in some instances as long as twenty years after their unfitness had become evident, because the rent was low and they could find nowhere else to go. He mentioned the mass of migrants from the South who, because of their ignorance of conditions in Chicago as to what was desirable and what was to be had for a given sum, fell an easy prey to unscrupulous owners and agents. Mr. Crew's description said:

> With the exception of two or three the houses are frame, and paint with them is a dim reminiscence. There is one rather modern seven-room flat building of stone front, the flats renting at $22.50 a month and offering the best in the way of accommodations to be found there. There is another makeshift flat building situated above a saloon and pool hall, consisting of six six-room flats, renting at $12 per month, but in a very poor condition of repair. Toilets and baths were found to be in no condition for use and the plumbing in such a state as to constantly menace health. Practically all of the houses have been so reconstructed as to serve as flats, accommodating two and sometimes three families. As a rule there are four, five, and sometimes six rooms in each flat, there being but five instances when there were more than six. It is often the case that of these rooms not all can be used because of dampness, leaking roofs, or defective toilets overhead.

The owners are in most instances scarcely better off than their tenants and can ill afford to make repairs. One house in the rear of another on Federal Street near Twenty-seventh had every door off its hinges, water covering the floor from a defective sink, and windowpanes out. A cleaning of the house had been attempted, and the cleaners had torn loose what paper yielded readily and proceeded to white-wash over the adhering portion which constituted the majority of the paper. There were four such rooms and for them the family paid $7 a month.

In 1920 a cursory examination by investigators from the Commission showed that the only change in the situation was further deterioration in the physical state of the dwellings. . . .

The Pathology of Race Prejudice

E. Franklin Frazier

"The Negro-in-America, therefore, is a form of insanity that overtakes white men." — *The Southerner,* by Walter Hines Page.

Although the statement above makes no claim to technical exactness, it is nevertheless confirmed by modern studies of insanity. If, in developing this thesis, we consider some of the newer conceptions of mental processes as they apply to abnormal behavior, we shall find in each case that the behavior motivated by race prejudice shows precisely the same characteristics as that ascribed to insanity. This does not refer, of course, to those phenomena of insanity due to abnormalities of the actual structure of the brain, nor does it refer to the changes that come in dementia. We are concerned here chiefly with the psychological approach to the problem of insanity, — for race prejudice is an acquired psychological reaction, and there is no scientific evidence that it represents the functioning of inherited behavior patterns. Even from a practical viewpoint, as we shall attempt to show, we are forced to regard certain manifestations of race prejudice as abnormal behavior.

The conception used to explain abnormal behavior which we shall consider first is dissociation of consciousness. Normally, the mental life appears to be a "homogeneous stream progressing in a definite direction toward a single end," as Dr. Hart puts it. That this apparent homogeneity is deceptive, even in normal minds, is shown by a little observation. Every one has had the experience of performing a task while engaged in an unrelated train of thought. In cases such as this the dissociation is temporary and incomplete, while in insanity the dissociation is relatively permanent and complete. Automatic writing in cases of hysteria, somnambulism, dual personality, and delusions are cases of the splitting off of whole systems of ideas. The conclusion of Hart that "this dissociation of the mind into logic-tight compartments is by no means confined to the population of the asylum" will lead us to those manifestations of race prejudice that show the same marked mental dissociation found in the insane. Herbert Seligman, in his book on the Negro, suggests the insane nature of Southern reactions to the blacks when he says, "The Southern white man puts certain questions beyond discussion. If they are pressed he will fight rather than argue." Southern white people write and talk about the majesty of law, the sacredness of human rights, and the advantages of democ-

E. Franklin Frazier "The Pathology of Race Prejudice," *Forum,* Vol. 77, June 1927, pp. 856–862.

racy, — and the next moment defend mob violence, disfranchisement, and Jim Crow treatment of the Negro. White men and women who are otherwise kind and law-abiding will indulge in the most revolting forms of cruelty towards black people. Thus the whole system of ideas respecting the Negro is dissociated from the normal personality and, — what is more significant for our thesis, — this latter system of ideas seems exempt from the control of the personality.

These dissociated systems of ideas generally have a strong emotional component and are known as complexes. The Negro-complex, — the designation which we shall give the system of ideas which most Southerners have respecting the Negro, — has the same intense emotional tone that characterizes insane complexes. The prominence of the exaggerated emotional element has been noted by Josiah Royce in contrasting with the American attitude the attitude of the English in the West Indies, who are "wholly without those painful emotions, those insistent complaints and anxieties, which are so prominent in the minds of our own southern brethren." Moreover, just as in the insane any pertinent stimulus may arouse the whole complex, so any idea connected with the Negro causes the whole Negro-complex to be projected into consciousness. Its presence there means that all thinking is determined by the complex. For example, a white woman who addresses a colored man as mister is immediately asked whether she would want a Negro to marry her sister and must listen to a catalog of his sins. How else than as the somnambulism of the insane and almost insane are we to account for the behavior of a member of a school board who jumps up and paces the floor, cursing and accusing Negroes, the instant the question of appropriating money for Negro schools is raised? Likewise, the Negro-complex obtrudes itself on all planes of thought. Health programs are slighted because it is argued Negroes will increase; the selective draft is opposed because the Negro will be armed; woman suffrage is fought because colored women will vote. In many other cases the behavior of white people toward life in general is less consciously and less overtly influenced by the Negro-complex. Bitter memories quite often furnish its emotional basis while the complex itself is elaborated by ideas received from the social environment.

There is a mistaken notion, current among most people, that the insane are irrational, that their reasoning processes are in themselves different from those of normal people. The insane support their delusions by the same mechanism of rationalization that normal people employ to support beliefs having a non-rational origin. The delusions of the insane, however, show a greater imperviousness to objective fact. The delusions of the white man under the influence of the Negro-complex show the same imperviousness to objective facts concerning the Negro. We have heard lately an intelligent Southern white woman insisting that nine-tenths of all Negroes have syphilis, in spite of statistical and other authoritative evidence to the contrary. Moreover, just as the lunatic seizes upon every fact to support his delusional system, the white man seizes myths and unfounded rumors to support his delusion about the Negro. When the lunatic is met with ideas incompatible with his delusion he distorts facts by rationalization to preserve the inner consistency of his delusions. Of a similar nature is the argument of the white man who declares that white blood is responsible for character and genius in mixed Negroes and at the same time that white blood harms the Negroes! Pro-slavery literature denying the humanity of the Negro, as well as contemporary Southern opinion supporting lynching and oppression, utilizes the mechanism of rationalization to support delusions.

Race prejudice involves the mental conflict, which is held to be the cause of the dissociation of ideas so prominent in insanity. The Negro-complex is often out of harmony with the personality as a whole and therefore results in a conflict that involves unpleasant emotional tension. In everyday life such conflicts are often solved by what, — in those following contradictory moral codes, — is generally known as hypocrisy. When, however, the two systems of incompatible ideas cannot be kept from conflict, the insane man reconciles them through the process of rationalization. Through this same process of rationalization, the Southern white man creates defenses for his immoral acts, and lynching becomes a holy defense of womanhood. That the alleged reasons for violence are simply defense mechanisms for unacceptable wishes is shown by a case in which a juror was lynched for voting to exonerate a Negro accused of a crime! The energetic measures which Southerners use to prevent legal unions of white with colored people look suspiciously like compensatory reactions for their own frustrated desires for such unions. Other forms of defense mechaisms appear in the Southerner's sentimentalizing over his love for the Negro and the tendency in the South to joke about him, — which has a close parallel in the humor of the alcoholic. At the basis of these unacceptable ideas, requiring rationalizations and other forms of defense mechanisms to bring them into harmony with the personality, we find fear, hatred, and sadism constantly cropping out.

When one surveys Southern literature dealing with the Negro, one finds him accused of all the failings of mankind. When we reflect, however, that the Negro, in spite of his ignorance and poverty, does not in most places contribute more than his share to crime and, — even in the opinion of his most violent disparagers, — possesses certain admirable qualities, we are forced to seek the cause of these excessive accusations in the minds of the accusers themselves. Here, too, we find striking similarities to the mental processes of the insane. Where the conflict between the personality as a whole and the unacceptable complex is not resolved within the mind of the subject, the extremely repugnant system of dissociated ideas is projected upon some real or imaginary individual. Except in the case of those who, as we have seen, charge the Negro with an inherent impulse to rape as an unconscious defense of their own murderous impulses, the persistence, — in the face of contrary evidence, — of the delusion that the Negro is a ravisher can only be taken as a projection. According to this view, the Southern white man, who has, — arbitrarily without censure, — enjoyed the right to use colored women, projects this insistent desire upon the Negro when it is no longer socially approved and his conscious personality likewise rejects it. Like the lunatic, he refuses to treat the repugnant desire as a part of himself and consequently shows an exaggerated antagonism toward the desire which he projects upon the Negro. A case has come to the attention of the writer which shows clearly the projection of the unacceptable wish. A telephone operator in a small Southern city called up a Negro doctor and told him that someone at his home had made an improper proposal to her. Although the physician protested that the message could not have come from his house the sheriff was sent to arrest him. His record in the town had been conspicuously in accord with the white man's rule about the color line. He had consistently refused to attend white men, not to mention white women, who had applied to him for treatment. Unable, in spite of his record, to escape arrest, he sought the aid of a white physician. The whole matter died down suddenly, the white physician explaining to his colored colleague that he had gone to the operator and found that she was only "nervous" that day. To those who are acquainted with the mechanism of projection, such a word as "nervous" here has a deeper significance.

The mechanism of projection is also seen in the general disposition of Southern white men to ascribe an inordinate amount of fear to Negroes. That the Negro has no monopoly of fear was admirably demonstrated in Atlanta, where, a year or so ago, white people were fleeing from a haunted road while Negroes were coolly robbing graveyards! This same mental process would explain why white men constantly lay crimes to Negroes when there is no evidence whatever to indicate the race of the criminal. Can we not find here also an explanation of the unwarranted anxiety which white men feel for their homes because of the Negro? Is this another projection of their own unacceptable complexes? In the South, the white man is certainly a greater menace to the Negro's home than the latter is to his.

We must include in our discussion two more aspects of the behavior of the insane that find close parallels in the behavior of those under the influence of the Negro-complex. We meet in the insane with a tendency on the part of the patient to interpret everything that happens in his environment in terms of his particular delusion. In the case of those suffering from the Negro-complex we see the same tendency at work. Any recognition accorded the Negro, even in the North, is regarded as an attempt to give him "social equality," the personal connotations of which are familiar to most Americans. In the South, Negroes have been lynched for being suspected of such a belief. Misconstructions such as are implied in the Southern conception of social equality are so manifestly absurd that they bear a close resemblance to the delusions of reference in the insane. Perhaps more justly to be classed as symptoms of insanity are those frequent hallucinations of white women who complain of attacks by Negroes when clearly no Negroes are involved. Hallucinations often represent unacceptable sexual desires which are projected when they can no longer be repressed. In the South a desire on the part of a white woman for a Negro that could no longer be repressed would most likely be projected, — especially when such a desire is supposed to be as horrible as incest. It is not unlikely, therefore, that imaginary attacks by Negroes are often projected wishes.

The following manifestation of race prejudice shows strikingly its pathological nature. Some years ago a mulatto went to a small Southern town to establish a school for Negroes. In order not to become *persona non grata* in the community, he approached the leading white residents for their approval of the enterprise. Upon his visit to one white woman he was invited into her parlor and treated with the usual courtesies shown visitors; but when this woman discovered later that he was colored, she chopped up the chair in which he had sat and, after pouring gasoline over the pieces, made a bonfire of them. The pathological nature of a delusion is shown by its being out of harmony with one's education and surroundings. For an Australian black fellow to show terror when he learns his wife has touched his blanket would not evince a pathological state of mind; whereas, it did indicate a pathological mental state for this woman to act as if some mysterious principle had entered the chair.

From a practical viewpoint, insanity means social incapacity. Southern white people afflicted with the Negro-complex show themselves incapable of performing certain social functions. They are, for instance, incapable of rendering just decisions when white and colored people are involved; and their very claim that they "know" and "understand" the Negro indicates a fixed system of ideas respecting him, — whereas a sane and just appraisal of the situation would involve the assimilation of new data. The delusions of the sane are generally supported by the herd, while those of the insane are often antisocial. Yet, — from the point of view of Negroes, who are murdered if they believe in social equality or are maimed for asking for an ice cream soda, and of white people, who are threatened with similar violence for not subscribing to the Southerner's delusions, — such behavior is distinctively antisocial. The inmates of a madhouse are not judged insane by themselves, but by those outside. The fact that abnormal behavior towards Negroes is characteristic of a whole group may be an example illustrating Nietzsche's observation that "insanity in individuals is something rare, — but in groups, parties, nations, and epochs it is the rule."

La Bourgeoisie Noire

E. Franklin Frazier

Radicals are constantly asking the question: Why does the Negro, the man farthest down in the economic as well as social scale, steadily refuse to ally himself with the radical groups in America? On the other hand, his failure so far to show sympathy to any extent with the class which *a priori* would appear to be his natural allies has brought praise from certain quarters. Southern white papers when inclined to indulge in sentimental encomiums about the Negro cite his immunity to radical doctrines as one of his most praiseworthy characteristics. Negro orators and, until lately, Negro publications, in pleading for the Negro's claim to equitable treatment, have never failed to boast of the Negro's social behavior in terms of hereditary qualities, have declared that the Negro's temperament is hostile to radical doctrines. But the answer to what is a seeming anomaly to many is to be found in the whole social background of the Negro. One need not attribute it to any peculiar virtue (according as one regards virtue) or seek an explanation in such an incalculable factor as racial temperament.

The first mistake of those who think that the Negro of all groups in America should be in revolt against the present system is that they regard the Negro group as homogeneous. As a matter of fact, the Negro group is highly differentiated, with about the same range of interests as the whites. It is very well for white and black radicals to quote statistics to show that ninety-eight per cent of the Negroes are workers and should seek release from their economic slavery; but as a matter of fact ninety-eight per cent of the Negroes do not regard themselves as in economic slavery. Class differentiation among Negroes is reflected in their church organizations, educational institutions, private clubs, and the whole range of social life. Although these class distinctions may rest upon what would seem to outsiders flimsy and inconsequential matters, they are the social realities of Negro life, and no amount of reasoning can rid his mind of them. Recently we were informed in Dr. Herskovits' book on the Negro that color is the basis of social distinctions. To an outsider or a superficial observer, this would seem true; but when one probes the tissue of the Negro's social life he finds that the Negro reacts to the same illusions that feed the vanity of white men.

What are some of the marks of distinction which make it impossible to treat the Negro group as a homogeneous mass? They are chiefly property, education, and

E. Franklin Frazier, "La Bourgeoisie Noire," V. F. Calverton, ed., *Anthology of American Negro Literature,* New York: Random House, 1929, pp. 379–388.

blood or family. If those possessing these marks of distinction are generally mulattoes, it is because the free Negro class who first acquired these things as well as a family tradition were of mixed blood. The church in Charleston, South Carolina, which was reputed not to admit blacks did not open its doors to nameless mulatto nobodies. Not only has the distinction of blood given certain Negro groups a feeling of superiority over other Negroes, but it has made them feel superior to "poor whites." The Negro's feeling of superiority to "poor whites" who do not bear in their veins "aristocratic" blood has always created a barrier to any real sympathy between the two classes. Race consciousness to be sure has constantly effaced class feeling among Negroes. Therefore we hear on every hand Negro capitalists supporting the right of the Negro worker to organize — against white capitalists, of course. Nevertheless class consciousness has never been absent.

The Negro's attitude towards economic values has been determined by his economic position in American life. First of all, in the plantation system the Negro has found his adjustment to our economic system. The plantation system is based essentially upon enforced labor. Since emancipation the Negro has been a landless peasant without the tradition of the European peasant which binds the latter to the soil. Landownership remained relatively stationary from 1910 to 1920, while the number of landless workers increased. If this class of black workers were to espouse doctrines which aimed to change their economic status, they would be the most revolutionary group in America. From ignorant peasants who are ignorant in a fundamental sense in that they have no body of traditions even, we cannot expect revolutionary doctrines. They will continue a mobile group; while the white landlords through peonage and other forms of force will continue to hold them to the land.

Another factor of consequence in the Negro's economic life is the fact of the large number of Negroes in domestic service. One psychologist has sought to attribute this fact to the strength of the "instinct of submission" in the Negro. But it has represented an adjustment to the American environment. Nevertheless, it has left its mark on the Negro's character. To this is due the fact that he has taken over many values which have made him appear ridiculous and at the same time have robbed him of self-respect and self-reliance. This group is no more to be expected to embrace radical doctrines than the same class was expected to join slave insurrections, concerning which Denmark Vesey warned his followers: "Don't mention it to those waiting men who receive presents of old coats, etc., from their masters, or they'll betray us."

Even this brief consideration of the social situation which has determined the Negro's attitudes towards values in American life will afford a background for our discussion of the seeming anomaly which he presents to many spectators. We shall attempt to show that, while to most observers the Negro shows an apparent indifference to changing his status, this is in fact a very real and insistent stimulus to his struggles. The Negro can only envisage those things which have meaning for him. *The radical doctrines appeal chiefly to the industrial workers, and the Negro has only begun to enter industry.* For Negroes to enter industries which are usually in the cities and escape the confinement of the plantation, they have realized a dream that is as far beyond their former condition as the New Economic Order is beyond the present condition of the wage earner. It has often been observed that the Negro subscribes to all the canons of consumption as the owning class in the present system. Even here we find the same struggle to realize a status that he can envisage and has a meaning for him. Once the Negro struggled for a literary education because he regarded it as the earmark of freedom. The relatively segregated life which the Negro lives makes him struggle to realize the values which give status within his group. An automobile, a home, a position as a teacher, or membership in a fraternity may confer a distinction in removing the possessor from an inferior social status that could never be appreciated by one who is a stranger to Negro life. Outsiders may wonder why a downtrodden, poor, despised people seem so indifferent about entering a struggle that is aimed to give all men an equal status. But if they could enter the minds of Negroes they would find that in the world in which they live they are not downtrodden and despised, but enjoy various forms of distinction.

An interesting episode in the life of the Negro which shows to what extent he is wedded to bourgeois ideals is the present attempt of the Pullman porters to organize. Some people have very superficially regarded this movement as a gesture in the direction of economic radicalism. But anyone who is intimately acquainted with the psychology of the Negro group, especially the porters, knows that this is far from true. One who is connected with the white labor movement showed a better insight through his remark to the writer that the porters showed little working class psychology and showed a dispostion to use their organization to enjoy the amenities of bourgeois social life. The Pullman porters do not show any disposition to overthrow bourgeois values. In fact, for years this group was better situated economically than most Negroes and carried over into their lives as far as possible the behavior patterns which are current in the middle class. In some places they regarded themselves as a sort of aristocracy, and as a colored woman said in one of their meetings recently, "Only an educated gentleman with culture could be a Pullman porter." The advent of a large and consequential professional and business class among Negroes has relegated the Pullman porters to a lower status economically as well as otherwise. Collective bargaining will help them to continue in a role of the colored group which is more in harmony with their conception of their relative status in their group. It is far from the idea of the Pullman porters to tear down the present economic order, and hardly any of them would confess any spiritual kinship with the "poor whites." The Pullman porters are emerging, on the other hand, as an aristocratic laboring group just as the Railroad Brotherhoods have done.

The Negro's lack of sympathy with the white working class is based on more than the feeling of superiority. In the South, especially, the caste system, which is based on color, determines the behavior of the white working class. If the Negro has fatuously claimed spiritual kinship with the white bourgeois, the white working class has taken over the tradition of the slave-holding aristocracy. When white labor in the South attempts to treat with black labor, the inferior status of the latter must be conceded in practice and in theory. Moreover, white labor in the South not only has used every form of trickery to drive the Negro out of the ranks of skilled labor, but it has resorted to legislation to accomplish its aims. Experience, dating from before the Civil War, with the white group, has helped to form the attitude of Negro towards white labor as well as traditional prejudices.[1]

In the February number of the *Southern Workman* there appears an article in which the psychology of the Negro is portrayed as follows. The discovery is made by a white business man in Chicago:

The average working-class Negro in Chicago earns $22 a week. His wife sends her children to the Day Nursery or leaves them with relatives or friends, and she supplements the family income by from $10 to $15 or more per week. The average white man of the same class earns $33 per week and keeps his wife at home. This colored man will rent a $65 per month apartment and buy a $50 suit of clothes while the white man will occupy a $30 per month apartment and buy a $25 suit of clothes. This average white man will come into our store to buy furniture and about $300 will be the limit of his estimated purchase, while the colored man will undertake a thousand dollar purchase without the least thought about meeting the payments from his small income.

To the writer of the article the company's new policy in using colored salesmen is a wonderful opportunity for colored men to learn the furniture business. The furniture company is going to make Negroes better citizens, according to the author of the article, by encouraging them to have better homes. This situation represents not only the extent to which the average Negro has swallowed middle-class standards but the attitude of the upper-class Negro towards the same values.

There is much talk at the present time about the New Negro. He is generally thought of as the creative artist who is giving expression to all the stored-up aesthetic emotion of the race. Negro in Art Week has come to take its place beside, above, or below the other three hundred and fifty-two weeks in the American year. But the public is little aware of the Negro business man who regards himself as a new phenomenon. While the New Negro who is expressing himself in art promises in the words of one of his chief exponents not to compete with the white man either politically or economically, the Negro business man seeks the salvation of the race in economic enterprise. In the former case there is either an acceptance of the present system or an ignoring of the economic realities of life. In the case of the latter there is an acceptance of the gospel of economic success. Sometimes the New Negro of the artistic type calls the New Negro business man a Babbitt, while the latter calls the former a mystic. But the Negro business man is winning out, for he is dealing with economic realities. He can boast of the fact that he is independent of white support, while the Negro artist still seeks it. One Negro insurance company in a rather cynical acceptance of the charge of Babbittry begins a large advertisement in a Negro magazine in the words of George F. Babbitt.

A perusal of Negro newspapers will convince anyone that the Negro group does not regard itself as outcasts without status. One cannot appeal to them by telling them that they have nothing to lose but their chains. The chains which Negroes have known in the South were not figurative. Negro newspapers are a good index of the extent to which middle-class ideals have captured the imagination of Negroes. In one newspaper there is a column devoted to What Society Is Wearing. In this column the apparel of those who are socially prominent is described in detail. The parties, the cars, the homes, and the jewelry of the élite find a place in all of these papers. In fact, there is no demand on the part of the Negro leaders to tear down social distinctions and create a society of equals. As the writer heard a colored editor tell a white man recently, "the white people draw the line at the wrong point and put all of us in the same class."

Negro schools in the South furnish an example of the influence of middle class ideals which make Negroes appear in a ridiculous light. These schools give annually a public performance. Instead of giving plays such as Paul Green's folk plays of Negro life, they give fashion shows which have been popularized to boost sales. Negro students appear in all kinds of gorgeous costumes which are worn by the leisured middle class. One more often gets the impression that he has seen a Mardi Gras rather than an exhibition of correct apparel.

Even the most ardent radical cannot expect the Negro to hold himself aloof from the struggle for economic competence and only dream of his escape from his subordinate economic status in the overthrow of the present system. A Negro business man who gets out of the white man's kitchen or dining room rightly regards himself as escaping from economic slavery. Probably he will maintain himself by exploiting the Negro who remains in the kitchen, but he can always find consolation in the feeling, that if he did not exploit him a white man would. But in seeking escape from economic subordination, the Negro has generally envisaged himself as a captain of industry. In regard to group efficiency he has shown no concern. For example, a group isolated to the extent of the Negro in America could have developed cooperative enterprises. There has been no attempt in schools or otherwise to teach or encourage this type of economic organization. The idea of the rich man has been held up to him. More than one Negro business has been wrecked because of this predatory view of economic activity.

Many of those who criticize the Negro for selecting certain values out of American life overlook the fact that the primary struggle on his part has been to acquire a culture. In spite of the efforts of those who would have him dig up his African past, the Negro is a stranger to African culture. The manner in which he has taken over the American culture has never been studied in intimate enough detail to make it comprehensible. The educated class among Negroes has been the forerunners in this process. Except, perhaps, through the church, the economic basis of the civilized classes among Negroes has not been within the group. Although today the growing professional and business classes are finding support among Negroes, the upper classes are subsidized chiefly from without. To some outsiders such a situation makes the Negro intellectual appear as merely an employee of the white group. At times the emasculating effect of Negro men appearing in the role of mere entertainers for the whites has appeared in all its tragic reality. But the creation of this educated class of Negroes has made possible the civilization of the Negro. It may seem conceivable to some that the Negro could have contended on the ground of abstract right for unlimited participation in American life on the basis of individual efficiency; but the Negro had to deal with realities. It is strange that today one expects this very class which represents the most civilized group to be in revolt against the system by which it was created, rather than the group of leaders who have sprung from the soil of Negro culture.

Here we are brought face to face with a fundamental dilemma of Negro life. Dean Miller at Howard University once expressed this dilemma aphoristically, namely, that the Negro pays for what he wants and begs for what he needs. The Negro pays, on the whole, for his church, his lodges and fraternities, and his automobile, but he begs for his education. Even the radical movement which had vogue a few years back was subsidized by the white radical group. It did not spring out of any general movement among Negroes towards radical doctrines. Moreover, black radicals theorized about the small number of Negroes who had entered industry from the security of New York City; but none ever undertook to enter the South and teach the landless peasants any type of self-help. What began as the organ of the struggling working masses became the mouthpiece of Negro capitalists. The New Negro group which has shown a new orientation towards Negro life and the values which are supposed to spring from Negro life has restricted itself to the purely cultural in the narrow sense.

In his article the writer has attempted to set forth the social forces which have caused the Negro to have his present attitude towards the values in American life. From even this cursory glance at Negro life we are able to see to what extent bourgeois ideals are implanted in the Negro's mind. We are able to see that the Negro group is a highly differentiated group with various interests, and that it is far from sound to view the group as a homogeneous group of outcasts. There has come upon the stage a group which represents a nationalistic movement. This movement is divorced from any program of economic reconstruction. It is unlike the Garvey movement in that Garvey, through schemes — fantastic to be sure — united his nationalistic aims with an economic program. This new movement differs from the program of Booker Washington, which sought to place the culture of the Negro upon a sound basis by making him an efficient industrial worker. Nor does it openly ally itself with those leaders who condemn the organization of the Pullman porters and advise Negroes to pursue an opportunistic course with capitalism. It looks askance at the new rising class of black capitalism while it basks in the sun of white capitalism. It enjoys the congenial company of white radicals while shunning association with black radicals. The New Negro Movement functions in the third dimension of culture; but so far it knows nothing of the other two dimensions — Work and Wealth.

Note

[1] E. Franklin Frazier, "The Negro in the Industrial South," *The Nation,* Vol. 125, No. 3238.

The Plantation during the Depression

Charles S. Johnson

What Is a Tenant?

A farm tenant, in the widest meaning of the term, is any person who hires the farm which he operates, paying for the use of the land either by a share of the crop which he raises or by cash rental or both. Now the renting of land is not in itself a bad thing; it is customary in other parts of America and to a limited extent in Europe. It is a simple means of getting access to land by persons who have not capital enough to purchase farms. Normally it is regarded as a step on the road to independent ownership. The evil is not in renting land but in the traditions and practices which have grown up about it in the South.

Tenants may be divided into three main classes: (a) renters who hire land for a fixed rental to be paid either in cash or its equivalent in crop values; (b) share tenants, who furnish their own farm equipment and work animals and obtain use of land by agreeing to pay a fixed per cent of the cash crop which they raise; (c) share-croppers who have to have furnished to them not only the land but also farm tools and animals, fertilizer, and often even the food they consume, and who in return pay a larger per cent of the crop.

In considering cotton tenancy, the first group may be almost ignored. Those who have definite agreements with landlords as to exact rental prices are few in number and their status is so independent as to remove them from the system of subservient tenancy. The share tenants and share-croppers are the two great subdivisions of the dependent workers in the cotton belt. The difference between these two classes is simply one of degree. The share tenants, since they supply much of their own equipment, are able to rent the land on fairly good terms, usually on the basis of paying to the owner not more than one-fourth or one-third of the crop raised. The share-croppers, on the other hand, having almost nothing to offer but their labor, must pay as rent a higher share of the product, usually one-half of the crop. In addition, of course, both tenants and croppers must pay out of their share of the crop for all that is supplied to them in the way of seed, fertilizer, and food

From Charles S. Johnson, Edwin R. Embree, and Will Alexander, *The Collapse of Cotton Tenancy*, Chapel Hill: University of North Carolina Press, 1935, pp. 6–33. Reprinted by permission of the publisher.

supplies. "Tenancy," as used in the present report and as commonly applied in the South, is a general term covering both the share tenants and the share-croppers, but not the renters. As a matter of fact, over one-third of all tenants in the South, and over half of the Negro tenants are croppers, that is, in the lowest category of poverty and dependence.

The risk of the tenant increases, of course, in proportion to what he is able to contribute to the contract. There is almost no financial risk assumed by the share cropper who furnishes only his labor (and that of his family), who receives his equipment and supplies and even his food, from the owner. The share tenant, who supplies his own tools and work animals, assumes more risk, and in return expects a larger share of the earnings. The renter of course assumes much greater risk. In turn the landlord's potential profits increase as he assumes more and more of the risk. Therein lies a danger to the tenant. It is to the advantage of the owner to encourage the most dependent form of share cropping as a source of largest profits. And he wishes to hold in greatest dependence just those workers who are most efficient. A shiftless and inefficient cropper is of little value to the owner and is expelled, unless, in a serious labor shortage, absence of any worker is even more costly than the presence of an incompetent one. The industrious and thrifty tenant is sought by the landlord. The very qualities which might normally lead a tenant to attain the position of renter, and eventually of owner, are just the ones which make him a permanent asset as a cropper. Landlords, thus, are most concerned with maintaining the system that furnishes them labor and that keeps this labor under their control, that is, in the tenancy class. The means by which landowners do this are: first, the credit system; and second, the established social customs of the plantation order.

As a part of the age-old custom in the South, the landlord keeps the books and handles the sale of all the crops. The owner returns to the cropper only what is left over of his share of the profits after deductions for all items which the landlord has advanced to him during the year: seed, fertilizer, working equipment, and food supplies, plus interest on all this indebtedness, plus a theoretical "cost of supervision." The landlord often supplies the food — "pantry supplies" or "furnish" — and other current necessities through his own store or commissary. Fancy prices at the commissary, exorbitant interest, and careless or manipulated accounts, make it easy for the owner to keep his tenants constantly in debt.

The plight of the tenant at annual settlement time is so common that a whole folklore about it has grown up in the South.

A tenant offering five bales of cotton was told, after some owl-eyed figuring, that this cotton exactly balanced his debt. Delighted at the prospect of a profit this year, the tenant reported that he had one more bale which he hadn't yet brought in. "Shucks," shouted the boss, "why didn't you tell me before? Now I'll have to figure the account all over again to make it come out even."

Of course every story of this kind, and such stories are innumerable, can be matched by tales of unrealiability and shiftlessness on the part of the tenant. The case against the system cannot be rested on any personal indictment of landlords any more than it can be vindicated by stories of the improvidence of tenants. The fact is that landlords generally act as they find it necessary to act under the system; tenants do likewise. The development of bad economic and social habits of whatever kind on the part of both landlords and tenants is direct evidence of a faulty system.

Even more than the credit system, the traditions of the region hold the tenant in thrall. The plantation system developed during slavery. It continues on the old master and slave pattern. For many years, even after Emancipation, black tenants were the rule in the cotton fields and the determination to "keep the Negro in his place" was, if anything, stronger after the Civil War than before. Although white families now form the great majority of the cotton tenants, the old "boss and black" attitude still pervades the whole system. Because of his economic condition, and because of his race, color, and previous condition of servitude, the rural Negro is helpless before the white master. Every kind of exploitation and abuse is permitted because of the old caste prejudice. The poor white connives in this abuse of the Negro; in fact, he is the most violent protagonist of it. This fixed custom of exploitation of the Negro has carried over to the white tenant and cropper. Yet it has been impossible to bring about any change, even to get the poor white workers to take a stand, since any movement for reform is immediately confused with the race issue. Because of their insistence upon the degrading of three million Negro tenants, five and a half million white workers continue to keep themselves in virtual peonage.

What the Tenant Earns

The average American farm family in 1929 earned $1,240, and this was about a third of the average for non-farm families. The lowest general earnings were in the southern states. The Carolinas, Mississippi, Arkansas, Alabama, Georgia, and Tennessee, the states of the old cotton belt, stood at the bottom of the list. Here, even at the period of national prosperity, a vast farm population barely earned subsistence.

Every study of wages and income in the South makes perfectly clear the low economic position of the rural South. Clarence Heer's exhaustive study of wages and income, covering a period of thirty years, showed that southern agriculture had provided its farmers just about half the per capita income of farmers in other sections. This includes all the "independent farmers, plantation owners, tenants, and share croppers." When tenants alone are considered, the family earnings slump distressingly below the level of decent subsistence.

The debts are a part of the system and are of two kinds: those accumulating from year to year; and current debts arising from the "furnishing" system. More than a third of the tenants have debts of more than a year's standing. In six widely differing counties included in the field studies of our Committee, 43.4 per cent of the tenants were in debt before they planted their 1934 crop. The average indebtedness, according to the Alabama tenants who were able to keep any record of their accounts, was $80.00.

As to current earnings or deficits, a study of Negro tenant farmers in Macon County, Alabama, in 1932, published in *Shadow of the Plantation,* showed that 61.7 per cent "broke even," 26.0 per cent "went in the hole," and 9.4 per cent made some profit. Of this latter group the total income ranged from about $70 to $90 per year. The special inquiry into tenant farmer earnings by this Committee, which covered some 2,000 families in 1934 and 1935 in Mississippi, Texas, Alabama, and South Carolina, found variations in earnings according to soil fertility and types of management, but universally a sub-standard. Inseparable from the small gross earnings of these farmers was the stern factor of landlord policy, prerogative, alleged supervision charges, and interest rates. It must be remembered that the tenant's actual income is very different from the earnings of his farm as listed in agricultural reports. The landlord's share is taken from the earnings together with the operator's gross expenses.

For the small number of all these 2,000 tenant families who received a cash income in 1933, the average was $105.43. The actual earnings per family, when distributed among five persons, would give a monthly income per person of $1.75. And these incomes, theoretically at least, were benefiting from the federal program of aid to farmers as administered in 1933.

Tenants in general have to consider themselves fortunate if they can farm for subsistence only. One cropper complained dismally: "For 18 years we ain't cleared a thing or made any real money." Another had received his cash in a manner which made it difficult to remember the amounts: "I couldn't possibly go to task and tell you. I got it in dribbles and couldn't keep a record of it, but it wasn't over $75.00." Still another farmer "cleared $45.00 last year; nothing the year before and no settlement; cleared $117.00 the year before that. The most I ever cleared was $260.00 — just before the war." Few of the tenants interviewed had cleared cash incomes since 1921, and many had made nothing since the World War.

There could, perhaps, be some compensation for low incomes if the farms were supplying food for the families. But the production of a cash crop rules out the raising of general produce. This much is obvious: if there is any advantage in cotton farming as a profitable business, the tenant does not share it.

How the Tenant Lives

Cotton has always been a cheap-labor crop; its development has rested on keeping this labor cost low. In fact many declare that profit is impossible "if all the labor it requires were paid for." The results appear in the living standards of the millions of families whose men, women, and children produce the crop.

The cultural landscape of the cotton belt has been described as a "miserable panorama of unpainted shacks, rain-gullied fields, straggling fences, rattle-trap Fords, dirt, poverty, disease, drudgery, and monotony that stretches for a thousand miles across the cotton belt." It used to be said that "cotton is and must remain a black man's crop, not a white man's, because the former's standard of living has always been low, and his natural inferiority makes it unnecessary to change it." Now that white families make up nearly two-thirds of the workers, it is clear that meager and pinched living is not a racial trait but a result of the system of cotton tenancy. Submerged beneath the system which he supports, the cotton tenant's standard of living approches the level of bare animal existence. The traditional status of the slave required only subsistence. The cotton slave — white or colored — has inherited a rôle in which comfort, education, and self-development have no place. For the type of labor he performs, all that is actually required is a stomach indifferently filled, a shack to sleep in, some old jeans to cover his nakedness.

This age-old condition of the cotton worker and the necessity to keep it unchanged, lead to some interesting rationalizing by supporters of the existing order. Serious statements about the happiness of the tenant in his dependent rôle are taking the place of the earlier stories of the contentment of the slaves. Anecdotes of ludicrous spending whenever he gets his hands on money are used to justify the regular condition of poverty. Shiftlessness and laziness are reported as reasons for the dependent state, whereas, in fact, in so far as they exist, they are not necessarily inherent, but are caused by the very conditions of the share-cropping system.

The studies made of tenant families confirm the indignant assertion of a writer in the Dallas, Texas, *News* that "the squalid condition of the cotton raisers of the South is a disgrace to the southern people. They stay in shacks, thousands of which are unfit to house animals, much less human beings. Their children are born under such conditions of medical treatment, food and clothing, as would make an Eskimo rejoice that he did not live in a cotton growing country."

The drab ugliness of tenant houses might be condoned if they were comfortable. Many of them are old, some have actually come down from the period of slavery, and all of them, unpainted and weather-beaten, appear ageless. They are crudely constructed, windows and doors are out of alignment, they leak even while still new. Family size and size of house have no relationship. Whatever the number in the family it must occupy the customary three rooms. In fact a family of any size may live in a two-room house; as many as thirteen have been found living in a single bedroom and kitchen.

A Children's Bureau study of the welfare of children in cotton-growing areas of Texas, showed 64 per cent of the white and 77 per cent of the Negro families living under conditions of housing congestion, and this in spite of the common belief that over-crowding is a phenomenon of the city. Another study of white tenant families in Tennessee estimated an average value of all personal belongings of tenants at less than a hundred dollars. In one cotton-growing county of Alabama, reported in *Shadow of the Plantation,* over half of the families lived in one- and two-room cabins, and the comment on the character and inadequacy of these by one of the tenants does not exaggerate the lot of this majority: "My house is so rotten you can jest take up the boards in your hands and cromple 'em up. Everything done swunk about it."

Although living on abundant land in the south temperate zone, tenant families have probably the most meager and ill-balanced diet of any large group in America. Devotion to the single cash-crop, and the fact that food crops mature during the same season as cotton, make it virtually impossible under the system to raise subsistence crops. Because the growing of household produce does not fit into the economy of a cash-crop, it is not encouraged by landlords, whose prerogative it is to determine the crops grown. As a result the diet is limited largely to imported foods, made available through the commissaries and local stores. This diet can be, and commonly is, strained down to the notorious three M's, — Meat (fat salt pork), meal, and molasses. Evidence of the slow ravages of this diet are to be found in the widespread incidence of pellagra, which Dr. Joseph Goldberger of the United States Public Health Service bluntly attributes to lack of proper food. This diet is a part of the very culture of tenancy, supported by habit, convenience, and cheapness. A dietary survey reported by Rupert B. Vance revealed significantly that the maize kernel constituted 23 per cent of the total food intake of white Tennessee and Georgia mountaineers, 32.5 per cent of that of southern Negroes, chiefly tenant farmers, but only 1.6 per cent of that of northern families in comfortable circumstances. Pork — chiefly fat salt pork — makes up 40 per cent of the food of southern tenant farmers.

Food is the largest item in the tenant's budget, and since almost no food is produced, it must be purchased. In six counties, the average monthly expenditure for food in 1934 was $12.34, or about $3.08 per week for the average family of five. As small as these amounts seem, they consume the major portion of the tenant's income.

Furnishing

The current credit used by share tenants is commonly known as "furnishing." The landlord furnishes his tenants with food and other necessities during the crop production period and is paid for these advances out of the tenants' share of the crop in the settlement at harvest time. The usual rationing consists of furnishing groceries from the commissary to a tenant and his family. The tenant does not know the money value of what he is receiving or, to be more exact, he does not know what he is being charged for it. Variations of furnishing are the less frequently used "account" from which the tenant makes purchases with some knowledge of what he is being charged, and the "limit," whereby the landlord allows the tenant commodities up to some fixed amount.

Under the "rations" system the tenant receives little, and often suffers rank exploitation. In some instances large plantations allot to each laborer two pecks of meal and four pounds of fat back pork every two weeks. Some of the landlords are even more niggardly, providing tenants only meal and leaving them to provide meat as best they can. The testimony of tenants, supported by the observation of bare cupboards, points to extreme meagerness.

We can't get any flour, snuff, shoes, sugar, coffee, thread or anything from the landlord but meat and meal. We have a divil of a time. No soap, soda, or salt. Can't borrow a dime, not a damn cent. If this ain't hell, I'll eat you. We work our damn heads off and git nothing. The harder we work, the deeper in debt we gits.

The restriction of the landlord's advance does not, however, prevent a heavy debt at the close of the year.

Boss said after we's gathered the crop last year, I still owed him $130.00. Sometimes we got less than 15 pounds of meat and two bushels of meal every two weeks.

A Negro woman reported her conversation with her landlord, about furnishing, and his sympathetic response:

Yesterday, Mr. ——, the boss man, came through the field and asked me how I feel. I just stopped my hoeing and said, "Mr. ——, I just don't know how I feel." He says, "What's the trouble, Julia, don't you feel well?" I say, "I'm just hungry, Mr. ——." "Ain't you got nothing to eat at your house, Julia?" "I ain't got nothing but fat back and corn bread, and I done eat that so long that I believe I got the pellagacy, Mr. ——." His face turns red when I say that, and he said, "Well, Saturday I'm gonna give you some flour too. Just come by the office."

The amounts allowed tenants under the several systems of furnishing and the period over which the credit extends are determined by the landlord. The "margin of progress" possible to the tenant is generally so small that he is constantly dependent upon credit at any terms. The amounts croppers receive are not sufficient for a family by any standard of adequacy. The fact that millions live and work under these conditions offers little ground for national pride when death and sickness rates are included in the picture.

No Incentive to Improvement

Since the tenant has no legal claims on any improvements he may make, he has no interest in conserving or improving either the land or the buildings. On the contrary, just as it is to his advantage to rob the soil of its fertility, so he is tempted to burn for firewood rails from any nearby fence or planks from the porch floor or from an outhouse — if the place happens to be distinguished by having any movable materials that have not already succumbed to the ravages of time and tenants. The tenant is not likely to trouble to make any repairs that are not absolutely necessary, and these few will be so made as not to outlast his stay on the place.

Under a system which does not encourage labor and thrift men easily develop habits of improvidence. As matters now stand, the tenant who really works on his place, who labors to restore the soil, who repairs and builds, is merely inviting his landlord to raise his rent. If he should use all his time and energy in improving the place on which he lives, with the hope of ultimately raising his own status, the tenant would have no recourse if his landlord demanded a higher rent or notified him that he would have to leave the next year. It may be argued that landlords generally would not follow any such course; but the absence of any laws on the statute books of the southern states protecting tenants in improvements made by them is a final answer to such arguments. Those who say that legal protection for the tenant is unnecessary, that we have too many laws, will have difficulty in justifying the crop lien laws which protect the immediate interests of the merchants and landlords, but ignore the immediate interests of the tenants and the long-time interests of everyone in the region.

Is it any wonder, then, that the soil is exhausted, buildings not fit for habitation, and the tenants themselves thoroughly inured to habits and attitudes that, if undisturbed, will keep them impoverished? There can be no general prosperity among any class for long in such an environment.

What the Status of Tenancy Means

It is a notorious and shameful fact that the stock arguments employed against any serious efforts to improve the lot of the cotton tenant are based upon the very social and cultural conditions which tenancy itself creates. The mobility of the tenant, his dependence, his lack of ambition, shiftlessness, his ignorance and poverty, the lethargy of his pellagra-ridden body, provide a ready excuse for keeping him under a stern paternalistic control. There is not a single trait alleged which, where true, does not owe its source and continuance to the imposed status itself.

The status of tenancy demands complete dependence; it requires no education and demands no initiative, since the landlord assumes the prerogative of direction in the choice of crop, the method by which it shall be cultivated, and how and when and where it shall be sold. He keeps the record and determines the earnings. Through the commissary or credit merchant, even the choice of diet is determined. The landlord can determine the kind and amount of schooling for the children, the extent to which they may share benefits intended for all the people. He may even determine the relief they receive in the extremity of their distress. He controls the courts, the agencies of law enforcement and, as in the case of share-croppers in eastern Arkansas, can effectively thwart any efforts at organization to protect their meager rights.

The present system is so constructed that the landless remain landless and the propertyless remain propertyless. To accumulate property, to increase independence, is to oppose the system itself. In a plantation area it is easier to be a cropper and conform to the system than to be a small owner or renter. For a share tenant to rise above his status he must overcome insuperable obstacles: (1) the agriculture that he knows fits only the old system, (2) the banks cannot finance him because they are geared to finance the plantations, (3) the cost of merchant credit dissipates his accumulated working capital, and (4) the crop lien credit system has destroyed his independence in the marketing of his crop.

Neither ambition, nor thrift, nor self-respect can thrive in such a climate. Not only is it impossible to develop a hardy stock of ambitious farm owners — the persistent American ideal — but it is impossible to avoid physical and moral decadence.

If the tenant is lazy, this is a result of his mode of life. As a Mississippian, H. Snyder, writing candidly in the *North American Review,* observes: "Certainly the common run of people in the South are poor, and we are told this poverty is born of their laziness. But this is upside down, as their laziness is born of their poverty."

Attempts to justify the existing system of tenure on the score that it is an adaptation to the latent and innate characteristics and capacities of the southern farm population are as baseless as they are vicious. All such observable characteristics can be traced directly to the system of tenure and the mode of livelihood that it promotes. The system, says Arthur N. Moore of the Georgia Experiment Station, does not provide ". . . a friendly atmosphere for the development of latent capacities."

Such in brief detail is the life of the tenant — drear, meager, and changeless. Upon this is reared an agricultural system which custom and a temporary federal subsidy are holding together against the insistent need of complete reorganization.

Let us now look for a moment at certain other central features of the industry of cotton culture.

A Precarious Credit System

Louis XIV of France observed with a grim irony that "credit supports agriculture, as a cord supports the hanged." For sixty years cotton culture has been strangling under an impossible system of finance. Only a very favorable world market for this staple has permitted survival of the system and the complex of social institutions bound up with it. Now, with the great and growing competition of other cotton-growing areas in the world, and newer problems of production and consumption, the cotton system faces finally and perhaps fatally the consequences of unsound credit.

Even under slavery the chief capital supporting cotton cultivation was not available in the South, a situation which kept the whole area in a secondary slavery to the capital of the North. In 1850 when the total cotton, rice, and sugar sales amounted to $119,400,000, the total bank deposits in the South were around $20,000,000. In 1860 when the value of crops reached $200,000,000, less than $30,000,000 was in southern banks. There has been a continuing lack of short-term credit to finance annual operations, for both productive and consumptive purposes. Bank credit in the South has been inadequate, and this has made necessary reliance upon other and costly sources.

In the cotton belt there is a high seasonality of both agricultural loans and bank deposits. The volume of loans is highest at precisely the time when deposits are lowest. In a one-crop system the bulk of farm income is in the fall and early winter months. The need for loans is in the spring and summer. Since cash deposits provide the body of lendable funds, it is impossible to meet demands of farmers for current financing, and, at the same time, maintain adequate reserves for safety.

Most loans on cotton crops are essentially speculative and this risk increases their cost. The hierarchy of these loans, with risk and service charges, results in an insupportable accumulation of credit costs for the groups lowest down. The credit merchant becomes an almost inescapable part of the credit structure, and is a response to the erratic nature of farm income under the exclusive one-crop economy. These credit costs, on the basis of studies made by the Department of Agriculture, have been shown to drain off 25 to 50 per cent from the operating capital of the small dependent farmers.

The three most important sources of credit for the small farmer in the South, before introduction of the federal credit agencies, have been (1) the landlords, (2) the merchants and dealers, and (3) the local commercial banks. The high cost of merchant and landlord credit, when this includes both the tangible and intangible costs, has been a retarding factor in the progress of the tenant and small owner classes of both white and Negro farmers. A mortgage or lien on the crop is regularly given as security. This gives the creditor domination over the debtor and final control of the cotton crop. As long as the crop lien is given as security for a loan and all financing is done through the agency which holds this crop lien, there is little chance of improvement in the short time credit conditions of farmers.

There is little hope of any economic progress for the tenant farmer generally, under the old credit system. What has actually happened is that the landlord and credit merchant, instead of promoting advancement in agricultural and social development, have been financing economic stagnation and backwardness. Where credit costs cut out the *margin of progress,* or the small accumulations by which ownership is eventually acquired, there can be no economic growth.

The Credit Merchant

Closest to the share tenant and cropper is the credit merchant. He may be a merchant only or he may be a landlord controlling the business, not only of his own tenants, but of any other renters and small owners who need to be "furnished." Through his own farming operations he can secure from one-half to two-thirds of the tenants' productivity, and through his commercial operations he can, and often does, secure the rest. As the system is at present organized he is essential to his own tenants and to croppers and share tenants on the plantations of absentee and non-furnishing landlords. In such a position he can and often does exact a high and exhausting tribute. He justifies his interest charges and time prices on the ground of risk. The method in practice, thus, is to sell on credit to the farmer "all that the trade can carry" and charge as much as the borrower can bear.

The credit merchant's security is the entire crop, which when harvested and ginned, must be turned over for disposal by the creditor in payment of the debt. The merchant keeps the books and sets the interest and time prices. Even if the merchant is fair and does not charge exorbitant prices and extortionate interest, there may be no balance or there may be a debt for the tenant. In any case, the tenant rarely if ever gets a detailed statement of his debits and credits. He has no choice but to accept the settlement given him. In earlier times the prestige of the white merchant or planter forbade any questioning of the account by the Negro tenant; today the prestige of the established credit system forbids questioning of accounts by either black or white tenants. Sentiment can play but small part in such a system and where "reasonable profits" mean bare subsistence for the workers, few favors and no questioning can be indulged. These merchants, when they are candid with themselves, see the viciousness of the system of which they are a part. One justification is that the excesses are necessary for survival in competition on a low level. A South Carolina merchant, who had changed his own practices and abandoned the prevailing customs, said:

We used to do a general credit business carrying many accounts. We charged interest plus a time price which amounted to 50 per cent. Thirty per cent was supposed to cover costs of operating the store, and supervision of farms, and 20 per cent was supposed to cover losses on accounts. We went bankrupt on this basis and changed our practice when my brother and I started this store. We now select very carefully those tenants that we "furnish" and charge them only a flat rate of 10 per cent which is assessed upon the account as it stands on September 30th.

I think the old credit system is wrong. Any system of "furnishing" which expects a 20 per cent loss is wrong. The old system is extortionate and too great a burden for the farmer to bear. We pick our risks and try to deal fairly with them. You won't find this a general practice.

This statement illustrates clearly the dilemma facing everyone who lives in the region. The merchant who chooses his risks carefully can abandon the prevailing customs. But what would happen if all merchants did this? Who would take the chances on the bad risks? We can be sure that no other agency could take the same chances of loss on a purely commercial basis without at the same time exacting the same terms and securing the same chances for profit. There is no reason to believe any other commercial agency would do this better than it is now done.

Because of the prevailing customs, the merchant or planter may exact exorbitant charges without feeling that any injustice is being done the tenant. It is possible to avoid the laws regulating interest charges by levying service charges and management costs. As one planter bluntly stated:

There are more ways of whipping the devil than around the stump. We don't charge interest. We charge a 25 per cent manager's fee, that pays for the rider, manager service, and supervision costs.

Even when a merchant wants to be fair to his tenants he is promptly placed at a disadvantage in competition with less scrupulous ones. A south Texas merchant complained about a group of competitors:

They advance a man cash or furnishings and in most cases they tie the man up so he never pays out of debt, which keeps the farmer forever using the furnishings of their stores. There are all sorts of unfairness in this type of business. A tenant of mine came to me and said that — promised that he would give him a certain price for his cotton on payment of his account. When the cotton was delivered — had reduced the price to another figure. . . . That shows you just how tenants are cheated out of their incomes and are kept perpetually in debt.

It is not that merchants are always cruel to their tenants. A common figure in the cotton belt is the paternalistic planter-merchant who renders kindly services and is in turn the only person of influence to whom dependents can turn in distress. The seriousness and tragedy of the situation lie in the fact that the merchant is virtually forced to exploit the tenant if he is himself to survive. For the credit merchant and the planter himself are in turn supported by the commercial banking system. And although merchants and landlords may even help to control the banks, banking capital is scarce because the masses of the people have little savings. The bulk of the savings among the rural population belongs to the landlords, and this is not enough.

The simple per annum interest rates in 1934 in three selected cotton counties studied in Mississippi and Texas varied from 16.1 per cent to 25.3 per cent. In addition to this, however, were credit prices. In these same communities the excess of the credit price was found to be greater even than the interest charges, and the total cost to the tenant for his supplies averaged more than 50 per cent per annum.

With a systematic charge of 50 per cent for production and consumption credit, the tenant fails to accumulate capital or even to get out of debt; and the small farm-owner is in constant danger of falling into the tenant class. The census figures on the startling increase in tenancy indicate that this is exactly what is happening.

Concentration of Land Ownership

The outcome of the precarious credit structure, which seems to have escaped general attention, is the quiet concentration of land in impersonal ownership. The Civil War and the following period of disorganization of southern agriculture witnessed a progressive breaking up of many large cotton plantations into small holdings. This trend continued until the decade of the 80's. With the turn of the century, conditions changed. The South now is experiencing a re-concentration of tenant farms under corporate ownership. In 1900 the census of agriculture shows the number of rented farms possessed by landlords owning five or more rented farms in Mississippi as 53.1 per cent. In 1920 the Bureau of Agricultural Economics found, in a study of five selected areas of the Mississippi Delta, that 81.2 per cent of the rented farms were so possessed. Although the areas are not strictly comparable, similar differences are found in other states between 1900 and 1920, when compared with the selected areas studied by the Bureau of Agricultural Economics. Such indications led Dr. Rupert Vance to conclude that "even before the disasters of 1920–1925 the trend toward land concentration was resumed." It is estimated that areas amounting to 30 per cent of the cotton lands of various states are owned by insurance companies and banks.

It is apparent that during times of normal prosperity in the cotton planting industry, since about 1880, the better lands of the South have been progressively concentrated into large plantations under central management. Many of these plantations have fallen into the hands of large creditor institutions, and at the present time enormous holdings are in the hands of a few of these institutions. Whether or not this concentration will continue, will depend upon the future prices of cotton, the continued profitableness of the plantation type of farm organization, the success of plantation owners in liquidating the present mortgage indebtedness without dissolution, and the ability of others to recover property they have lost. But whatever view one takes of the system, it is certain that it has not operated to the benefit of those living under it, and future prospects, unless the system is altered, are even darker than the past. In the past the tenant has paid with his labor and his life; later the landlord has paid with his land and his capital.

The Etiquette of Race Relations — Past, Present, and Future

Bertram W. Doyle

Social control, it is generally admitted among sociologists, is a focal problem of sociology. Yet, to Herbert Spencer, writing his *Principles of Sociology,* government was the center, if not the basis, of social control. Said he:

The earliest kind of government, the most general kind of government, and the government which is ever spontaneously recommencing, is the government of ceremonial observances. This kind of government, besides preceding all other kinds, and besides having in all places and times approached nearer to universality of influence, has ever had, and continues to have, the largest share in regulating men's lives.[1]

Ceremonial observances, he notes, comprise: (1) forms that express loyalty, respect, and worship, such as, obeisances, prostrations, bowing, salaams, uncoverings of the head; (2) forms that express subjection or, in many cases, prestige, such as, the use of titles, giving or receiving presents, extravagant compliments, exaggerated eulogies; (3) forms developing from emotional excitement, such as kissing, embracing, vocal expressions of joy or pleasure; (4) forms "not originating directly . . . but by natural sequence rather than intentional symbolization," such as making visits, the use of badges and costumes, and class distinctions that may be exhibited in differences in cut and quality of clothing, in the shape or ornamentation of houses, and in methods of transportation.[2]

William Graham Sumner, seeking controls more informal, and yet more binding than police, laws, courts, and formal government, has established the thesis that the *mores*[3] are of the former type of controls, and has indicated that etiquette — the equivalent of Spencer's "ceremonial government" — is "in the mores."[4]

Students of society, moreover, have shown that ceremonial observances are not confined to any one social group, but, differing in form and degree, are universal.

Bertram W. Doyle, "The Etiquette of Race Relations — Past, Present, and Future," *Journal of Negro Education,* V, April 1936, pp. 191–208. Reprinted by permission of the publisher.

They agree, generally, that fundamental patterns of life and behavior are everywhere the same, and they recognize that similarities of culture are due to the nature of man, which "is everywhere essentially the same and tends to express itself in similar sentiments and institutions."[5]

It has been widely noted that ceremonial observances, generally deemed proper to the association of white persons and Negroes, exist in the South. A survey of the literature of the period prior to the War between the states will confirm the observation that such observances were formulated into a code[6] which included, on the one hand ceremonial forms used by all persons, and on the other, forms resorted to white persons and Negroes — slave and free — associated (sic). In addition, a cursory glance into the literature of relations between the races, for the period since 1865, will give the impression that a code still exists which, barring some exceptions, is a reminder, if not a heritage, of the antebellum period.[7] It is, however, doubtless true that small attempt has been made to analyze the etiquette of race relations from the standpoint of social control.

It might then be profitable to seek to discover: (1) the social usages or the etiquette[8] customarily employed in social contacts and relations of white persons and Negroes; (2) how these have operated to control those relations; and (3) what effect the success or failure of the control has had upon the ability of the two races to enter into, and to cooperate in, an effective corporate life. If these objectives were realized, it might again be profitable to discuss certain educational implications involved in the question of etiquette and race relations.

The Code of Interracial Etiquette

The Golden Age of etiquette in race relations might with a degree of accuracy be placed in the period of American Negro slavery. Politeness on the part of Negroes, especially, was during that period remarked by more than one traveller and generally attributed to innate disposition.[9] Where slaves met white persons publicly, the men touched or removed their hats — in those cases where they actually wore hats — or would nod and bow, and women slaves would curtsy. Shaking hands, regulated by local custom, might or might not be appropriate, but kissing, especially when indulged in by "Black mammy" was not entirely tabooed.[10]

Masters were addressed as "massa" or "marster," and mistresses as "missis" by slaves on the plantations and in the homes, but favorite slaves were occasionally granted the privilege of addressing the mistress as "Miss" with the Christian name, or of using "Missy" without the Christian name. The master's children were addressed as "Young Massa" or "Young Miss," perhaps from the cradle.

"Mistis," "Madam" or "Captain" and "Boss" were forms widely used by slaves to address white persons with whom they were not intimately acquainted, and whom they met publicly. "Buckra," or the variant, "Buckraman," were forms employed by slaves of the South Carolina Sea Islands to refer to non-slave-owning white men; and "poor white trash," or "mean white men," were widely used to refer to poorer white persons.

Ceremonial forms were also a part of the equipment of white persons used to address, and to refer to Negroes, slave and free. "Mammy" was perhaps the title of highest respect bestowed upon slaves, with "uncle" and "auntie" ranging respectively a shade lower[11] "Old man" — not referring to age — and "daddy" seemed to be a bit more respectful than just the Christian name, which was generally used, and "boy" or "girl" when used in terms of address seemed to border on familiarity, although they were also used as terms of reference. Legal records of the colonial period refer to "Negro Sam" or "Negro Mary" where slaves are mentioned at all, with the "N" widely capitalized until about the middle of the nineteenth century. Yet, the literature of the entire period is replete with "nigger" used as a form of address, as a term of reference, as a noun, and as an adjective.

If, having addressed one another in appropriate ways, a conversation were necessary between a white person and a slave, the latter either removed his hat, or touched it, as though he might remove it, at the end of every sentence. If he had no hat, he pulled at his forelock, kept his eyes on the ground while the conversation lasted, and uttered "sir" or "ma'am" at least once in every complete sentence.

On the plantation or farm, and within the home, or "big house" other forms appeared. "No slave," says Steward, "was ever allowed to sit down in the presence of master or mistress."[12] If he were sitting when addressed, he would stand; and, if out of doors, would remove his hat. The errand-boy stood behind the master's chair; and the waiters or waitresses, of course, stood while serving meals.

Although intercourse was not prohibited between master and slave in the "big house" and though white persons might, in the presence of slaves, discuss their own or some particular slaves, yet, except infrequently, the good servant did not initiate a conversation, nor enter into one, unless first addressed.[13]

On the small farms, and perhaps in the case of house servants on the large plantation, slaves ate in the kitchen. On the large plantations, there was perhaps a cookhouse for the field hands, or they might be expected to prepare their own meals in their cabins. On the larger estates, master and mistress visited the slave cabins or "quarters" on Sunday; while the children might visit some favored slave in the quarters at any time. The ceremonial character of the visit is attested to be a frequent giving, and an occasional interchanging of gifts, such as cakes, eggs, and the like.

The etiquette was apparently more precise when it came to matters of contact in the pastimes of hunting and fishing. At these times, status was indicated by who rode a horse, a colt, or a mule, and who walked; or who walked first and who walked last.[14]

When Christmas came to the plantation a set of forms, adequate for the occasion, was observed. The time for celebration, while not uniform, generally lasted "as long as the yule log burned." At any rate, on Christmas day, it was the custom to surprise another by calling "Christmas gift" before the other could say it. The one who first called must then receive the present. Holding this in mind, the slaves would lie in wait, in order to pounce upon the first white person and to call "Christmas gift." If they received small gifts, they would respond by bowing, by pulling at their hats, or by pulling the forelock. In some localities the slaves would line up to receive gifts of knives, tobacco, dolls, handkerchiefs, pieces of money, and occasionally such useful articles as shoes. As each slave received his present, he would call out, "Merry Christmas." After luncheon, a meal would be served for the slaves in the back yard, at which the master's family would be interested spectators. The latter, however, would stand while the slaves sat, or vice versa.

If the slaves wished to hold either a picnic, or a barbecue, or to combine business with pleasure at a corn-husking, they first sought the master's permission. If the answer were favorable, they invited the master and his family to attend, and reserved seats for them at the grounds. Before the actual festivities began, the slaves would march by the master, perhaps for inspection, and during the procession or festivities, would find some occasion to extol the master's virtues, perhaps by an extemporaneous song. When the time came to dine the white persons present, who either stood while the slaves sat, or vice versa, were served first; visiting slaves were served next, house slaves next, and field hands last of all.

House-servants seemed generally to attend the weddings of their young masters and mistresses. Thus, when a young master, who had married away from home, returned with his bride, he was expected to present her first to his parents, then to his kinspeople, and finally to the house-servants.

Marriage ceremonies were occasionally observed for favored slaves of the household, although it appears that such unions were neither legally binding nor recognized. However, whether a slave married or was merely *joined,* the first step was to procure the master's permission. If the slave, bride or groom, were a house servant, the young men and women of the master's family would assume charge of the proceedings, frequently providing suitable finery for the groom, or making a trousseau for the bride, and occasionally bedecking her at the ceremony with the family jewels.[15] For the actual "ceremony" the slaves would appear at the Great House, where the ceremony might be said by a white minister, or a colored minister, or by the master, in the dining-room or hall. After the ceremony, a wedding supper might be held on the back porch, or in the kitchen, and occasionally there would be a dance, on the back porch.

Field hands seemed not to fare so well as house servants in this matter. They were *married* in the cabins or quarters, by the master, or by a colored preacher. One master in performing the ceremony used an "old copy of an English reader" for a prayer-book; another said:

'Come on in de house chillum.' . . . He set down an' look at us. 'Now,' he say, 'I don' want no fussin' ner fightin.' De way ter live happy is ter be forgivin' an' not start no ruckus. I hopes you have a long life togedder, an' if'n de Lawd send little niggers, dey'll be mos' welcome."[16]

On the larger plantations, perhaps, even this latter procedure was neglected, and the slaves needed to resort to the "blanket-wedding." This type of "marriage" was described by one slave as follows: "We come togedder in de same cabin an' she brings her blanket and lays it down sides mine, an' we gits married dat way."[17]

If, on the other plantations where there was more or less intimate relationship, the owner were perchance sick unto death, the slaves would be called to the bedside to receive a parting blessing and to bid the master, or perhaps the mistress, farewell. After death came, the slaves might attend the master's funeral, but favored places in the procession or at the service would be given to the house servants.

However, when a slave died, a colored or white minister might officiate at the services, and occasionally both racial groups might attend. The slave was then buried in a section reserved for slaves — on the plantation in the "plantation ceme- tery," but in "slave cemeteries" in the cities.[18]

One interesting development of ceremonial observances came in the association of whites and blacks in matters of religion. From 1619 to about 1641, while inden- ture was becoming slavery, Negroes who were baptized and who thus became Christians were released from such slavery as then existed for the current belief was that Christians could not rightfully, nor righteously, be enslaved. Later, however, the notion developed that bondage was a small price for the Negro to pay for the benefits of Christianity. Baptism, formerly a means of manumission, then became merely a preliminary to membership in the churches.

It thus happened, that, through the eighteenth century, though the develop- ment is difficult to trace, Negroes were generally attached to churches or denomina- tions, in which might be also found white persons.[19] By the beginning of the nine- teenth century, they were members of churches along with and frequently in greater numbers than white people, and were also found in separate organizations.[20]

Good form seemed to require separation of the racial groups in the church services proper. In the older and more established churches, perhaps, such as the Episcopalian, the Negroes sat in the galleries; while on the other hand, and until the insurrection of Nat Turner, about 1831, separation was generally not practiced in the churches affiliated with the Methodist and Baptist denominations. By 1835, race distinctions were clear, for slaves might be seen seated in galleries, or at the sides of churches, in separate sections, and occasionally even in separate churches.

Generally the whites and blacks partook of the Lord's Supper separately, and were also baptized separately, although in the latter ceremony, at least until Negro preachers were ordained, white ministers officiated. However, before a slave was baptized he needed to obtain permission from his master. Christening and naming of slave babies, by white persons, was not an unheard of phenomenon. In fact, some observers seem to believe that many classic, if not serio-comic, appellations of Negroes — such as Plato, Lily, Madame de Stael — were acquired in this manner.

How slaves were received as members into the churches of mixed membership is not clear. In the instance related by Frederick Douglass, of his conversion in a camp-meeting, he came from behind the minister — where the slaves *stood* — and stopped, *still standing*, half-way to the "mourners" pen, where white converts *sat.*

As slaves became members of the regularly established churches in increasing numbers, there grew up, in the cities especailly, the practice of holding separate services for white and black members. At first special services for slaves were held by the white minister in the white church; but later, separate churches for slaves were established with white pastors. The latter development, however, tended to be an outgrowth of an organization of slaves within the general church, in which the slaves exercised much the same powers over their members as did the white persons over their members. Complete separation ensued when slaves were assigned to separate churches, over which Negro ministers officiated. This situation was generally, but not altogether, delayed until after 1865.

Negro ministers were perhaps not accepted in large numbers until after the beginning of the nineteenth century. In some instances, they were "graduates" of the plantation, where they had either been supervised or subject to the censorship of the master, or, in other instances were talented persons who had, in company with some white person, previously travelled about preaching to white and black alike; although in many instances they spoke only to white audiences. As a matter of fact, unless a Negro preacher had some white person to "speak for him," and to guarantee his orthodoxy, it appears that he might be whipped or otherwise punished.[21]

Separate phases of this development appear, about 1858, in Macon, Georgia, where according to report there were three churches for Negroes — one of which had a white minister, the others Negro ministers. Moreover, the congregation with the white minister was paying him a regular salary and had erected and paid for its building.

In formal and public relations, forms were sufficiently distinct to be noted. White persons and slaves seldom, almost never, walked in public together. Yet, it appears, free Negroes were not always required to observe the rule. Meeting a white person on the street, Negroes, as in Richmond, Virginia, were "required to give the wall," and if necessary to get off the walk into the street. However, even though Negroes did not get off the walk, white persons were not expected to push them off. Public conversation was also thought improper unless the relationship between white and black were known as that of master and slave. Moreover, the responsibility of beginning a conversation always rested with the white person.

On the other hand, evidence appears that Negroes frequently served as musicians for dances and balls given by white people. Others might even attend, and stand around on the floor, or at the windows. Body-servants occasionally attended their masters and mistresses to the theatres. Public funerals of local or national characters would witness a gathering of both whites and blacks.

Travel conditions of the period were not so complex as they were later. Moreover, slaves seldom had any occasion to travel, and practically none to travel alone. The private travelling arrangement of a large slaveowner throws some light on the general situation. In this case negro outriders would come first, then the master, later the family carriage, and behind that slaves ranged in the order of their status, with the most lowly, of course, bringing up the rear.

On the stage-coaches, until about the fourth decade of the nineteenth century, Negroes rode inside unless the coach was overcrowded with white people. On the trains, body-servants and occasionally free Negroes rode in the "first-class," or "ladies' coach," but unattached slaves rode in the "second-class" car next to the engine, along with smokers from the ladies' car. The evidence, not precise and taken for what it is worth, indicates that there were no special accommodations in stations and depots for Negroes.

On the steamboats, of which there were many during the period of slavery, white persons of the wealthier classes commonly rode on the main deck, while slaves and poorer whites commonly rode "forward of the shaft" or on a lower deck. A body-servant could, however, remain on the main deck with his owner, and might sleep outside the owner's cabin door. Free Negroes rode on the main deck, but were apparently not given staterooms in which to sleep. In one instance, they seemed to sleep on the floor of the lounging room.

Meals on a steamboat brought all the matter of rank and precedence to the fore. At this time the captain and white passengers would dine first; after them came the white members of the crew, and then the Negro crew members and slaves. Free Negroes offered a problem in such circumstances. In one instance, since they could neither dine with free whites nor slave blacks, they took their meals in the pantry. In another instance, they dined after the white crew but before the negro crew.

Clothing as a class distinction, and considered as a derived form of etiquette, showed inter-, and intra-group delineation. The slave's outer garments were commonly made of cotton osnaburg, known as "Negro cloth." In very few inventories of slave clothing was underclothing mentioned at all. Slave children, some thought, ran around naked until later they were given a "negro shirt," — described as a "cross between a gent's undergarment and an ordinary potato-bag."

When dey big 'nough ter put on *anything*, it's a shirt. Boys and gals de same. Run 'roun in dat shirt-tail. Some de gals tie belt 'round de middle, and dat's de only diffrunce. . . . Dis hyar shu't wuh made jes like a sach. Got hole in de top fo' de haid, an' holes fo' de arms. Pull it ovah youah haid, push yo' arms t'rough de side holes, and dar yo' is.[22]

In the cities, however, slaves generally dressed in the cast-off clothing of white persons, or occasionally purchased clothing for themselves. Olmsted remarks that "the finest French clothes, embroidered waistcoats, patent leather shoes, brooches, silk hats, kid gloves, and *eau mille fleurs*[23] were by no means absent. Livery, in the instances where it was used at all, was generally confined to the cities.

The city slave also enjoyed a degree of association with white persons quite different from the field hand. Masters, in the cities and towns, frequently owned more servants than they could profitably employ at household tasks. These latter were often allowed to "hire themselves" to persons who either needed more help, or to persons who, unable to purchase thier own slaves, nevertheless sought the status of slave-owners. When persons are mobile, as in the city, relations are more impersonal. Again, attempts to maintain social distance and to preserve the superficial signs of status evoke newer and more multiplied forms. These reasons, among others perhaps, explain why the etiquette of the city and among city slaves was more complex and more formal than that common to the plantation and field hands.

There is reason to believe that cities and towns, during the slave period, contributed more than their share of the free Negro population, and certainly more independent Negroes than the rural sections. Some city slaves learned trades, others engaged in small businesses, or became self-supporting, or accumulated money sufficient to purchase their own freedom or that of some kins-person. These conditions also developed "exceptional slaves"; that is to say, slaves who had achieved independence, if not freedom. From among many instances, we might mention that one Cato, of Darien, Georgia, was allowed to carry a gun, in violation of the law; C. G. Hall saw a slave, travelling from Montgomery to New Orleans, who "was frequently entrusted with large sums of money and business of importance." One Frank, of Macon, Georgia, "had become rich, was the owner of considerable town property, carried on a mercantile business with great success, and was respected and esteemed by everyone who knew him."[24]

Slaves practiced distinctions and observed an etiquette among themselves. "Uncle" and "Auntie" were, among them, terms of respect, and "de nigger" was a term of contempt. In their own gatherings, they adopted the customary salutations of "sir" and "madam" and referred to themselves as "ladies" and "gentlemen." House servants looked down on field hands, and considered field labor a disgrace. The field hand responded with a defense mechanism of pretending to hate house servants, but considered an assignment to the household as a distinct promotion. Slaves, of whatever rank, considered their lot more perfect in proportion to the wealth and influence of their owners. The status-complex, indicated among the white people where it was said that a judge owned a house with two chimneys, and a colonel owned one with three, was reflected on the plantation where the washerwoman, the cook, the butler and the carriage-driver all had understudies, "to do the dirty work." At White Sulphur Springs, for example, a resort for upper class planters, precedence and rank were seen in the morning airing of babies, where nurses and "mammies" sat on the hotel veranda in order of the social consequence attached to their own owners. At Beaver Dam Springs, in Tennessee, Ingraham observed that:

After the masters and mistresses have left the dining room, the long table is relaid, and they who whilom served are now feasted. I have been twice to look at them.

Not less than one hundred Ethiopian and Nubian ladies and gentlemen were seated in the places occupied an hour before by their masters and mistresses. There were servants of "de lower class," — scullions, ostlers, and bootblacks, — to wait on them.[25]

Evidence points to the fact that, with the possible exception of certain exceptional slaves who had had contact with abolitionists, or with anti-slavery agitators, the majority of the slaves were thoroughly accommodated to their status as inferiors. Older slaves would show the child "a nigger's place," perhaps through slaps and whipping, but most likely through their own accommodations. In due time the etiquette and status common to slaves would then become entirely accepted.

Yet, the slave was not entirely without controls of his own, nor was he altogether a passive factor in the process of adjustment. Etiquette is in fact a reciprocal act. That is to say, a gesture or an observance on the part of one person calls out the complement of that observance or gesture on the part of the other person. Slaves early learned this, and would either laugh, or grin, when they committed breaches of etiquette, or when they did not know precisely how to act. As a consequence the laugh and grin came to be known as signs of "right attitudes." Likewise, the slave occasionally quoted Scripture to emphasize a point that otherwise would be considered impudent. But, it is in his interest in imitating the manners of white persons, in the incorporation of these forms into his own life, especially in the cities and among the houseservants, that we discern the extent of the assimilation of the slave to the institution of slavery.

Generalizing at this point upon some of the statements and materials hitherto presented, it would seem accurate to state that: (1) There was a code of etiquette in slavery that covered practically the whole of relations existing between persons of the white and Negro groups; (2) The code was different in different places and at different times, and reflected the changes that occurred in the social organization; (3) the forms had become inculcated into the attitudes of both white and black, free and slave, and were generally accepted and expected. To the extent that it was thus universally accepted and universally practiced, we may say that the code exercised a form of social control over interracial relations, and one that Spencer and Sumner were wont to call elementary.

Testing the Control of Etiquette

A test of the foregoing generalizations could be obtained if instances were discovered where etiquette was neglected, was unobserved, or had not developed, between whites and blacks. A situation, where etiquette did not control, is in fact found in the relation of free Negroes with white persons.

The free Negro class had developed from several sources. There were those who had originally served their terms of indenture, and who had left a heritage of freedom to their descendents; others who had acquired freedom by becoming Christians before restrictions were placed upon this course and method; still others who had been manumitted individually or in groups by masters who believed slavery incompatible with the theory of democracy, or with the principles of Christianity. Still others, and perhaps the greatest number, had been manumitted by masters for personal or sentimental reasons, — among which we might mention cohabitation, blood relationship, a feeling that certain individual Negroes were above a slave status, or even a conviction that long and faithful service deserved some reward. As a consequence of these and other factors, the free Negro class increased constantly in total numbers, if not in rate, from 1790 to 1860, and amounted to approximately one-tenth of the Negroes in America at the Emancipation.

When a slave was manumitted, his legal status was fixed, so far as the ex-master was concerned. There remained, however, the definition of his social status, both by himself and by others. Having acquired a new *legal* status, it was natural for the free Negro to see his condition in a new light, and to conceive his adjustments in terms of attitudes adopted by white freemen. On the other hand, it was difficult for white persons to treat him as free; moreover the hostility which ensued was not submerged in any discovered social ritual. "Indeed," says Wright, "if any change at all resulted from the rise of the new class, it caused a more strict definition of class boundaries, a more firm repulsion of the Negro, and an outcasting of any white man who went across to the Negroes."[26]

On the legal side, the restrictions on free Negroes passed by the several state legislatures over the entire period of slavery, and the movements designed to colonize them in Africa or in some separate section of the United States, all attest to the problem created by the rise of the class. The first half of the nineteenth century witnessed a rather continual debasement of the free Negro's legal status to that of the slave. By the later fifties, indeed, the almost universal sentiment was that the class constituted a distinct menace, as criminals, as possible inciters of insurrection, and as object lessons of the benefits, and sometimes of the disadvantages, of freedom for slaves. By indirection, then, we arrive at the conclusion that something was lacking in the relations of free Negroes and white persons that was present in the relations of slaves and white persons. Shall we then assume that the social ritual was the missing factor?

What, then, were the adjustments made by the free Negroes to their anomalous situation? On the one hand, they entered occupations requiring personal service, or became tradesmen, or semi-skilled and, in some instances, even skilled workers. this occupational specialization doubtless relieved the friction that would have resulted had they entered more widely into competitive relations, even provided they had had either means or opportunity. On the other hand, there were the "exceptional" free Negroes who were occasionally teachers, some planters, a physician or so, and several inn-keepers. Some among them, accumulated slaves, and were known as slaveholders, not of kinsmen, but for commercial purposes.

Since however, relations between white and black were largely personal with an etiquette based upon personal relations, free Negroes tended, on the one hand, to settle in communities where white people seldom intruded; or to go, on the other hand, into the cities, where contacts were more impersonal, and where they could move as symbols, rather than as persons. They could never completely cut off communication and contact with white people. Their presence in the cities, while reducing personal relations to a minimum, nevertheless implied some intimate contacts. The adjustment that was expected of them under such circumstances is expressed in the Black Code of Louisiana as follows:

Free people of color ought never to presume to conceive themselves equal to the white; but, on the contrary, they ought to yield to them in every occasion, and never speak or answer to them, except with respect.[27]

An analysis of the attitudes of free Negroes, who attained places of respect and influence in communities where they dwelt with white persons, forces upon us the conclusion that they conformed, in spirit, to this code, and that they attained their positions not because they were free, but because they either reverted to, or never departed from, the etiquette considered proper to the association of all white persons with all Negroes, slave or free.[28]

In other words, the free Negro could adjust himself to his new status, either by betaking himself to a place where no white persons were present, or by adopting the etiquette common to slavery, if and when he associated with white persons at all. If he did neither, the only outcome of association with white persons would be friction, disharmony, conflict.

Summarizing, we see the relations and the etiquette commonly accepted between slaves and whites reflected among the free Negroes. We also see further evidence of a caste system sustained by legislation. But, perhaps, what appears most significant is that the Negro was able to adjust himself to circumstances, and to gain a modicum of security and recognition even in the face of excessively restrictive formal regulations. The adjustment — or if you wish, the accommodation — was facilitated when, as, and if, the free Negro retained a conception of himself, and the white man's conception of him, as subordinate in the social scale. The adjustment, generally present when the etiquette of race relations was resorted to, or absent when it was not utilized, might then be understood as a function of that etiquette.

But, perhaps in view of the purposes at hand, and considering the confusion that resulted from attempts of white persons and free Negroes to accommodate themselves to the anomalous situation, what is more significant is that we begin to arrive at a conception of the problem that arose later, when, by emancipation, all Negroes had become free; and when *presumably,* the moral controls of the slave had been superseded by legal and political enactments.

The last generalization may be further elaborated. We might, to the already numerous and confusing interpretations of the period of Reconstruction, add another to the effect that the period, stripped of its legal and political implications, was one in which adjustment between the races could, and did, not proceed for the reason that (1) the controls, characteristic of ceremonial government, had been overthrown and (2) that no basic controls had replaced them. Negroes seemed to believe that change in legal or political status was synonymous with, and equivalent to, change in social status. Southern white people, on the other hand, generally denied the assumption. No basis of agreement was reached until the Negro, disillusioned with his freedom, began to revert to the attitudes and the etiquette that had been characteristic of slavery; and that seem to be characteristic of social relations wherever social superior and social inferior meet.

Thenceforward, to compress a period of history into one sentence, interracial friction has been relieved by the simple process of reverting to the etiquette of the period of slavery. Where this adjustment has been accomplished relative harmony prevails. In those instances where etiquette has not developed, or where for whatever reason it is neglected, friction, and occasionally conflict, arises.

Interrelation of Etiquette and Education

Considering the facts and interpretations so far advanced, the question arises whether or not formal education, recognizing a code of interracial etiquette that is based upon the assumption of the inferiority of the Negro, should attempt to offer substitutes. The question becomes important in proportion as the notion of innate inferiority of races is rejected,[29] or as it is recognized that increasingly large nunbers of Negroes become restive when social inferiority is assumed. Stated, for example, as a phase of the "cardinal principles of secondary education" the question would be: should education seek to undermine, or to strengthen the etiquette of race relations in order to develop high citizenship and ethical character? Efforts to answer the question must inevitably seek to rationalize values, may lead to prophecy, and undoubtedly will arouse controversy.

However, among the arguments advanced to support the question, there is the thesis which regards education as a means of providing techniques with which to meet the conditions of life. Those who accept this philosophy seem also to admit that the present code offers a definite handicap to Negroes who would improve their social status. Moreover, they point out that Negroes should be prepared for the good life, and should be taught radical self respect and race consciousness. In no way, they say, might these objectives be attained more quickly than in a complete overthrow of any system that proposed to keep Negroes in a permanently inferior position.

Education from this point of view, should evaluate the *status quo* and should indicate the positively hurtful, or dangerous, social tendencies. Social planning, as an outgrowth of education, could then develop a rational statesmanship for race problems that confront us. Since appreciation of the worth of the individual is a cardinal principle of education and a value of American society, education should then seek to obliterate artificial differences among men, and to change the attitudes that have arisen to fortify the belief in differences. Recognizing these goals education will go far toward realizing the democratic social order to which we already lay claim.

A more militant stand holds that recognition of Negroes as equals of all other racial groups should be forced. If then in the social organization inequality of the Negro is assumed, Negro students should read Negro history, should study and interpret the Constitution, and should acquire in these ways a sense of race pride, and a familiarity with the devices that may be used to force equality before the law. Although this philosophy takes no direct stand on etiquette, it seems to hold that, along with all other assumptions of inferiority, the interracial code should be charged, if not actually overthrown.

Advocates remind us that etiquette is taught in the "finishing" schools. Then they ask: "If etiquette can be taught in one type of institution, why not in another? Why then should not all schools seek to teach a new code of manners, especially when it may be admitted that such a code would effect more amicable interracial relations?"

There is some disagreement among the proponents of this latter point of view. However, Negroes seem generally to expect the reorganization of etiquette to begin in the colleges — those institutions that propose, and are expected, to furnish leadership for the Negro group. Since college-trained persons are those from whom complaints on the score generally come, and if those who would be free must themselves strike the blow, there seems to be ground for the contention that colleges, so far as educational institutions attempt such at all, should make the first assault upon inferior status.

In this regard, however, it must be noted that Negroes exhibit mutually antagonistic attitudes. When and if college students show any desire or tendency to break away from custom, it is quickly charged that colleges are radical and that students are irresponsible. On the other hand, those same people who make these charges, also presume to believe that only through the efforts of the intelligentsia — college students and graduates — will there come any assault upon the customs that bind them to an inferior status. Occasional complaints decry the conformist tendency in Negro colleges. The objection is offered that these latter teach the same subjects in the same way as the white colleges when, as a matter of racial necessity, they should be preparing Negroes to break the chains of social thralldom.

Taking the opposite view, however, there are those who point out that the etiquette of race relations is "in the mores"; that the mores change slowly; and that they perhaps cannot be changed at all by taking thought.[30] The implication of this point of view, occasionally coming by actual declaration, seems to be that there is little that education can do to answer the question of etiquette in interracial relations. Some advocates go so far as to show that with all the schools in America, the code of etiquette and relations of the races are about what they would be if there were no schools at all.

Still others have indicated that the mores, when they change at all, do so as a result of some change already inaugurated in the field of material culture. Indeed, Ogburn points out that change in the material culture precedes change in the non-material culture, of which latter etiquette is a part. Moreover, he shows that a "cultural lag" exists since industrial and economic development not only precede, but also outstrip, development in the social attitudes and organization.[31] If then, as indicated by this theory, a change of status for groups might result from invention more frequently than from education and legislation, it could readily be conceded that the invention of a new machine — say the cottonpicker — might effect greater changes in the status of the Negro than college degrees, or even a congressional enactment.

A corollary of this hypothesis is that conscious attempts to change the mores generally result in revolution.[32] There then remain two possible courses of action: (1) to expect inventions, when and as they come, to effect changes in the social order; or (2) to seek to change conditions immediately, and thus bring about revolution.

The social psychologists insist, however, that education brings new status. Moreover, when a person attains a new status, he experiences changes in attitudes. In consequence he expects no longer to be bound by an old code of social relationships, but adopts newer forms toward others, and expects them to use different forms toward him. Hence, this theory goes: when a Negro has become educated, and has attained a new status, old forms reminiscent of an inferior status will neither be used by, nor toward, him; and his status will be a function of his change in attitude, or vice versa.

The explanation is, however, too simple. Says Park:

As far as the South is concerned, it is where racial prejudices and the social order which they perpetuated, are breaking down that racial animosities are most intense. It is when the Negro invades a new region that a race riot occurs; it is when he seeks a new place in a new profession or new occupation that he meets the most vigorous opposition; it is when he seeks to assume a new dignity that he ceases to be quaint and becomes ridiculous.[31]

Wrenched from its background, this statement may be taken to mean that, to the extent that it breaks down the social order, or gives Negroes new conceptions of themselves, or stimulates competition, or changes the status of Negroes, education will result in widespread racial animosity, and perhaps in racial conflict.

The effect is occasionally noted when Negroes take only a normal interest in changing their social status. But when education does cause a Negro to become "bumptious," "arrogant," or "contentious," it is confidently expected that race conflict will result. If then both a non-assertive, and a "bumptious" Negro may stimulate race friction, by seeking a changed status, and even though neither is *taught* to neglect the interracial etiquette, friction may be expected to be increased by teaching them to neglect the expected and accepted forms. Those who hold this latter view occasionally suggest that the lesson of the Reconstruction Period and race relations has been lost.

Finally, it is shown, etiquette is a form of social control. Developing unconsciously, it comes to be accepted and expected in the association of social beings, and eventually exerts a very effective control over the relations of groups and individuals. Persons who behave in entirely undetermined ways, are considered insane and are institutionalized; children who have not learned what is expected are tolerated; boors, who neglect the etiquette, are shunned; and rebels who disparge the code, are suppressed. These are normal results and expectations in the world of men, for when persons act in ways that cannot be understood, communication is broken, adjustment is hampered, and confusion results. Considering these hypotheses, then, conscious disregard of the etiquette of racial relations may generally be expected to bring confusion, and perhaps conflict, between the two groups in America.

Moreover, the men become free by observing the forms of behavior expected of them. Having done what is expected, they may think what they please, and they may, in fact, use the etiquette as a mask to hide what they are thinking. It then becomes no longer necessary to know what to think, but only what to do. Hence, having learned what to do through long drill, men may apply their minds to other problems even while they are associating together.

Lastly, no person who is party to an interchange of social gestures has less control than any other, for the association is reciprocal, and effects adjustment in the interest both of peace and of harmony. Again, the forms of behavior expected of, and exhibited with regard to, a person are a function of his status. If then he has control; if securing of status precedes change in forms, the man who wishes to change the forms will consider the loss of control that he will suffer when and if he seeks to change these before he gains a new status. In other words, if through education, the status of the Negro were changed, a change in the etiquette of race relations would be expected to follow. We may not expect a change in the status of the Negro from a change in etiquette.

Conclusion

A solution of the difficulty encountered in postulating a philosophy of the relation of education and etiquette, especially with regard to the Negro in America, seems then to be impossible. A summary of the phases of the code, and a study of the development, show (1) that, over a period of over three hundred years, an etiquette of race relations has governed the association of Negroes and white persons; and (2) that the etiquette has, in some respects, changed but that in many other respects it remains practically intact. The basis of the code is admittedly the inferiority of the Negro, and the superiority of the white group. A change would in many ways be acceptable, and in many other ways would be desirable. However, if one advocates conscious change in the etiquette, one looks down a road that bristles with friction, conflict, perhaps revolution. If one accepts the situation, expecting that, as always, it will take a change for the better, one seems to adopt too fatalistic an attitude. One certainly does in that way deny the claims of Negroes, who, having become both race conscious and self-conscious, chafe under the status of inferiority in a land of democracy. The weight of evidence seems to be with Sumner and Spencer, but the claim of humanity seems to be with the Negroes. The solution of the matter is doubtless a matter of social philosophy, and one that must be rationalized in terms of circumstance, necessity, and social progress. Until this is done, and in the presence of the two opposing views, one can only emulate the farmer who sought to select the shell under which there was a pea. He was invited to "pay your money, and take your choice."

Notes

[1] Herbert Spencer, *Principles of Sociology*, (London, 1882) Vol. II, p. 3.

[2] *Ibid.*, pp. 12–13, 30–5.

[3] See: W. G. Sumner, *Folkways* (New York, 1910), pp. 34–35.

[4] *Ibid.* See especially the chapter on Social Codes.

[5] R. E. Park and H. A. Miller, *Old World Traits Transplanted* (Chicago, 1925), pp. 1–2.

[6] The use of the term "code" does not here refer to any formal organization or formulation of rules to be observed, but to those codes whose value, according to Sir Henry Maine, "does not consist in any approach to any symmetrical classification, nor to terseness and clearness of expression, but in their publicity, and in the knowledge which they furnish to everybody as to what he was to do, and what not to do."*Ancient Law* (New York, 1888, 3rd American edition from the 5th London edition), p. 25.

[7] Within the last decade, the code has been made the subject of an occasional article. See, for example, G. S. Schuyler, "Keeping the Negro in His Place," *American Mercury*, XVII, 68 (August, 1929) pp. 469 ff.

[8] We shall consider etiquette, or the code of social usages, to be the forms required by custom and tradition to be observed in contact and association of white persons and Negroes; as the ceremonial side of race relations; as the behavior that is expected and accepted when white and black associate.

[9] Nehemiah Adams, *A Southside View of Slavery*, (Boston, 1854) p. 18; and William Ferguson, *America by River and Rail*, (London, 1856), p. 128.

[10] T. D. Ozanne, *The South As It Is, or Twenty-one Years' Experience in the Southern States*, (London, 1863), pp. 75–76; Thomas N. Page, *The Old South; Essays Social and Political*, (New York, 1892), 165; F. L. Olmsted, *A Journey Through the Seaboard Slave States*, (New York, 1861), Vol. I, p. 150; F. D. Srygley, *Seventy Years in Dixie*, (Nashville, 1891),

p. 48; Frances Anne Kemble, *Journal of Residence on a Georgia Plantation in 1838–1839*, (New York, 1863), p. 59; Frederick Bremer, *Homes of the New World*, (New York, 1853), Vol. II, p. 99.

[11] Not all old slaves were so addressed. The terms carried with them something of respect, of dignity, and frequently of responsibility. See: W. R. Vance, *Slavery in Kentucky*, (Lexington, Va., 1895), p. 62; R. R. Moton, *What the Negro Thinks*, (Garden City, New York, 1929), p. 190; Ingraham, *op. cit.*, p. 68; Hundley, *op. cit.*, p. 88; J. D. Long *Pictures of Slavery in State Church*, (Philadelphia, 1857), p. 21.

[12] Austin Steward, *Twenty-two Years a Slave and Forty Years a Freeman* (Rochester, 1857) p. 26. See also J. W. Loguen, *As a Slave and a Freeman* (Syracuse, 1859) p. 154.

[13] *Cf.* Harriet Martineau, *Society in America*, (New York, 1837), Vol. I, p. 123. Olmsted, *Seaboard States*, etc., Vol. I, 49–50; Ferguson, *op. cit.*, p. 111.

[14] See Ingraham, *op. cit.*, p. 26; and Hundley, *op. cit.*, pp. 33, 37.

[15] See on the point, James B. Avirett, *The Old Plantation; How We Lived in Great House and Cabin Before the War* (New York, 1901), p. 124; W. L. Fleming, Home Life in Alabama During the Civil War, *Southern History Association Publications*, VIII (1904), p. 99; Ingraham, *op. cit.*, 144; Page, *op. cit.*, p. 183; MacDonald, *op. cit.*, p. 96

[16] O. K. Armstrong, *Old Massa's People* (Indianapolis, 1931), p. 164.

[17] J. Redpath, *The Roving Editor, or Talks with Slaves in the Southern States*, (New York, 1859), p. 164.

[18] See Phillip A. Bruce, *An Economic History of Virginia in the 17th Century*, etc., (New York, 1896), Vol. II, pp. 38–39. Legislative provision to the effect that no slave should be buried in a private place, "but in public cemeteries provided for the purpose," for example, was found in Virginia as early as 1664.

[19] See W. M. Gewehr, *The Great Awakening in Virginia* (Durham, N.C., 1930) pp. 72, 237, 249.

[20] The literature on this point is voluminous, but see C. G. Woodson, *The History of the Negro Church* (Washington, 1921), *passim*.

[21] F. L. Olmsted, *A Journey in the Seaboard Slave States; with Remarks on their Economy*, (New York, 1856), ii, 34–35.

[22] Armstrong, *op. cit.*, 72–73.

[23] Olmsted, *The Cotton Kingdom*, Vol. I, p. 46 (New York, 1861).

[24] Mrs. A. Royall, The Black Book, Vol. I, p. 110 (Washington, 1830).

[25] J. H. Ingraham, *The Sunny South*, pp. 209 210 (New York, 1854.)

[26] James M. Wright, *The Free Negro in Maryland*, (New York, 1921) pp. 346–347.

[27] G. McD. Stroud, *A Sketch of the Laws Relating to Slavery in the Several States* (Philadelphia, 1827), p. 68. The original is found in *Martin's Digest*, I, 640–642.

[28] The evidence, while not cited here, for reasons of brevity, is sufficiently general to warrant the conclusion, and will perhaps be published in another form soon.

[29] See: Otto Klineberg, *Race Differences*. (New York, 1935), pp. 341–349.

[30] See a particularly illuminating statement to this effect in Sumner's *Folkways* (New York, 1910), pp. 77–78.

[31] W. F. Ogburn, *Social Change* (New York, 1922) *passim*.

[32] L. P. Edwards, *The Natural History of Revolution* (Chicago, 1927) p. 8.

[33] R. E. Park, Bases of Race Prejudice, *Annals*, CXXX (Nov. 1929) p. 15.

The Black Matriarchate

E. Franklin Frazier

Only women accustomed to playing the dominant role in family and marriage relations (if we may regard the slaves as having been married) would have asserted themselves as the Negro women in Mississippi did during the election of 1868. We are told that,

if a freedman, having obtained [a picture of Grant], lacked the courage to wear it at home on the plantation in the presence of "ole marsa and missus" or of the "overseer," his wife would often take it from him and bravely wear it upon her own breast. If in such cases the husband refused to surrender it, as was sometimes the case, and hid it from her or locked it up, she would walk all the way to town, as many as twenty or thirty miles sometimes, and buy, beg, or borrow one, and thus equipped return and wear it openly, in defiance of husband, master, mistress, or overseer.[1]

These women had doubtless been schooled in self-reliance and self-sufficiency during slavery. As a rule, the Negro woman as wife or mother was the mistress of her cabin, and, save for the interference of master or overseer, her wishes in regard to mating and family matters were paramount. Neither economic necessity nor tradition had instilled in her the spirit of subordination to masculine authority. Emancipation only tended to confirm in many cases the spirit of self-sufficiency which slavery had taught.

When emancipation came, many Negro mothers had to depend upon their own efforts for the support of themselves and their children. Their ranks were swelled by other women who, in seeking sex gratification outside of marriage, found themselves in a similar situation. Without the assistance of a husband or the father of their children, these women were forced to return to the plow or the white man's kitchen in order to make a livelihood for their families. From that time to the present day, as we have seen in the preceding chapter, each generation of women, following in the footsteps of their mothers, has borne a large share of the support of the younger generation. [Today in the rural sections of the South, especially on the

From E. Franklin Frazier, *The Negro Family in the United States* pp. 125–145, Copyright © 1939 by The University of Chicago. All rights reserved. Published July 1939. Reprinted by permission of the publisher.

remnants of the old plantations, one finds households where old grandmothers rule their daughters and grandchildren with matriarchal authority. Sometimes their authority dates from the days following emancipation when, in wandering about the country, they "found" their first child.]

It is, of course, difficult to get a precise measure of the extent of these maternal households in the Negro population. The 1930 census showed a larger proportion of families with women heads among Negroes than among whites in both rural and urban areas.[2] Moreover, it also appeared that in the cities a larger proportion of Negro families were under the authority of the woman than in the rural areas. In the rural-nonfarm areas of southern states from 15 to 25 per cent of the Negro families were without male heads; while in the rural-farm areas the proportion ranged from 3 to 15 per cent. In the rural-farm areas tenant families had a much smaller proportion with woman heads than owners, except in those states where a modified form of the plantation regime is the dominant type of farming. For example, in the rural-farm area of Alabama between 13 and 14 per cent of both tenant and owner families were without male heads. Although rural areas showed a smaller proportion of families without male heads than urban areas, still it is in the rural areas of the South that we find the maternal family functioning in its most primitive form as a natural organization. In spite of the fact that official statistics on the marital relations of these women are of doubtful accuracy, a closer view of census materials on the families in three southern counties in 1910 and 1920 throws additional light on the extent and character of these maternal households in this region.[3]

Table 1 indicates that from a fifth to a fourth of the families in the three counties — two in the Black Belt and the third in the coastal region — were without a male head. In each of the counties in 1910 the families in which the wife was a mulatto had a smaller proportion without a male head than the families with a black wife or mother.[4] The smaller proportion of families without a male head among

Table 1: Number and Percentage of Negro Families with Female Heads in Three Southern Counties

County	Color of Woman	1920			1910		
		Total Number Families	Families with Woman Head		Total Number Families	Families with Woman Head	
			Number	Per Cent		Number	Per Cent
Hertford County, N.C.	Black	1,270	243	18.9	1,093	266	24.3
	Mulatto	796	122	15.9	788	154	19.5
Macon County, Ala.	Black	939	274	29.1	840	240	28.5
	Mulatto	101	30	29.8	110	27	24.5
Issaquena County, Miss.	Black	1,940	372	19.1	2,595	636	24.5
	Mulatto	94	23	23.4	331	67	20.2

the mulattoes was doubtless due to the relatively higher economic and cultural status of this class, which had less illiteracy but a higher rate of homeownership than the blacks. In 1920 the mulattoes in the North Carolina county still showed a smaller proportion of families without male heads; while in the Black Belt counties the standing of the mulattoes was reversed in one instance and was the same as the blacks in the other. The migrations during the war might have been responsible for the change in the relative position of the two classes in the Black Belt counties, since the population of both counties decreased between 1910 and 1920. This much, at least, is true: the increase in the proportion of families without a male head among the mulattoes in these latter counties was accompanied by a decrease in the number of homeowning families among this class.

We can get a better conception of the relation of homeownership to stable and normal family relations by examining the marital status of these women who are heads of families. Although our figures are not absolutely accurate, they reveal to a much greater extent the real nature of the conjugal relations of these women than the published statistics.[5] We have, in addition to the two usual classifications — widowed and divorced — two others: women who apparently had been married but were separated from their husbands and women who had had only irregular relations with men. For example, we find that in Issaquena County, Mississippi, in 1910, of the 671 women heads of families, 159, or 21 per cent, were separated from their husbands and 66, or about 10 per cent, had had only irregular relations with men. In Hertford County, North Carolina, for the same year, 14.1 per cent of the women heads of families were separated, and 34.6 per cent had had only irregular relations with men; while the separated and the irregular unions each comprised about 14 per cent of the women heads of families in Macon County, Alabama. After making allowance for the separated and those who have had only irregular associations with men, the majority of these women are classified as widows. This is true of the blacks as well as the mulattoes and of the tenants as well as the homeowners. But an important difference appears between the women who own their homes and those who are renters or whose home tenure is unknown. Among the homeowners from 80 to 100 per cent of the women are included under widowhood, whereas for the renters and those of unknown tenure only from 50 to 70 per cent were in this class. This was true of both the blacks and the mulattoes and seems to indicate that widowhood among the homeowners was generally real widowhood.[6]

That these figures represent more truly the conjugal relations of these women than published statistics is apparent from the histories of their marital experiences. The divorced, and in some cases the widowed, in published statistics are often in fact merely separations, since divorce is regarded by many of these people as an individual affair not requiring legal sanction. As we shall see below, "divorce" in one case consisted in giving the man a "scrip." On the whole, these simple folk have vague notions concerning the legal requirements for divorce. One man said that he did not need a divorce from his wife because "she was in one county and me in another."[7] Another man considered himself divorced when his wife was sentenced

Table 2: Marital Status of Women Heads of Families According to Tenure of Homes in Three Southern Counties, 1910 and 1920

Tenure of Homes	To-tal Fami-lies	1920				To-tal Fami-lies	1910			
		Sepa-rated	Wid-owed	Di-vorced	Irreg-ular		Sepa-rated	Wid-owed	Di-vorced	Irreg-ular
Hertford County, N.C.										
Owners	63	3	53	2	5	74	2	60	2	10
Renters	133	24	77	3	29	112	9	63	4	36
Unknown	165	30	119	3	13	126	33	127	4	62
Macon County, Ala.										
Owners	15	0	15	0	0	15	1	13	0	1
Renters	161	20	121	2	18	142	22	86	20	14
Unknown	127	20	100	3	4	108	15	62	11	20
Issaquena County, Miss.										
Owners	31	1	29	0	1	20	1	18	1	0
Renters	239	60	140	1	38	316	81	208	3	24
Unknown	118	28	82	1	7	340	77	211	10	42

to jail for cutting a woman. Many of the women who were heads of families have been married and in some cases often married. They have often broken marital ties and remarried without a legal divorce. On a plantation in Alabama a woman near sixty, who worked a "one-horse farm" with her son, recounted the story of her three marriages. Her father, who had been "raised up under the hard task of slavery," had sent her as far as the fourth grade. Then her marriage career began. Of the first two husbands she said:

Me and him separated and he divorced me. Me and the second one got married and come down here. Then he fought me when this boy [her son] was six months old. We fought like cats and dogs. One night I had to call Uncle R—— P——. He asked me for his 'vorce and I gi' it to him. I just wrote him a "scrip." I got a man to write it for him.

Her third husband, who had been dead seven years, died, according to her testimony, of high blood pressure, leakage of the heart, and kidney trouble. Another old woman had a similar story to tell. When she announced "all my children done married off," she was speaking of two sets of children — one by her husband and another by the man with whom she lived after having "divorced" her husband. According to her story, her husband had told her that he wanted a divorce, and she had replied that he was welcome to it. But as to the reason back of the breaking of the marriage bond, she explained: "He didn't work to suit me, and I didn't work to suit him."

This last naïve statement concerning divorce reveals much in regard to the nature of marriage and its dissolution among these simple folk. Among these people we come face to face with marriage as it probably existed in the early stages of social development. Marriage as an institution rooted in the mores does not exist in many places. Where it has developed any degree of permanency and the couples are seemingly bound by conjugal affection, more fundamental interests than mere sentiment have been responsible in the beginning for the continuance of the association in marriage. When one woman was asked whether she was married, her reply was: "Me and my husband parted so long, done forget I was married." What marriage means to many of these women was expressed by a woman who spoke of herself as "Miss," although she had been married twice, and wanted another husband to help her work. Her first husband, whom she had married when she was fifteen, was killed by lightning after they had been together twelve years. A second husband had been dead two years, and at present she was making a living by "hoeing and fertilizing" on a place that, she said, "they tells me it was here in slavery times." Her only idea indicating preference in regard to a husband was that he must be dark, for "if he is most too light, he looks too much like white folks." But the main factor in regard to the partner in marriage was that he should co-operate with her in farming. As she remarked, "I am looking for someone to marry, so I can get on a farm and kinda rest." She had hoped that her son in Cleveland, who had served in France during the war, would relieve her from going into the field each day in the hot sun; but he had written that he was sick, and she had sent for him to come home.

Where marriage is regarded chiefly as a means of co-operation in the task of making a living and does not rest upon an institutional basis, it is not surprising to find some of these women speaking of "working with a man" as a sufficient explanation of their living together. This was the explanation offered by an illiterate buxom black woman of forty or more who had been farming "right round twenty-five acres" for two years with a man who was separated from his wife a quarter of a mile away because they "just couldn't get along and separated." She had had several children without being married, the only living one being cared for by her mother. But some of these cases of irregular unions are not the result of the naïve behavior of simple folk. We have seen in the preceding chapter how in one case both the parents of the unmarried mother and the unmarried mother herself attempted to represent the man in the house as a "boarder."[8] Wherever we find this consciousness of the violation of the dominant mores or a certain sophistication, the couples will attempt to represent their union as some socially approved relationship or as conventional marriage. This was the case with a brickmason, forty-seven, who had been educated at Tuskegee Institute. He was living with a woman, twenty-two, on a "patch" of five acres for which they were paying sixty dollars rental a year. The woman was a mulatto who thought that she had some Indian blood. Her mother was farming with eight children, while her father had deserted the mother and gone to Detroit. This irregular union was especially convenient for the man, since it was outside the public opinion and censure of the group with whom he spent much of his time in town.

Some of these irregular unions are due to the association between white men and colored women. The prevalence of these associations is determined by several factors. They are found more frequently in the small towns of the South than in the isolated rural regions where large numbers of Negroes have been concentrated for nearly a century or longer. The proportion of mulattoes in the Negro populaton is a measure of the isolation of the Negro and of the amount of contacts between the races. In Issaquena County in the Yazoo-Mississippi Basin only 10 per cent of the families were mulattoes in 1910, while in Hertford County, North Carolina, 40 per cent of the families showed mixed blood. In Hertford County, where in 1910, as we have seen, about 35 per cent of the women who were heads of families had had only irregular relations with men, the association between white men and colored women continued on a large scale for a long period after slavery. These irregular unions were generally formed by white men and mulatto women. According to our figures, 28 of the 108 women heads of families who had carried on irregular relations were mulattoes. In 1920 there were 19 mulattoes among the 47 women in this class. The change in these figures is indicative of an actual decrease in these types of associations; for in this community there has been a conscious effort on the part of the colored population to repress such associations and enforce conventional standards of conduct.[9]

A minister, who established a school in this county and has worked there nearly a half-century, related the following concerning these associations when he began his work there:

When I first came here I often heard mulatto women say that they would rather be a white man's concubine than a nigger's wife. The mulatto women and white men claimed that since the law did not allow them to marry and they had only one wife that it was all right. Conflict over this almost broke up P—— P—— Baptist Church. There was a scattering of families, many going north and passing for white. The feeling was such between mulattoes and blacks that they wanted me to place the mulattoes on the second floor and the blacks on the third floor of the school dormitory. I mixed them up in the school purposely and got black evangelists for the church.[10]

Although frequently the white man was not married and lived with his mulatto concubine as his wife, this was not invariably the case. It is also true that in many instances the economic advantages which these mulatto families enjoyed were due to the provision which the white father had made for his concubine and his mulatto children. In the following document, which was furnished by a woman who was born before emancipation, we have the case of a white man with a white family as well as a colored family. In this case, the white father made no provision for his colored family:

I wanted to be somebody and some account. I was ashamed of my back family [family background]. I hated that my mother did not marry a colored man and let me live like other folks with a father, and if he did not make much he could spend

that with us. I despised my white father and his folks. I might have loved him if
he had noticed and treated us like other folks. His wife died after a while, but she
never fussed as I know of about his colored family. He had large children, some
grown. He did not stay at home. He would have the work done by Negro slaves.
He had lots of slaves and families of slaves. He must have had, with the children,
fifty or seventy-five slaves in all. He was right good to them. He would eat at my
mother's house. She called him "the man," and we called him "the man." He would
come in at bed-time; and even before his wife died, he would come and stay with
my mother all night and get up and go to his house the next morning. His children
despised us and I despised them and all their folks, and I despised him. We had
to work hard, get no education, and but a little to live on. He had plenty of property
but didn't give mother one thing. Her uncle gave her home and field and we had
to work it.[11]

The disgust which this woman felt toward her home life caused her to leave
it and establish one based upon conventional moral standards. Referring to her
home, she said, "It was so ugly and common that I meant to get married and leave
that hateful place. It is true I loved the man I married; but I had as much in mind
in getting married to leave that place as I had in marrying for love."[12]

While the association between white men and colored women in this community has been on a larger scale than in most southern communities, it is similar to
many other areas in the South where there has been a long history of such associations dating from slavery. Just as the phenomenon in this community has declined
because of the growing sentiment against it on the part of both blacks and whites,
it has decreased in other areas of the South.

Let us turn our attention to these women in their role of mothers and as heads
of their families. Some of the separated and widowed in Issaquena County in 1910
had given birth to as many as twenty children or more. Even among those who had
only irregular relations with men there were women with from ten to twelve children. But the actual number of children in these families was often small because
of the numerous miscarriages and stillbirths and the high infant mortality which
we find among them.[13] The following case of a woman who had two stillbirths and
three miscarriages was not unusual, for some women had lost as many as nine or
ten children.

This woman had no conception of her age for she thought that she might be
about 20, although later she said that her husband had been dead nearly 20 years.
She was living in a one-room shack, covered with sheet iron, with a daughter's
illegitimate 12 year old son, and her own illegitimate 14 year old daughter. These
two children were helping her to hoe and plow a "one-horse farm on halves," instead
of attending school. The family was receiving an "advance" of $4.00 a month.
Another daughter, who "had taken sick with a misery in the head and breast," died
suddenly during the past year. The mother tried to get a doctor; but as she said
concerning her landlord, "Dis white man don't gi' you doctor like talking." Al-

though it was difficult to get a clear history of her pregnancies and children, it appeared that she had had three children while married and three illegitimate children after the death of her husband. Two of these latter children were stillborn and in addition she had three miscarriages. These still-births and miscarriages were evidently due to syphilitic infection since she showed a positive Wassermann reaction.

This woman and her children had been on the present location for three years; and, although she had moved away from her former landlord because she "got tired of working for nothing," she "hadn't seen a nickel for a year." With her "advance" of four dollars a month, she and the children were living on "dry meat and corn bread," with an occasional dinner of greens from her garden on Sundays. Her situation was not unlike that of many other women who were heads of families.

The struggle of these women to get a living for themselves and the children who are dependent upon them is bound up with the plantation system in the South. Most of the mothers, as we have seen (Table 2) are tenants; and many of the relatively large group of unknown home tenure are either living with their parents who are tenants or are themselves mere farm laborers. They work from year to year "on halves" or are supposed to pay a stipulated amount of cotton and receive in return an "advance" in food, and, occasionally, clothes at the store. Mothers living with their parents and mothers with grown sons to aid them are able to work larger farms than women depending solely on their own labor. Consequently, mothers with young children are generally only able to work a "patch," comprising four to six acres. The "advances" in food, which often consist of corn meal and fat bacon, are correspondingly small. They supplement this with vegetables from their gardens when the dry weather does not destroy them. As the result of this restricted diet, we find both mothers and children suffering from pellagra. Statistics indicate that eight Negroes in Macon County died in 1930 of pellagra, but we know little concerning the numerous cases that did not result in death.[14]

One could scarcely find a more depressing picture of abject poverty and human misery than that presented by a young black woman, who had had two illegitimate children by different fathers, living in a one-room shack on a plantation in Alabama not many miles from Tuskegee Institute. The father of one child was somewhere over the creek, while the father of the other was "in Montgomery or somewhere." One child had evidently died of undernourishment and neglect. The young mother sat on a broken stool in the middle of the room furnished only with an iron cot covered with filthy rags. From her dried-up breast a baby, half-strangled by whooping cough, was trying to draw nourishment. Barefooted and clothed only in a cotton waist and dress pinned about her, she was rocking the child as her body swayed listlessly to an inarticulate singsong tune. On the cold embers in the fireplace lay a skillet containing the remnants of corn bread made only with water, because the landlord had refused fat meat as a part of her "advance." That same morning he had driven her with blows from her sick child to work in the field.

Not all mothers with children depending upon them for support sink to the level of poverty and misery of the woman portrayed above. Although as tenants they receive no accounting from their landlords, many of them manage to get adequate clothing and food of sufficient variety to keep them in health. In the plantation area the relatively few owners are better off so far as the necessities of life are concerned. But ownership of land is not always an infallible sign of independence and comfort. The system of credit and the relations of the races in the former stronghold of slavery cause even landowning mothers to lead a precarious existence. In regions like the North Carolina county outside of the area where agriculture is still dominated by the plantation system, homeownership signifies much more independence and comfortable living. No single crop dominates the agricultural activities; and, consequently, even during times of economic stress there may be an abundance of food for consumption. Moreover, in situations like that in the North Carolina county, where colored women have lived with white men, the struggle for existence has been relieved by the provision which the white fathers often made for concubines and children.

The maternal family is not held together solely by the co-operative activities incident to farming; it is also a natural organization for response. Although some women, after a brief marriage career, return to their mothers' households in order to work with them at farming, many others return to the family group for satisfactions of an emotional nature. There was, for instance, a thirty-eight-year-old woman who had left her husband after five years of marriage, because, as she said, she "got tired of staying with him" and preferred to "be with mamma and them." She was working on a "two-horse farm" with her brother, who took care of her until the settlement was made at the end of the year. That she usually received nothing at the end of the year was of no importance to her as long as she lived with her mother and brother and sister. The same valuation which she placed upon the intimate and sympathetic contacts afforded by the family group was expressed by a man, when he remarked: "I'm rich; when you have mother and father, you're rich." In fact, in the relatively isolated world of these black peasants, life is still largely organized on the basis of the personal and sympathetic relations existing between the members of the various family groups.

As a rule, the mothers show a strong attachment for their children. This is evident even in the young mothers whose offspring could be mistaken for younger brothers or sisters and are frequently regarded as such. In fact, in this world where intimate and personal relations count for so much, the relation between mother and child is the most vital and is generally recognized as the most fundamental. The rumor that even a starving mother was giving up her children was received by some women as an unpardonable crime against the natural dictates of the human heart. The intense emotional interdependence between mother and child that one so often finds is encouraged by a long nursing period. According to their own testimony, some women have nursed their children until they were three or four years old. Of course, these elemental expressions of love and solicitude for their offspring are often detrimental to the welfare of the children. Many a woman who "jes lives and wuks to feed her chillen" will give her child meat and bread when it is a few days old. This is done, they say, "to strengthen their stomachs." When one mother pointed to her overfed nineteen-year-old daughter as proof of the efficacy of such treatment, she never thought of the possible relation of such treatment to the death of ten of her children during infancy.

The dependence of the child upon the mother, who is the supreme authority in the household, often creates a solidarity of feeling and sentiment that makes daughters reluctant to leave home with their husbands and brings sons back from their wanderings. During the World War Negro soliders who had been drafted in these rural areas and sent to camps often complained in the manner of children of being torn from their mothers. The mothers on their part show equally strong attachment for their grown sons and daughters. The reason which mothers frequently give for not permitting their daughters to marry the fathers of their illegitimate children is that they were unwilling to part with their daughters. No matter how long a wandering son or daughter has been away from home, mothers rejoice in their return; and, if they hear that their children are sick, they will make great sacrifices to bring them back in order that they may have the ministrations that only a mother can give, or that they may die in the arms of the one who bore them.

As a rule, where we find mothers who do not want their children or neglect them, the sympathetic basis of family relations has been destroyed through the mobility of the population, or life and labor have made children a burden and a hardship. The isolation of these simple communities is being broken down, and "overproduction" in agriculture is sending women and girls to seek a living in town. The old relationships and traditional values are being destroyed, and new wishes, generally indicating an individualization of life-pattern, are becoming dominant. Sometimes children are left at home to be cared for by grandmothers. In spite of these changes, a large proportion of each generation of Negro mothers in these rural areas continue to bear patiently the burden of motherhood and assume responsibility for the support of their children. Their daughters still follow in their footsteps and bring their offspring to the maternal household. Then these mothers are elevated to the dignity of grandmothers, a position which gives them a peculiar authority in family relations and places upon them the responsibility for keeping kindred together.

Notes

---

[1] A. T. Morgan, *Yazoo; or, on the Picket Line of Freedom in the South* (Washington, D.C., 1884), p. 232.

[2] The 1930 census gave an enumeration of families with woman heads. The general situation in regard to Negro families may be briefly summarized as follows: (1) the proportion

of families with woman heads is higher in the South than in the North or West; (2) in all three sections it is higher in urban areas than in either rural-farm or rural-nonfarm areas; (3) it is higher among tenants than among owners in the urban areas but shows the opposite tendency in rural areas; and (4) it is lowest in the rural-farm areas of the North and the West.

³ Statistical data on the families in these three counties represent approximately 100 families from each of the ten precincts in Macon County, Ala., and practically all the Negro families in Issaquena County, Miss., and Hertford County, N.C. These families were taken from the original census returns. They were not the "families" or households as defined by the census but included the following types of relationships: (1) a married couple and their children, adopted, and step-children, if any; (2) a married person whose spouse is not living at home and the children of that person if any; (3) a widowed or divorced person and the children, if any; (4) a single man and woman who, from the information in the "relation to the head of the house" column, or from other information on the schedule, appear to be living as man and wife; and (5) a single girl who has an illegitimate child where this was clear. These families have been classified according to the color of the wife. The families in which no woman was present have been classified in the totals according to the color of the male head of the family.

⁴ The writer is aware of the criticism which can be brought against the use of the census classification of blacks and mulattoes as an index to the extent of the mixed-bloods among the Negroes. At the census of 1910 the term "black" included all persons who were "evidently full-blooded Negroes," while the term "mulatto" included "all other persons having some proportion or perceptible trace of Negro blood" (Bureau of the Census, *Negro Population, 1790–1915* [Washington, 1918], p. 207). The same definition of mulattoes and of full-blooded Negroes was used in 1920. Although the Census Bureau admits the uncertainty of the classification, since the distinction "depends largely upon the judgment and care employed by the enumerators," the classification probably contains on the whole as much accuracy as one could obtain.

⁵ The Census Bureau made the following statement concerning the accuracy of data on marital condition of Negroes: "It is recognized that the error attaching to the return of marital condition may be considerable. In some cases males who are or have been married, but are living apart from their families, may return themselves as single; females who have never been married, especially mothers with young children dependent upon them, may return themselves as either married, widowed, or divorced; married females deserted by their husbands may return themselves as widowed, the deserting husbands returning themselves as single; widowed males may return themselves as single; divorced males may return themselves as either single or widowed; and divorced females may return themselves as widowed. Where the return of marital condition is made by a third person, who does not know the facts, it is probably commonly presumed, and in some cases erroneously, that persons living apart from their families, especially males, are single. The result of these errors in combination would be, as regards the classification of males, overstatement of the number single and understatement of the number married, widowed, or divorced, and as regards the classification of females, overstatement of the number married, and widowed, and understatement of the number single or divorced" (*Negro Population, 1790–1915*, p. 235).

⁶ Concerning the accuracy of statistics on the widowed in the federal enumeration of 1900, the Census Bureau states that "among 1,000 negroes at least 15 years of age, 345 are single and 539 are married, while among 1,000 whites of the same age, 14 more are single and 20 more are married, the total difference of 34 being almost balanced by the fact that among the negroes 31 more in each 1,000 are widowed than among the whites. The relatively short life of the negro population would lead one to expect a rather large number in this class, but the difference between the two races seems to be too great to be accounted for in that way. One is disposed to believe that no small number of the 565,340 negro widows or widowers were persons whose conjugal relations had been ended by separation rather than by death and whose conjugal condition, therefore, has been inaccurately described" (Bureau of the Census, *Negroes in the United States* [Bull. 8 (Washington, 1904)], p. 48).

⁷ Nearly a half-century ago Bruce made the same observations concerning the breaking of family ties among the plantation Negroes: "The instance very frequently occurs of a negro

who has deserted his wife in one county getting, by false statements, a license to marry in another county, and there establishing a new home with as much coolness as if he had been single when he obtained the second license; but so accustomed are the whites to the sexual freedom of their former slaves that when it comes to their ears that a certain negro who resides in their vicinity has two wives to whom he is legally bound, living, the rumor, however capable of substantial proof, is almost always winked at or not considered worthy of investigation" (Phillip A. Bruce, *The Plantation Negro as a Freeman* [New York, 1889] p. 22).

[8] Bishop Coppin related the following concerning marital relations after the Civil War and attempts on the part of the church to break up such irregular unions: "Then there were other kinds of irregular living by Church members when there was no one to prefer 'charges and complaints,' and bring the transgressor to book. A man might be a member of the Church, and yet be 'stopping' with a woman to whom he was not married. Or, in the irregular union, the woman might be the Church member. These are cases where even Common law marriage was not claimed. Both parties going for single. The man just a 'star boarder.' But, in this general clean-up at Friendship, under the new regime, such parties had to choose between getting married, or facing charges for immoral conduct. Dear old Friendship now became the Ecclesiastical Court House, as well as the Church. For any of the above named lapses, hitherto unnoticed, a member was liable at any 'Quarterly meeting' to be called to face charges and complaints" (L. J. Coppin, *Unwritten History* [Philadelphia, 1920], pp. 126–27).

[9] Bishop Coppin (*op. cit.*, pp. 130–31) recites the following typical case in which a white man forced the Negro community to accept his colored concubine: "The father being a man of means and influence, defied public sentiment, and held family number one in servile submission. But his influence did not stop there; he would have it understood that his mistress must not be Churched, but rather must be regarded as a leading spirit at the Church to which she belonged, and which he gave her means to liberally support. If he had power enough to enslave his own legitimate family, forcing even the wife into unwilling silence, and besides, to so maintain himself in society as to prevent a general protest, it is not to be wondered at, that the Colored Community, dependent, perilous, would also hold its peace."

[10] Manuscript document.

[11] Manuscript document.

[12] Manuscript document.

[13] A study of Negroes on a plantation in Louisiana in the early part of the present century showed the following: "Of these 80 women 58 have had children. These 58 have had 268 children, or an average of 4.62 per woman, of which 154, or 57.5 per cent, are still living. In 34 cases out of 58, or 59 per cent, the first child is living. All those who were questioned on this subject, and who have lived with the Negroes all their lives stated that the birth rate is diminishing rapidly and that stillbirths and miscarriages are becoming much more common" (J. Bradford Laws, *The Negroes of Cinclaire Central Factory and Calumet Plantation* [Louisiana Department of Labor Bull. 38 (January, 1902)], p. 103).

[14] See Elbridge Sibley, *Differential Mortality in Tennessee* (Nashville, Tenn., 1930), pp. 91–95, concerning high death-rates among Negroes from pellagra in the cotton areas of Tennessee.

Patterns of Negro Segregation

Charles S. Johnson

The most elementary form of racial segregation is the reservation, or preserve, which in American history is associated with the development of the frontier. This form may be distinguished from that involved in the more complex social processes observed in the spatial distribution of urban populations which, in the growing community, is occasioned by the inevitable division of labor. Both forms of segregation are based upon difference. The basis of the difference in the first instance is in respect to kind, and in the second, in respect to function.

Incompatibility of groups, whatever the cause, is a basis for segregation. The most familiar type of inharmonious contact leading to segregation is found in the relations between a dominant and a subordinate group competing as groups rather than as individuals within the same area. Examples of this appear at one stage or another in every instance of the association of alien groups. Culture, religion, and physical characteristics all play an important part in defining the group relations. The Indian reservations in North America, the kampongs of Java, the compounds of South Africa, the Jewish ghettos of Europe, the Chinatowns and "Little Italys" and "Black Belts" of the United States are all expressions of the social or racial policy of the dominant society.

Segregation may be described as a form of partial ostracism. The ostensible purpose of this ostracism may be the protection of one group or the other from the consequences of contiguity and physical contacts, or the artificial limitation of economic competition, or the isolation for whatever reasons, religious or personal, of the social worlds of the groups in contact. In a fluid and unstable society such as that of the United States segregation may be, for a period at least, a partial substitute for caste.

There are forms of segregation or group isolation which are self-imposed. The purpose of such self-segregation may be to protect the group from the infection of strange or incompatible ideas and customs, or to achieve freedom in the exercise of some social functions, as in the case of a religious cult. Where there is no external compulsion, the limits and duration of the segregation can be regulated by the group itself, and no invidious distinctions of the segregated group need be implied.

Excerpts from pages 3–7, 44–47, 49–50, 56–59, 72–75, 316–17, 318 in *Patterns of Negro Segregation* by Charles S. Johnson. Copyright 1943 by Harper & Row, Publishers, Inc. Reprinted by permission of the publishers

A segregated immigrant community may perform the function of a cultural enclave in which the immigrant is at home and in which assimilation to the larger culture proceeds slowly. When cultural assimilation is achieved, the individual is less at home in this "cultural island" and in a generation or two may be lost in the larger society. This is the history of the European immigrant in the United States. But assimilation among the various racial and national groups in America proceeds at an unequal rate; and this diversity is due largely to differences in the culture and economic status of the groups and to the interest of the dominant or minority group in maintaining these distinctions. In the case of the white and Negro populations of the United States, the patterns of racial segregation and the intensity of the supporting sanctions vary markedly in different regions, in response to population ratios, and according to the historical and cultural backgrounds of the groups involved.

It is obvious that the policy of segregation which the American system of values proposes, merely to separate and to maintain two distinct but substantially equal worlds, is a difficult ideal to achieve. Any limitation of free competition inevitably imposes unequal burdens and confers unequal advantages. Thus, segregation or any other distinction that is imposed from without almost invariably involves some element of social discrimination as we have defined it. Residential segregation enforced by law is an obvious instance.

It is not enough for the purpose of the present study, however, to limit the concept of segregation merely to physical or spatial separation. Occupational segregation can be just as effective in maintaining an invidious distinction, but the separation is not necessarily spatial. So it is with many other types of relationships having the effect of restricting or qualifying communication between groups in contact. In order to distinguish and analyze certain less obvious aspects of the policy and practice of racial segregation in the United States, the term "segregation," as here used, includes all conventions and social ritual designed to enforce social isolation and social distance, and for this reason embedded in racial traditions.

The most distinct and clearly defined racial segregation is in the South. Bound as it is by its static economy and its racial traditions and ideologies, it presents an environment which resists, with a considerable expenditure of human energy, the incorporation of the Negro population into the total life of the area. In the early years of the present century an experienced and discerning journalist from the Middle West traveled over portions of the southern and northern states for the purpose of recording, as objectively as possible, the exact present conditions and relationships of the Negro in American life."[1] This was a period slightly more than a generation removed from the abolition of slavery and Reconstruction in the South. The older patterns of race relations, rooted in slavery and temporarily disturbed by the collapse of the formal structure of the institution, were apparently being restored and maintained with increased vigor. This is substantiated by Bertram Doyle who notes, in discussing the restoration of the etiquette of slavery in the South, that in a given locality both whites and Negroes have discovered and continue to observe the forms expected.[2] This appears to be the easiest adjustment making for tolerable relations. At the time of Baker's visit every southern state had enacted legislation requiring physical separation of the races in public and private institutions. Economic competition between the Negro and the emerging white worker, who was supported by the ballot, was acute in the cities. Atlanta, the most prosperous and promising of the cities of the "New South," had just experienced a most disastrous race riot which unquestionably had its roots in the economic competition of white and Negro workers. A new brand of politician had emerged from the ranks of the poor whites, long submerged by the planter-slave domination of the cotton kingdom; and these leaders were stimulating the emotions of the masses with bitter eloquence of speech with reference to a threatened "white supremacy." There was an outburst of overt conflict in the form of lynching. The average number of Negroes lynched each year in the first decade of this century was 115, with two peak years of 1255.[3] The ties between master and slave, which in numerous individual cases had persisted for nearly a generation after the collapse of slavery, were rapidly disintegrating under the new order, without a reassuring remedy or substitute.

There had been no great migrations to the North, but a steady small stream of migrants out of the South to the larger cities. Although the Negro population in these northern cities was negligible when compared with the population in the South, these migrants found themselves inexorably pressed together in more and more exclusively Negro blocks and residence areas. They found better wages but also higher living costs. In contrast to the positive opinion of virtually every white man in the South the average white man in the North knew little, and cared less, about the Negro and rarely, if ever, discussed him. There was little professed segregation, but a subtle and persistent discrimination in practically all areas of life and particularly in the economic sphere.

There have been important changes over the past forty years in the basic economy and also in the cultural life of the people in all sections of the country. The changes have affected the Negro as well as the other elements of the population. The broad structure of race relations, with its separate social categories, is deep-set in the mores and has changed more slowly than other conventional social practices. Within the framework and policy of racial segregation are wide variations in local practice. In fact, the items of behavior demanded of Negroes and of whites in relation to Negroes, in order to conform to the conventions, have become so complex that it is difficult at times to follow them. This very complexity and uncertainty has become, for the Negro in particular, abundant source of confusion and discontent. It is what a Negro traveler, Albon L. Holsey, had in mind when he described himself as "zig-zagging through the South."

Those states lying between the southern and northern states, and referred to as border states, play an interesting role in the realm of race relations. There are to be found many of the traits of the racially "solid South" and at the same time many of the practices of the northern states which violate the southern racial conventions and taboos. While practicing both segregation and nonsegregation, these areas are usually most explicit in labeling the segregation where it does exist. It is in these areas that attempts to reinforce custom with legal support have been most frequent, as, for example, in the matter of separate residential areas and a different scale of salaries for white and Negro teachers.

Since the border cities vary among themselves almost as widely as their practices vary internally, it is difficult to describe a fixed pattern. There are cities in this area with more and with less pronounced traditions and ideologies. The patterns of segregation and discrimination represented here, however, are typical of this marginal area. In Baltimore and Washington, D.C., for example, there is more rigid segregation and rejection of Negro patronage in the large department stores than anywhere in the South. In Washington the theaters are completely segregated. No Negroes, except those who pass as whites, can attend the theaters used by whites in the nation's capital. More of the government offices separate Negro workers and exclude them from the restaurant concessions in the buildings than accept them. There have been more changes in this practice since the beginning of the New Deal government under President Roosevelt than had occurred over a full generation before. There is segregation in the public schools, but none in local transportation, nor in the use of libraries, public buildings, and parks.

In such a border area, in which the institutional forces are so largely arbitrary and the total pattern of segregation so often broken by both planned and unplanned exigencies, the web of racial custom is confused and confusing. It is frequently necessary to be more explicit regarding segregative intent than in the South. Baltimore is one of the cities in which an attempt was made to effect complete residential segregation by race, only to have the law declared unconstitutional by the Supreme Court. Such a law is unnecessary in the South because the end is served by the fixed racial etiquette, as well as by the economic limitations of the Negro people.

In the northern cities there is no legalized and little overt racial segregation on a formal basis. In fact, however, there is considerable segregation and discrimination in this region.

If we attempted to classify institutions by degree of physical and spatial racial segregation, they would range themselves along a continuum, from those institutions in which complete segregation is supported by custom and prescribed by law to those institutions without differential treatment.

The most conspicuous forms of racial segregation are (1) in residential areas, (2) in educational, recreational, and other public institutions, (3) in quasi-public institutions or privately operated institutions under public control, such as railroads, steamship lines, streetcar and bus systems, and hospitals, (4) in private business establishments, such as hotels and restaurants under customary or legal mandate to prevent racial contact on a level implying social equality or permitting social intimacy, (5) in other private commercial and professional services, such as department stores, undertaking establishments, and doctors' offices. . . .

All southern states have laws separating white and Negro passengers in all land and water transportation. When the statutes were enacted there was no indication that the airplane would ever become a common medium of transportation and so no present laws regulate interracial association on air passenger lines. The Negro traffic, however, has not yet reached sufficient volume to create an issue in this new means of transportation.

Laws regulating racial separation in land and water transportation are similar throughout the South. These laws stipulate that the separate accommodations shall be similar, in the sense of being nondiscriminatory, and the intent of the policy is to achieve complete separation; but neither of these objectives is achieved. There is separation but it is seldom, if ever, complete; and accommodations are seldom equal or similar.

Railroads

The varying volume of both white and Negro traffic imposes a formidable cost hazard for the railroads. Above the level of the plain railroad coach, the "separate but equal" principle would become definitely costly, if carried out faithfully. On trains with sleeping, dining, and club cars it would be necessary to provide sections of these special facilities for both whites and Negroes despite the small volume of Negro patronage, if the spirit and letter of the laws were observed. It seldom happens, however, that these are observed or that the car, or section of a car, for Negroes is substantially the same as that for whites. In attempting to allow for variations in traffic some flexibility has been introduced in practice. Where the volume of Negro traffic warrants, an entire separate car may be assigned to Negroes; but white men have no scruples about riding in the open Negro coach for the purpose of smoking, or conveying a prisoner, or visiting with train officials, for the Negro coach is the favorite spot for the congregation of white train functionaries, including the news vendor.

Trains consisting of three or more cars set aside from one-half car to a whole car for Negro passengers. On trains containing coaches, chair cars, sleeping and club cars, and a diner, the front half or all of the first coach immediately behind the baggage and mail cars is usually set aside for Negroes.

Where traffic is light Negroes may ride in a separate section of a car occupied by white people, but may be asked to move if more space is needed for whites. The cars provided for Negroes are almost invariably older and less well equipped, and frequently in such condition as to defy cleaning. Trains engaged in interstate transportation usually employ the divided baggage and smoking car for Negro passengers. The newer streamlined trains have separate but more comfortable accommodations for Negroes.

Railroad stations and terminals vary widely in provisions for segregation. The waiting rooms and toilets are always separate and, except in a few instances, disparate in equipment. The typical station has the Negro waiting room adjoining the baggage room, with a window aperture to the ticket agent's office. Negroes are served when they can get the attention of the ticket agent. The entrance to the Negro section is generally on the side or back of the station. Some stations have separate entrances and exits from trains, but this is cumbersome. It is simpler to leave it to custom to enforce a sort of caste etiquette in passing through the gates to trains. The rules and expectations vary. For example, at the Union Station in Atlanta Negroes may leave the waiting room provided for them and patronize the newsstand and lunch counter in the white waiting room. At the Terminal Station in the same city they cannot enter the white waiting room for any purpose, and they are denied use of facilities other than those provided for them specifically. The stationmaster stands at the entrance to the white waiting room and directs Negroes away if any attempt to enter.

In Houston the new Grand Central Station has a well-appointed waiting room for Negroes with well-kept rest rooms and a capably operated lunch counter. Entrances to the street and the train sheds make contact with white travelers unnecessary. The check room, however, is in the white waiting room and Negroes with bags or parcels to check are directed there. The newsstand, from which Negroes make purchases, is also in the white waiting room. At the Union Station in Houston the Negro waiting room is an alcove off the white waiting room, with no separating doors between, but passage from the street to the waiting room is direct. While contact with white travelers is thus reduced, all entrances to trains are through the large white waiting room in which the ticket office is located, and to get to trains or to purchase tickets Negroes must go into the white waiting room.

In Richmond one railroad station provides a small waiting room for Negroes with a separate entrance at one side of the building. Negroes must use a long passageway to reach the gateway to trains. Another station has a bare and dirty little alcove, marked "For Colored," at the bottom of one stairway, so inadequate that little attempt is made to enforce the segregation. Negro passengers do not sit in the general waiting room upstairs, but await their trains standing near the train gates.

Only in exceptional cases are Negroes sold accommodations in Pullman cars; they are ordinarily obtained through some irregular procedure, such as having a white person purchase the reservation, or approaching a friendly railroad official who will sell the reservation without regard for the prohibition features of the laws. In some states legal provisions regulating accommodations for Negroes in Pullman cars are so phrased as to permit varied interpretation. Because of the heavy penalties imposed for violation of the explicit provisions of the state, trains entering Houston carry very few Negro Pullman passengers, and these only under most unusual circumstances. No Negro interviewed in Houston recalled an instance of Pullman accommodations being sold to a Negro leaving Houston; nor could informants who were interviewed in Birmingham recall any such sales. The late and distinguished James Weldon Johnson, a few years before his death in 1938, attempted to secure such accommodations. After engaging space over the telephone he called for the ticket and it was bluntly refused. No amount of argument or persuasion from him or several prominent citizens of the city could change, or obtain an exception to, the prevailing policy.

The Negroes who occasionally procure Pullman accommodations on trains entering Alabama are given "Lower 13," the drawing room; and this is interpreted as providing segregated quarters. Pullman accommodations are used without difficulty by Negroes entering Atlanta, probably because of the frequent use of this form of transportation by teachers in the various Negro colleges. The ticket offices in the Atlanta stations sell only coach accommodations to Negroes. Pullman accommodations are usually secured by telephoning the city offices of the railroad line on which passage is desired. The city office sells the reservation and instructs the station agent to deliver it when demanded. In Richmond Pullman accommodations are sold freely to Negroes.

When Congressman Arthur Mitchell was ejected from a Pullman car in Arkansas in 1937, he brought suit against the railroad and Pullman companies and eventually won a decision from the United States Supreme Court which, in effect, declared that the railroads would have to provide accommodations for Negro passengers in common Pullman and dining cars, if demanded, or provide a speccial Pullman and dining car. The practice of denying these accommodations has been considerably relaxed since this decision.

Meal service for Negroes varies on different railroad lines. In the recently inaugurated practice of serving Negroes in the dining cars on southern lines the separation is accomplished by curtaining off the two tables near the kitchen, and by making the call for Negro diners before the beginning or near the end of the regular meal hour. For example, some trains running through Alabama invite Negroes to the diner for the last service at each meal call. Trains in Texas have for some time served Negroes in the coaches where they ride, which practice is also observed in Georgia. . . .

Southern municipal ordinances require a separate section for Negroes in city streetcars and buses. The front seats in the car or bus are set aside "For White People" and the rear seats are assigned to "The Negro race." The operator is empowered to regulate the space occupied by each in accordance with the respective numbers of passengers. This system is subject to abuse since it permits the attitude of an operator to become a factor in segregation.

In Houston, as in many other cities, the buses have a movable sign designating the racial sections. In that city Negroes reported that they have had much greater freedom since buses were installed than when streetcars were in operation. There is a kind of customary arrangement which is expected not to be violated: In the Negro sections Negroes are assumed to have the whole bus with the exception of two seats in the very front. Often Negroes begin seating themselves just behind the two seats for whites. If it becomes apparent that the two seats will not suffice for whites, the Negroes will move a seat or two back, without being told by the operator of the bus.

The passengers on streetcars in Birmingham are segregated in a more definite manner. Large screens serve as partitions when clamped on the back of a seat to indicate the respective accommodations for white and Negro passengers. The unwieldy character of the screens and the reluctance of car operators to change them account for many abuses of this system.

In Richmond, Atlanta, and Nashville the personal inclination of the streetcar operator is eliminated from segregation. Signs in the cars notify white passengers to seat themselves from the front toward the rear, and colored passengers from the rear toward the front. The number of passengers by a sort of automatic process determines the line of separation. In Atlanta racial distinctions are also made in boarding the trolleys. The cars are operated by one man and, while all passengers enter from the front, Negroes are supposed to leave by the rear door only. A Negro going to the front door is usually told to go to the rear, but some operators of cars serving in Negro communities will allow Negroes to leave by the front door. Entering from one end only causes little friction or confusion. In fact, use of one-man cars has reduced friction; when the cars were operated by two men and the conductor attempted to take a hand in regulating the seating, there were frequent conflicts. . . . Everywhere in the South there is rigid segregation and traditional discrimination in hotels and restaurants, for these personal service establishments perform functions associated with strong racial taboos.

Hotels

No Negroes are accommodated in any hotel in the South that receives white patronage. As a rule there are no hotels for Negroes in small towns, but Negroes seeking lodging may find a Negro boardinghouse where rooms of a sort are available. In the cities there are usually several small but questionable hotels for Negroes, but nowhere in the South is the segregation pattern relaxed, except perhaps in the instance of a white person stopping at a Negro hotel.

Whether as a cause or as a result of the meager and unsatisfactory hotel accommodations available, most Negroes who travel in the South stop in private homes. On one social level private homes regularly accept a few transient lodgers and may rely on them as the chief source of income, but these are not always safe places because they have little or no supervision. Travelers exchange experiences, however, and recommend places that are more acceptable or agreeable than others. On another social level there is a mutual understanding of the problem of hotel accommodations, and when one has to visit a city, any friend or acquaintance in that city readily accepts the person as a guest; or he may be accommodated by a friend of a friend. Negro schools with eating and sleeping arrangements will usually accommodate a few visitors, whether their visit has to do with the school or not.

Hotel functions have expanded to include their general use for meetings of civic, business, and professional organizations. While the taboo against the association of Negroes and whites in hotels as lodging places is definite and strict, the pattern of exclusion is not so clearly defined on the more formal institutional level. As Negroes come to be included in civic and business organizations, a strain develops between the mores and a practicable pattern of behavior in a new situation. The traditional color line still is insisted upon; and even in the largest cities mixed meetings involve a compromise of custom, if not of law. Hotel managers are not always willing to compromise, nor are officers of the law always willing to look the other way while Negroes and whites assemble or eat together. For the sake of the patronage of such gatherings, however, the management may permit Negroes to attend general meetings, but usually on condition that they use side doors and freight elevators and do not loiter in the lobby.

A few of the hotels in the large cities of the South permit interracial dining in private dining rooms on such special occasions and at least one hotel has extended the privilege to the general dining room. This was doubtless due in part to the pressure and prestige of the Southern Sociological Society, which is made up almost entirely of northern social scientists and has a rule that, when its Negro members are excluded from dinner or luncheon meetings, these formal meetings will not be held.

The strict policy of segregation and exclusion of Negroes from the hotels of southern cities for many years prevented a meeting in the South of the National Conference of Social Work, with a membership reaching several thousands. When this organization finally decided to accept an invitation to meet in New Orleans, it was necessary in view of the Negro membership to insist on certain guarantees: (1) Negroes should attend all meetings freely; (2) there should be no separate entrances or elevators; (3) there should be no segregation in seating arrangements of delegates; (4) on the part of the organization, if meetings were to be held at a time when meals were being served and Negro members were not allowed to share the meals in private dining rooms, the meetings would be dispensed with. It was not expected that the Negroes would sleep in the hotels or eat in the general dining rooms.

When the National Education Association, whose membership includes several hundred Negro teachers, met in New Orleans in 1937, the headquarters hotel objected to use of the formal entrance by Negroes and to their passing through the lobby. As a solution the hotel proposed a temporary ladder or stair leading through a side window. The Negroes objected, and only a few attended. One special program on problems of Negro education was canceled.

In the border cities there are separate hotels for whites and Negroes. Each race uses the establishments provided for its use; and Negro hotels generally serve only Negroes.

In Baltimore at Community Chest banquets, meetings of the Junior Bar Association, and similar gatherings Negro and white members meet together in white hotels and are served together. No discrimination is felt in these meetings. It was reported that the city's largest hotel first opened its doors to mixed meetings several years ago. It received a large amount of trade as a result of this liberal policy and other hotels changed their policies of exclusion. According to a local Negro attorney, "mixed meetings" can be held at all the hotels in Baltimore.

The hotels in Dayton stringently discourage Negro patronage. The manager of the best of the local hotels, conscious of the civil rights act, said that he did not object to a few Negroes at meetings, but private lodgings are never offered except in rare cases. He said:

We recently let Marian Anderson stay here, but it was all arranged beforehand, so that when she came in she didn't register or come anywhere near the desk. She went right up the elevator to her room and no one knew she was around.

In the North many of the hotels belong to syndicates or chains, and their policies are remarkably consistent. One or two Negroes, usually of national distinction, are accommodated on occasions at the well-known hotels, but in most cases some special arrangement has been made with the management. When this concession is made, the facilities of the hotel are limited to the room. There is no effort to conceal the intent to exclude these special guests from the rest of the facilities. Negroes attend meetings in most of the hotels without difficulty and on occasion, as members of a convention predominantly white, may for a limited period be extended most of the privileges of the hotel, including the dining room and lobby.

An ordinary applicant for a room will be met with the statement that no rooms are available. Civil rights statutes permit court action for proved discrimination. In such cases, if one can prove by witnesses that he was refused accommodations after being accepted by mail, he may receive damages. However, with the still small number of suits it has been easier for the hotels to pay the comparatively small damages than to change the present policy of exclusion.

Restaurants and Cafés

Discrimination in eating places may be regarded as a reflection of the taboo against interracial dining which is so pronounced in the South and in the border states. The exclusion of Negroes from eating places in the South is based upon social implications and does not prevent white men, usually foreigners, from operating places strictly for Negro trade. In Birmingham, Memphis, and Atlanta there are several restaurants run by whites for colored patronage. These are inexpensive places where the quality of the food is of secondary importance in comparison with the quantity of liquor and beer that is dispensed. If such a place is of sufficient size to warrant additional help, some Negro who is known by the clientele is usually employed. Small cafés catering to Negro trade may also be operated by Negroes. Cafés catering to whites frequently have a side or back entrance for Negroes, and they are served at a table in the kitchen. At lunch counters and roadside stands they may buy a sandwich and a drink to be eaten some distance away.

In the business districts of northern cities Negroes usually eat in the more impersonal chain restaurants catering to large numbers of hurried workers; otherwise Negroes "pick their spots." The lunchrooms of department stores are as a rule open to Negroes. More expensive restaurants and the smaller and cheaper ones are likely to discourage Negro patronage in one way or another. Since it is a matter of individual management and the particular circumstances under which service is sought, it is never wholly possible to predict what may happen. Disagreeable incidents, especially if comparatively frequent, are enough to eliminate all except naïve or bold and aggressive Negro patrons. . . .

The chief amusement places in the South are the motion-picture theaters, swimming pools, skating rinks, bowling alleys, dance halls, and baseball parks. The exclusion of Negroes from most of these places patronized by whites is so universal and complete as to require no further elaboration. The issue of segregation arises only in the theaters and ball parks. There are segregated sections for Negroes in the ball parks — usually in the less favorable locations. Negroes may also rent parks in some places, for their own games. If they expect white spectators they must reserve a section exclusively for them, and this section must be in some desirable location. The same procedure is followed in the case of dance halls. Commercial dances with a Negro "name band," sponsored by Negroes, frequently advertise "A reserved section for whites."

Negroes attend the motion-picture theaters in all the towns visited, but are always segregated. The common attitude in this regard was expressed by a Negro businessman in Bolivar County:

If they did not let the Negroes go to shows here there would not be much for them to do, but go to church. They don't have anything to do. The Negroes can't even gamble like they used to do. This new mayor has closed all of that down. They make the Negroes go up in the balcony or "buzzard's roost," as they call it. It is close up there, and sometimes when the Negroes haven't had a bath yet, it is hard to stay up in some of them. They can go to all of the shows. The only other kind of thing they can go to here is the minstrel, and that doesn't come until the cotton picking season. Everybody goes then, but you have to sit in separate places. They always save the best seats for the white people. Even when these Negroes give something for themselves, they have a special section for the white folks, and do you know that they leave the best seats for them? These Negroes here have been kicked so much by the white folks that they like it, I believe. They would not know how to act, most of them, if they were not making the world comfortable for white folks. I know what I am talking about. That is so.

The town of Cleveland in Bolivar County has three motion-picture theaters. All of them have outside entrances for Negroes in the front of the building to the side of the white entrance. Each theater has a separate ticket window for Negroes, and in all cases Negroes are seated in the balcony. At one of the theaters visited in the course of this study, a white man frequently passed through the aisle of the balcony ordering Negroes to move to make room for others. This person always spoke gruffly and in a manner that would normally be considered discourteous. He would shout. "Move over there, boy, and give these girls some seats. Hey, you boy, did you hear what I said?" The "girls" referred to were middle-aged negro women.

While the color line is always drawn in theaters, it is sometimes of a tenuous and shifting character. Thus a domestic worker in Marked Tree, Arkansas, said:

Colored go upstairs in the movie here. It is either too hot or too cold up there. Colored buy tickets at the side window. You just stand there, as a rule, until all the white people go in. They had a colored picture here, and they were to let colored people have the whole theater. The white people wouldn't let the colored have the whole building, so they had three shows. Not many white people went to see it.

When they fill up downstairs some of the white fellows come up and sit with the colored. Most of the time they are just young fellows. Sometimes they come up with their girl friends. It's just like it always is — the white can come on your side, but you don't go on theirs.

In Johnston County, North Carolina, Negroes sit in a segregated section of the balcony, but they are separated from white balcony patrons only by an aisle. If the houses are crowded, Negroes and whites sit together wherever a seat can be found, but generally they seat themselves separately.

On "jack pot" nights, in one Mississippi town, Negroes are not admitted to the theater, although they may hold winning tickets for the money given away by the theater to attract patronage. After the jack pot a special picture is shown for whites and Negroes who want to come.

In all the cities visited the theaters either segregate Negroes or exclude them altogether. The usual pattern of segregation appears in the description provided by a Negro professional man:

In one of the oldest theaters half of the balcony is divided by a chain. When the white side fills up they push over into the colored side. They used to have special days for Negroes, but I understand now that it is open all of the time to Negroes. Negroes enter the theater from a side door, on a side street. They have a separate ticket window, and a colored girl selling tickets. Two of the large theaters have special midnight shows for colored people when a Negro stock company or some Negro movie comes here. They had a special show when Ivy Anderson was playing in some movie here not so long ago. She is a native of Houston. At one of the houses Negroes enter through a side door. At the newest theater they have to use the fire escape.

In some cases theaters have discontinued the "crow's roost" in the balcony and no longer accommodate Negroes, because of inability to compete with theaters operated by Negroes, or by whites for Negroes. A school official in Birmingham said:

There is one white theater that the Negroes can go to but must sit in the balcony. I never worry about going there. If I go, I am going to the Negro show. They don't have much like that in the way of amusement for Negroes around here. When you get away from the movies there is little that you can point out. They used to go in another show, where they had to go in through the back. That made the Negroes pretty mad, and they did not go very much. So few of them went that the management did not think it worth while to make arrangements for any of them.

In Richmond all-Negro houses have entirely displaced the attendance at white shows. This movement received its impetus in Richmond in 1934, when a Negro motion-picture house showing good pictures was opened. The situation is similar to that in Washington, D.C., where Negroes prefer the all-Negro theaters to the segregated sections of the larger white theaters. By 1937, when the last of five all-Negro theaters was opened in Richmond, the Negro population had been won from the white theaters altogether, and now no provision is made for Negroes to attend white motion-picture shows. The chain theaters for Negroes have been successful and are now found in many cities along the eastern seaboard.

In Baltimore Negroes generally attend all-Negro theaters, of which there are ten or more. Most of these are on Pennsylvania Avenue in the Negro residence section, and some of them are clean and attractive. None of the theaters are owned by Negroes. Negroes can go to three white theaters which have legitimate stage performances as well as motion-picture shows. In all cases they sit in the last rows in the balcony, but they use the common entrance to the balcony.

The local theaters in Dayton, Ohio, discourage Negro patronage. One theater manager said:

Of course, I have nothing against them, but I know that most of my patrons have. I don't want any migrant business, so I try to keep them from coming into my theater.

This theater has the general privilege of changing prices without notice, which is done if a Negro appears at the ticket window. If this fails to discourage their patronage, Negroes are ushered to an inconspicuous corner of the theater. On one occasion a Negro woman was pulled from the ticket line by an attendant. . . .

In one way or another, minorities are excluded from full participation in the life of the community and the conduct of the state. This immediately raises the question of the relation of this circumstance to the democratic theory of the state, which assumes complete participation of all who are capable of functioning economically or politically as members of society. The essential fact is that the actual practices of the dominant majority are, for whatever reason, in direct conflict with the ideals and professed objectives of the state. It is this fact that gives reality to the minority status of the Negro and other groups. It is the necessity for struggle that forces upon them the solidarity by which alone they can gain the status that is assured them.

The theory of the democratic state assumes, with respect to the different racial and cultural units of which it is composed, a degree of cultural assimilation corresponding to their equal status in citizenship. In actual fact, however, the democratic theory is frankly qualified by the dominant group's value judgment of assimilability. Racial groups that are physically and culturally similar to the dominant pattern or ideal are acceptable; racial groups which differ markedly from the norm are less acceptable. In their case adjustment or accommodation within the framework of the democratic society is demanded rather than assimilation. The policy of segregation and the permanence of the pattern differ for groups regarded as assimilable and unassimilable. . . .

The laws prescribing racial segregation are based upon the assumption that racial minorities can be segregated under conditions that are legally valid if not discriminating. Theoretically, a segregation is merely the separate but equal treatment of equals. In such a complex and open society as our own this is, of course, neither possible nor intended; for whereas the general principle of social regulation and selection is based upon individual competition, special group segregation within the broad social framework must be effected artificially and by the imposition of arbitrary restraints. The result is that there can be no group segregation without discrimination, and discrimination is neither democratic nor Christian.

Notes

[1] Ray Stannard Baker, *Following the Color Line* (New York: Doubleday, Page and Company, 1908).

[2] Bertram W. Doyle, *The Etiquette of Race Relations in the South* (Chicago: University of Chicago Press, 1937), p. 156.

[3] Arthur Raper, *The Tragedy of Lynching* (Chapel Hill: University of North Carolina Press, 1933), p. 480.

The New Negro Middle Class

E. Franklin Frazier

Thirty years ago I wrote for inclusion in *The New Negro* a short chapter entitled "Durham: Capital of the Black Middle Class." In that chapter I undertook to show how a small group of Negroes, practicing the philosophy of thrift, had built up businesses which indicated the emergence of the spirit of modern business enterprise. Moreover, I undertook to describe the patterns of behavior and general outlook on life of this new class among Negroes, which I regarded as representative of a new element that was appearing in the evolution of Negro life in the United States. The many changes which have occurred in the economic and social structure of American society since that chapter was written have brought about a transformation of Negro life. One of the most important aspects of this transformation has been the emergence of a sizeable middle class which has acquired a dominant position in the Negro community. It is my purpose in this paper to discuss the development of the new Negro middle class and its present status. But before entering upon the main emphasis of this paper I must say something of the character of the Negro middle class which I described thirty years ago.

The middle class of which I wrote was composed principally of teachers, doctors, dentists, preachers, trusted persons in personal service, government employees, and a few business men. At that time all persons in professional occupations comprised about two and a half per cent of all employed Negroes, while the percentage of all those gaining a living from business enterprises, including clerical workers as well as proprietors, was even smaller. When I speak of this group as a middle class group I am not referring simply to the source of its incomes. This group was distinguished from the remainder of the Negro population not so much by economic factors as by social factors. Family affiliation and education to a less degree were as important as income. Moreover, while it exhibited many middle class features such as its emphasis on respectabilitly and morality, it also possessed characteristics of an upper class or an aristocracy. To this extent the middle class group of which I wrote thirty years ago may be regarded as a caste in the Negro community. This leads me to say something of the sources of the traditions of this class.

From the standpoint of their cultural history, the Negroes in the United States

From E. Franklin Frazier, *The New Negro Thirty Years Afterward*. pp. 25–32. Washington, D.C.: Howard University Press, 1955. Reprinted by permission of the publisher.

have developed only two really vital traditions. The most important has been the folk tradition which gave the world the Spirituals and secular folk songs. The second, of less importance but of considerable interest from the standpoint of the stratification of the Negro population, is the tradition of the gentleman. The folk tradition developed out of the experiences of the Negro masses on Southern plantations. The tradition of the gentleman was developed as the result of the close association of negroes and whites, often in the same household, and led to the amalgamation of the two races. The assimilation of the patterns of behavior and values of upper class whites, mainly Southern aristocrats, established the tradition of the gentleman among a small class of Negroes. Of course, the traditions of the folk have often become mingled with the traditions of the gentleman. This is the reason for my statement in the chapter written thirty years ago that "the Negro has been a strange mixture of the peasant and the gentleman." This fact, as we shall see, has become especially significant in the growing importance of the new middle class today.

But let us return to the middle class of three decades ago. With few exceptions the representatives of the middle class were educated in the missionary schools which had been established by Northern missionaries after the Civil War. These missionaries had inculcated along with their pious teachings the idea of thrift. The influence of the missionaries extended to Tuskegee Institute and other schools under Negro administrations where the idea of thrift and the practice of piety were so conspicuous in the education of Negroes. In the schools of higher education founded by missionaries the teaching of piety and thrift was designed to build character and create a group of leaders with a sense of responsibility for the welfare and elevation of the masses. Moreover, these schools aimed to instill a certain love and appreciation of cultural things — music, literature, and art. The tradition of Yankee piety and thrift was often grafted onto the tradition of the aristocrat and gentleman.

The changes which occurred in the economic and social organization of the United States as the result of two world wars brought into existence a new middle class group among Negroes. The primary cause of this new development was the urbanization of the Negro population on a large scale. Prior to World War I about nine-tenths of the Negro population was in the South, and less than 25 per cent of Southern Negroes lived in cities. As the result of migrations to Southern as well as Northern cities about five-eights of the Negroes live in cities today. The migration to Northern cities was especially crucial since it created large Negro communities in an area that was relatively free from the legal and customary discriminations under which Negroes live in the South. One of the first effects of the migrations to Northern cities was that it gave Negro children access to a standard American education. Secondly, the entrance of the Negro into industrial employment and into occupations that had been closed to him in the South accelerated the occupational differentiation of the Negro population. The occupational differentiation of the Negro population was accelerated also by the new needs of the Negro communities which were served by Negroes. Finally, the migrations gave the Negro access to political power which helped him to improve his economic as well as his social position.

These changes provided, first, the economic basis of the new middle class. Whereas the middle class of thirty years ago, as we have seen, was composed of a few professionals, mainly teachers and a few persons in other occupations including a few business men, middle class Negroes are found today in a large variety of professional and technical occupations. And what is more important is the significant increase in the proportion of Negroes in clerical and other white collar occupations. This latter development has occurred in the North because whereas in the South Negroes in white collar occupations are restricted to employment in segregated Negro schools and Negro businesses, in the North Negroes have increasingly been employed in white collar occupations in both public services and private enterprises. Then, too, Negro business in the North has become more important than in the South. This has refuted the old belief that Negro business could thrive better in a section where the Negro was segregated and suffered discrimination. However, in discussing the development of Negro business one should remember that some of the most conspicuous successes of Negroes in business have been in the policy racket and other illegal enterprises.

The expansion of the Negro middle class and the change in its character are indicated by the change in its capital, so to speak. Thirty years ago Durham, with its flourishing business enterprises, was rightly regarded as the capital of the black middle class. But today one turns to the North in order to discover what might be regarded as the capital of the black middle class. Although both Chicago and Detroit lay claim to this distinction, the unbiased observer is inclined to regard Detroit as the new capital of the Negro middle class because it is in that city that he finds the most intense expressions of the character and values of the new Negro middle class. The outlook on life and patterns of behavior of the new middle class are not confined to any city, however; they have tended to permeate the new middle class wherever the economic and social conditions have favored the emergence of this new element among Negroes. In the remainder of this paper, I shall undertake to analyze the orientation of this new class and to assess its influence upon the adjustment of the Negro to American civilization.

Let us consider first the economic basis of this class in the light of economic realities. At the present time, about a fourth of the Negroes in the North and West and one-eighth of those in the South may be classed as of middle class status. This estimate is based upon the fact that around three per cent of the employed Negro men in the North and West gain a living in professional and technical occupations and the same percentage as managers, officials, and proprieters, exclusive of farm owners. Slightly more than eight per cent are employed in clerical occupations and as salesmen. To these groups are added the skilled craftsmen and foremen who comprise between ten and eleven per cent of the employed Negroes in the North and West. In the South there are half as many, proportionately, in these occupations.

From the standpoint of incomes, Negroes of middle class status have incomes ranging from between $2,000 and $2,500 upwards. In the South the majority of the Negro middle class do not have incomes amounting to $3,000. In the North and West the Negro middle class is better off since a half of the Negroes of this status have incomes between $3,000 and $4,000. But in any case the less than one per cent of Negroes in the country with incomes between $4,000 and $5,000, who are at the top of the Negro middle class, have incomes about equal to the medium incomes of white collar workers among whites. As we have seen, the group of managers, officials, and proprietors, excluding farm owners, comprise slightly more than two per cent of employed Negroes. It is in this group that belong the Negro business men who are the symbols of the Negro middle class and its aspirations and values. Therefore, it is necessary to say something concerning Negro business.

In our discussion we are interested in Negro business first from the standpoint of its economic significance and secondly from the standpoint of its social significance for the Negro middle class. From the first standpoint, it has little significance in the economic life of the United States and little significance in the economic life of the Negro. It is obvious to anyone that the infinitesimal accumulations of capital represented by all Negro business enterprises have no significance in the American economic system. One small bank in a small town in the state of New York, for example, has more assets than all the Negro banks combined. Then, from the standpoint of providing employment for Negroes, Negro businesses provide employment for less than one-half of one per cent of all the employed Negroes. On the other hand, Negro business has a social significance that can not be ignored or underestimated.

Negro business is not only an economic fact, however insignificant; it is a social myth. The social myth has a long history. It originated in the 1880's when Negro leaders in the South, seeing the Negro supplanted by white workers, began preaching the doctrine that Negroes would achieve economic salvation by building their own businesses. These business enterprises were supposed to give employment to Negro workers. The myth was institutionalized when the National Negro Business League was organized in 1900. Since then the doctrine of salvation through business has been preached in every Negro church and school. Despite the fact that Negro business is no more significant today in the American economy and in the economic life of Negroes than it was fifty years ago, the myth is still perpetuated among Negroes. It is dear to the heart of the Negro middle class and no argument based upon facts can change their faith in Negro business as the means to racial salvation. This is not strange because the Negro middle class lives largely in a world of delusions.

The world of delusions which the Negro middle class has created for itself is due partly to the fact that it has no integral body of traditions. Here, then, it is necessary to consider the social origins of this class and its education. Earlier it was pointed out that two distinct traditions had developed among Negroes: the tradition of the folk and the genteel tradition or the traditions of the gentleman. The small

Negro middle class of thirty years ago had its roots on the whole in the latter tradition. Most of the leaders among the Negro middle class were of mixed ancestry and had inherited the traditions of the upper class whites. The missionary education which they received tended to reenforce this tradition. As the result of the rapid social mobility which has brought into existence the new middle class, this tradition has been dissipated. Then, those with the traditions of the Negro folk who have risen to middle class status have shed their social heritage.

This may be seen if one views the changes which have occurred in Negro schools which provide education for the Negro middle class. Formerly, these schools were dedicated to the building of character or the making of men. As a part of this process the students of these schools were expected to become literate in the broadest meaning of the term and to develop some philosophy of life which included a sense of social responsibility. But today these institutions have become a sort of finishing schools for the children of the middle class. The term 'finishing school' is not exactly appropriate, since a finishing school is supposed to give a superficial culture, whereas the graduates of these schools lack even a superficial culture and are generally illiterate. This is not serious from the standpoint of the Negro middle class since these schools are no longer dedicated to the making of men but to the making of money-makers. The students are no longer taught habits of thrift and piety. They take as their models the successful members of the middle class who did not gain their money through such old fashioned virtues as thrift, and saving, but through clever manipulations, rackets, and gambling. Moreover, during their college life the students strive to emulate the conspicuous consumption in which their parents and other persons who provide models engage. They have little or no respect for knowledge and learning and often even exhibit a certain contempt for anything involving intellectual achievement. In this respect they tend to perpetuate the anti-intellectualism which sets the new middle class apart from the old middle class that had some respect for education and learning.

The general anti-intellectualism of the new middle classes was shown by the failure of the Negro Renaissance in the twenties, many of the fruits of which are contained in *The New Negro,* edited by the late Professor Alain Locke. The Negro Renaissance of the twenties represented a reevaluation of the Negro's past and of the Negro himself by Negro intellectuals and artists. It failed because at that time the new middle class which was growing in size and importance in the Negro community rejected it. The short stories, novels, and poems which expressed this new evaluation of the Negro and his history in America by his artists and intellectuals were unread and ignored by the new middle class that was eager to gain a few dollars. Instead of being interested in gaining a new conception of themselves, the new middle class was hoping to escape from themselves. Money appeared to them to provide this main avenue of escape. But the escape was to be into a world of make-believe and delusions.

The Negro press has been one of the chief agencies by which the Negro middle class has escaped from the realities of its position in American life. The Negro press has created a world of make-believe into which the middle class attempts to escape from the realities of its position in American life. Some of these realities have been described. But there is still an important fact concerning the middle class which has not been mentioned, namely, the inferiority complex from which the middle class suffers. During its rise to its present position, the middle class has broken with its traditional background and identification with the Negro masses. Rejecting everything that would identify it with the Negro masses and at the same time not being accepted by white American society, the middle class has acquired an inferiority complex that is reflected in every aspect of its life. In creating a world of make-believe for the middle class, the press has provided compensations for their inferiority complex.

Although the vast majority of Negroes of middle class status are in reality white collar workers who derive their incomes from salaries, the Negro press represents them as a wealthy group. The press constantly plays up fantastic stories of rich Negroes. From time to time the Negro millionaires are featured in the Negro press. It carries pictures of their richly furnished homes, their expensive automobiles, their gay and extravagant parties and debutante balls. Since there has been a movement toward integration and white people are increasingly reading about the Negro world behind the walls of segregation, white teachers are asking how Negro teachers can afford debutante balls. But they are only beginning to learn of the gaudy carnival in which the middle class Negroes find an escape from their inferior status in American life.

In fact, much of the news carried in the Negro press is concerned with status. Every bit of news concerning the Negro that indicates that he is given some recognition by whites is recorded as of great consequence. If a Negro has nearly completed his residence work for the doctorate in a Northern university, it is played up as a great intellectual achievement. If a Negro is elected or appointed as a mere police magistrate, he is heralded as a great jurist and is forever afterwards referred to as "Judge." Even if a Negro was supposed to have been intimately associated with some notorious white criminal, he becomes a figure of note. Sometimes a Negro woman gains fame because she was caught in an illicit love affair with a white man. Of course, some of the news showing that the Negro has achieved recognition is mere fiction. Negroes who travel abroad are usually received by royalty, or some count falls madly in love with a Negro woman. Sometimes one reads in the Negro press of some Negro who scarcely knows a word of a foreign language astonishing foreign scholars with his facility in the language as well as his erudition. Thus does any recognition, real or fancied, soothe the inferiority feelings of the Negro middle class.

Much of the world of make-believe created by the Negro press consists of the activities of "Negro society." Nearly everyone who is featured by the Negro press is a socialite. This seems to be the highest compliment conferred upon a person of middle class status, male or female. A very retiring, scholarly friend of mine about whom a notice of his participation in a scientific meeting was carried in the Negro press was surprised to read that he was a leading socialite. Inclusion in "society" implies that a person is wealthy and can engage in all kinds of conspicuous consumption and waste. For example, one hardly ever reads of a socialite getting into her automobile but of her getting into a "chauffeured Cadillac." Minute details are generally provided concerning the cost of a mink coat, the cost of a house, or the cost of a party. But extravagant expenditure is not the only feature of being a socialite. It involves exclusiveness, and exclusiveness is always a means of overcoming one's feeling of inferiority.

The attempt of the middle class Negro to escape from the realities of his position in American life is really an attempt to escape from himself. This is shown partly in the case of the religious life of the middle class. At one time the Negro middle class was identified with the Congregational, Episcopal, Presbyterian, and, in a few cases, the Catholic churches. When one acquired middle class status it often meant a change from membership in the Baptist or Methodist denomination to affiliation with one of the above churches. But today, the new middle class has lost much of its religion and is constantly seeking some new religious or quasi-religious affiliation. But since the middle class has no philosophy of life and can only draw upon scraps of a religious tradition which it has rejected, it seeks solutions of life's problems in spiritualism and other forms of superstition. In fact, the world has become a world of chance for the middle class. After all, don't most of the most successful prominent members of the middle class owe their achievement to chance? This accounts for its almost religious devotion to poker, horse racing, and other forms of gambling.

The middle class owes its growth and form of existence to the fact that the Negro has been isolated mentally, socially, and morally in American society. Therefore, in some respects, the Negro community may be regarded as a pathological phenomenon. It is not surprising, then, that the Negro middle class shows the mark of oppression, to use the title of a recent study of the Negro, in its mental and psychic make-up. The middle class Negro shows the mark of oppression more than the lower class Negro who finds a shelter from the contempt of the white world in his traditional religion, in his songs, and in his freedom from a gnawing desire to be recognized and accepted. Although the middle class Negro has tried to reject his traditional background and racial identification, he cannot escape from it. Therefore, many middle class Negroes have developed self-hatred. They hate themselves because they cannot escape from being identified as Negroes. This self-hatred is really the hatred of the Negro turned against themselves. The inefficiency of the middle class Negro in the running of businesses and the management of educational institutions is notorious, but he excuses his deficiencies by exaggerating the defects of the Negro masses. Yet the middle class Negro pretends that he is proud of being a Negro while rejecting everything that identifies him with Negroes. He pretends that he is a leader of Negroes when he has no sense of responsibility to the Negro masses and exploits them whenever an opportunity offers itself. As a result, the middle class Negro is often plagued by feelings of guilt. Much of the neurotic behavior of the middle class Negro is doubtless due to his self-hatred and guilt feelings.

The middle class Negroes are haunted by feelings of insecurity. None of the compensations of the world of make-believe can completely efface their deep feelings of insecurity. The reality of the world about them breaks through the pretenses about wealth and recognition and social status. These feelings of insecurity become more urgent as the walls of segregation cease to protect them from the competition and requirements of American society. While middle class Negroes are often vociferous in their fight against segregation, many of them are afraid of the competition and the demands of the larger community. Some hope to come to terms with the white world by shedding as far as possible the last vestige of their racial identification. But this will provide no solution of their problems which arise from their rejection of their racial identification and their refusal to accept their real role in the economic organization of American life. As they become integrated into American society, they can achieve personal dignity and peace within themselves only through acceptance of their racial identification and their real position in American economic life.

Black Metropolis: Sociological Masterpiece

3

The Measure of the Man

St. Clair Drake and Horace Cayton

As we have noted in the preceding chapters, Bronzeville judges its institutions and leaders in terms of "racial loyalty." To be called a Race Man is a high compliment. But "race-relations" is only one axis of life. People are also interested in "getting ahead," "having a good time," and "serving the Lord," and when people are choosing a church or social club or selecting a wife or a husband, they do not choose primarily according to how the organization or person "stands on the race question." There are other measures of the man. Yet, as we shall see, the shadow of the Job Ceiling and of the Black Ghetto falls on every activity, and all of Bronzeville's standards of appraisal are conditioned by the way Negro-white relations are organized.

Color of the Skin

White people with an interest in "Negro progress" sometimes profess shock at the distinctions Negroes make among themselves. Most disconcerting are color distinctions — the lines that Negroes draw between black and "light," "fair" and brown-skinned. "How," they ask, "can Negroes expect white people not to draw the color-line when they can do it themselves?" Negro leaders in Bronzeville usually throw the ball back to the whites by demanding in effect, "How can Negroes ignore color distinctions when the whole culture puts a premium upon being white, and when from time immemorial the lighter Negroes have been the more favored?" A Negro physician, for instance, told an interviewer:

"Any Negro who is honest will admit that he is dominated by the standards of the society he is brought up in. When we are little children we use story books in which all the characters have long blond hair. When we go to church we're taught that God is a white man. The Virgin Mary is white. What can you expect? All our early concepts of desirable physical attributes come from the white man.

It is a sociological rule that people are pulled into the standardized ways of thinking. The average Negro may say that he's proud to be black. This is more or less a defense mechanism. People in America don't black their faces and make their hair kinky. They would be laughed at; it would be too different from the American standard. The whole situation is easy enough to understand.

There is much truth in this argument. "Black" is a word loaded with derogatory implications in Anglo-Saxon linguistics. Things are "black as sin." When you don't like a person you give him a "black look." When trouble passes, you emerge "from darkness into light." Conversely, "That's damned white of you" is a compliment. To be "free, *white,* and twenty-one" is considered the ultimate in independence. White people will even sometimes compliment a Negro by unconsciously saying, "Good — you did it like a white man." Scant wonder that Negroes have picked up the idea that "black is evil."

The "Color-struck"

When "fair" (i.e., light-skinned) Negroes seem inordinately proud of their skin-color, or when darker Negroes have a predilection for associating with very light ones or encouraging their children to do so, Bronzeville calls them "color-struck." One color-struck woman told an interviewer that she liked dark-skinned people "in their places. . . . I mean I like them, but not around me. Their place is with the rest of the dark-skinned folks." Another woman says much the same: "I have no ill-feeling for the 'less fortunate,' but I don't care to entertain them outside of closed doors. I really feel embarrassed when people see me with black persons. I do have a friend who is quite dark. I love her and really forget that she is black until we start outdoors. I never go very far with her, though." Of such people, a dark-brown-skinned professional man observed: "Somewhere in their early childhood these light-skinned people who think they are better than the dark Negroes are taught that the nearer they are to white the better they are. They have a superiority complex. This attitude, just like the attitude of white people toward Negroes, is the result of the propaganda."

There are very few "fair" Negroes who will speak so bluntly as the two women quoted above. But there are clear indications that light people (especially women) have a tendency to form social cliques based upon skin-color. There are persistent rumors that certain formally organized voluntary associations, including one or two churches, are "blue-vein" — that is, will not accept any members whose skin is not light enough for the veins to show through. Though there is no evidence to indicate that any "blue-vein societies," as such, exist in Bronzeville, there are a few clubs like the one described by the organization's secretary:

Don't quote me in telling this. Of course it is an unwritten law in our club that all of the members range from light-brown to yellow. I think it's positively silly, because there are so many fine people who are darker.

The member of another club insists that such homogeneity is accidental:

> The club is over sixteen years old. The color pattern, I guess, would be light-brown to fair. I am the darkest member in the club. I have never paid any attention to that in any of the groups that I have been affiliated with. The question of a person's color or how much money he had or did not have has never arisen in any discussion that I can recall.

Being "Partial to Color"

When negroes show preferences or draw invidious distinctions on the basis of skin-color, Bronzeville calls them "partial to color." And "partial to color" always means "partial to *less* color" — to light color. The outstanding example of partiality to color is seen in men's choices of female associates. It is commonly charged that successful Negro men of all colors tend to select very light-brown and fair women. One cynical young man summed up the situation by declaring that "no man, irrespective of how dark or light he is, wants a dark woman." A prominent professional man, discussing two of his fraternity brothers, began with the usual "I don't want you to put this down," and then proceeded to name two men "who have gotten themselves white-looking women." One has "two of them — little white dolls." He also called attention to "a big black bandmaster who has got himself a little white-looking doll." A lawyer (himself married to a light-brown-skinned woman) expressed his disapproval of marrying "fair" women:

> I heard a University of Chicago girl say that an educated dark girl has a hard time trying to find herself a husband. Why did she say that? Because just like Dr. ——, our educated men will go and marry some pretty little light, senseless, and dumb chick. Well, I like brown-skinned girls. I started off in high school with one, and I married one. But when most of our educated men get well off, instead of finding themselves a woman that matches them they pick one of those little white chicks. [I.e., very light Negro girls.]

While the charge is made that successful Negro men put a premium on women that "look like white," it would be more accurate to say that they seem to put a premium on marrying a woman who is not black or very dark-brown.[1] Such mate-images are revealed when men are having "bull sessions" about women. Thus one young man tells his fellows:

> "I never go out with dark women because they just don't interest me. I prefer a light person for a sweetheart or a wife. They are more affectionate, lovable, and understanding. They are usually more attractive; they're prettier; they have good hair. They're more intelligent. I don't look for coal mines; I look for gold mines.

These attitudes toward "marrying light" are often implanted at an early age. One mother told an interviewer frankly: "I'm not prejudiced, but I don't want my children to marry dark people, because I feel they're hard to understand and I want my children to be happy. Of course, if they did marry someone dark-complexioned, I couldn't do anything about it. But I hope they don't."

Despite talk of not preferring a dark woman, hundreds of men do marry women darker than themselves. (There are not enough light-browns to go around.) But it is a rare man who will say, as did one young college fellow: "I would marry a dark girl if I loved her and she loved me. The same about a white girl if she loved me and I loved her. I am not prejudiced against race or color. It's the individual I'm interested in." (It isn't fashionable to say things like this except to interviewers.)

If male partiality to color constitutes a *social* handicap for the very dark woman, it may also be an *economic* handicap in seeking certain types of employment. Undoubtedly it is harder for a very dark woman to get a position as a stenographer or physician's attendant than it is for others. There is also some evidence to indicate that Negro restaurants and stores draw the color-line in hiring girls. The owner of one of the best-known restaurants in Bronzeville frankly stated that he was partial to color:

I have a policy of hiring only real light girls with good hair. I do this because they make a good appearance. The people of the sporting world who trade here will favor a light girl. A dark girl has no drawing power. The men who play in orchestras come here, and if I was to hire a dark girl she would be forced to stand around and do nothing while the other girls would be busy. I know this. I've even tried hiring brown-skinned girls, and they didn't make enough money to pay their carfare. Every girl who works as a waitress has got to depend to a certain degree on tips. The dark girls don't get 'em.

Another man, himself brown-skinned, said categorically, "Even the very blackest man would come into my restaurant oftener if light girls were employed." Probably any entrepreneur who is trying to be particularly "classy" feels that a bevy of light girls is desirable.[2]

Since very light women are a decided minority in Bronzeville, they are not always available for proprietors or professional men who would like to utilize their services. With a constantly growing pool of girls and young women with high school training, color-distinctions become less important. The proprietor of one employment agency reported in 1938: "The Negro employer used to ask for very light-skinned or very light-brown-skinned Negro girls, but since the Depression he is getting some sense — now he is asking for 'a well-qualified young woman.' This is better both for the young people and for us as an employment agency."

Many Negroes feel that white people, by favoring lighter Negroes, make it hard for dark-skinned Negroes to secure personal-service jobs as well as other types of employment. Even men make this complaint. One light-brown-skinned boy who had no grievance of his own said: "When it comes to finding a job with either whites or Negroes, they prefer light people. That is especially true of white people in the North. In the South it is exactly turned around: down there the blacker they are the better the white people like them."

There is some evidence, based on a study of newspaper advertisements and interviews, to substantiate the claim that upper-class and upper-middle-class white families and establishments in Midwest Metropolis do favor lighter-skinned servants,³ despite the observation of one Bronzeville man that:

White women don't like to have too light-colored girls working for them, or too pretty ones. It introduces an element of competition that they don't like. A light girl might look in the mirror and say, 'Well, I'm about as light as you are and maybe a lot prettier.' She'll feel just as good as her mistress. Dark women make better servants.

Escape from Shame

Two groups within the Negro community are sometimes made to feel "ashamed of their color" — the very dark and the very light. We mentioned above some common colloquial phrases derogating blackness, and cited examples of partiality to color on the part of Negroes and of whites. At the other extreme of the color-scale, the few Negroes light enough to pass for white are liable to obscene taunts about the way they acquired their white blood, or can be ridiculed as "rhinies" if they have reddish hair. It is this kind of ridicule that was referred to by a social worker in charge of placing children in foster homes when she reported: "We have the most difficulty in adjusting children at the two extremes. Brown-skinned children seldom seem to have conflicts over color."⁴ Yet, light-skinned Negroes often learn to adjust either by "passing" or by forming élite cliques. They can get a certain amount of satisfaction from the suspicion that the darker people who criticize them are envious; also they can retaliate by imputing all sorts of undesirable characteristics to darker folk. Thus, one light-skinned woman described a newly organized club:

We always had a lot of trouble with the darker women in clubs. We found them disagreeable — you had to be careful of every move you made. So we organized a club that we could enjoy. We went places and enjoyed a lot of opportunities we wouldn't have had if we had had a darker group with us.' I found that darker people don't know how to mix amiable. I don't care how cultured and educated they are, they feel they're being slighted by the lighter people.

Consciousness of having an undesirable skin-color comes very early. Hundreds of dark-skinned people in Bronzeville report experiences like that of a girl who said:

"My oldest sister, Lucy, was always calling me names and telling me that the buzzards laid me and the sun hatched me. I hate to say this, but she made me hate her." A young man reports his reaction to the discovery that his mother was "partial to color":

I knew that my light-skinned brother had always got the preference, but I accepted it because he was older. Whenever somebody went on a visit or to the store, he always went. Then one day — I must have been seven years old — I was left at home by myself. I was so lonesome that I went over next door to play. When my mother came home she was furious. She told me I was disgracing myself by playing with black children, that I was dark enough and should be satisfied. It was then that I became conscious of the reason I was never permitted to go places and do things like my brother.

Sometimes play groups drive the point home vigorously:

I was about ten or eleven years old when I began to learn what the different colors of Negroes meant. We were playing house. Some of us were very fair children; some were light-brown; and some were very dark. We were choosing up for playing house. We made the very fair person the father, and so on down the line until we came to the darkest children. We tried to make them the servants, but they refused. We couldn't get enough co-operation to play house that day.

One of the most baffling things to a dark person is his inability to tell when he is being discriminated against because of his skin-color. He is likely to be oversensitive and suspicious — to "smell a rat" that isn't there. One young man who has never finished high school owing to lack of money was sure that "light fellows get all the breaks." He said: "I've often wished to be real light. Those people always get the better breaks." (In this case other traits than color may have contributed to the boy's lack of success.)

Most dark Negroes, however, do not sit around wishing they were light. They are much more likely to develop a kind of belligerent and aggressive affirmation of their worth.[6] Some fortunate children have parents who encourage them to overcome their color handicap by striving for superior achievements. One physician who reports that he had been "conscious of color" all his life told how his family handled the color problem:

When I was a little boy — I guess about six years old — my uncle, who is very light, said to me, 'Boy, I believe you are getting blacker and blacker every day you live.' I was the darkest child in my family. My mother was brown-skinned and my father was very fair. My brothers and sisters used to call me 'tar baby.' That would hurt me, but my mother would say, 'You shouldn't mind — you have more brains than they have.' Sure enough, none of them went to school to make anything out of themselves. But it's just too bad to think that one must do extra work to be recognized just because he's a certain color.

Some parents not only spur the darker child on, but may also humor or spoil him. One woman stated: "I am about the darkest girl in my family. I was always sensitive about my color. Mother and my youngest sister are light-brown. My brother is medium-brown. Kids used to tease me about my color, and I'd come home crying. Mother would feel sorry for me and humor me." As Warner, Junker, and Adams have pointed out, the way parents handle this color question in the very young child may determine the set of his or her personality.

Bronze Americans

A light-brown-skinned mother surprised one of the interviewers with the frank statement of a wish:

I have five children, you know — all grown now — four girls and one boy. Three of the girls have decent light-brown skins, but the boy and the other girl are dark-brown-skinned. The Lord in Heaven knows that I love them all dearly, but He also knows that I wish the two dark ones were lighter.

Such a feeling is common among parents. They do not wish for "fair" children, but for "light-browns" or "smooth-browns." Men, too, often idealize the light-brown girl. A very dark-brown-skinned young man was being interviewed. At one point in the conversation he said earnestly: "To be frank with you, I am partial to light-brown-skinned girls. I don't mean yellow women. I think nothing is prettier than a good-looking brown-skinned woman." Another young man of like complexion described the kind of woman he wanted to marry: "I don't want her to be either yellow or too dark. If she is yellow, the first time she called me 'black' that would be the end. I don't want her too dark — just dark enough so she can't call me black."

Such comments are heard at all social levels in Bronzeville. There is a veritable cult of the brown-skinned woman[7] and a pronounced tendency to idealize "brownness" in contradistinction to "blackness." Negro journalists and publicists have popularized expressions such as "sepia artists," "The Tan Yanks," "Brown Bomber." The very name Bronzeville is, as we have mentioned, one of these euphemisms. Nowhere is the cult of the brown-skinned more vividly revealed than in newspaper advertisements for cosmetics and hair preparations. Today, the brown-skinned girl with "good hair" is the type.[8] A decade ago such ads featured the "white" type of Negro.

Race Leaders of all colors may orate about "the black hands that have built this country and fought for it." But in their *personal* choices of the "ideal female type" and also in many other contexts, Negroes reveal their preference for an in-between color that is neither black nor very light. The evidence from interviewer-observers is voluminous, but only a small number of illustrative examples can be presented here.[9]

On the level of nonverbal behavior: when a Negro artist decorates a church with colored angels and disciples, he paints *brown* ones. When a Negro storekeeper displays colored dolls, they are usually *brown* dolls. The most popular colored female movie stars are *brown*. Beauty contests and fashion shows are usually displays of *brown* beauty.

On the verbal level, comments on desirable boy-friends and girl-friends and children stress the brown-skinned type. One brown-skinned girl claimed to have been in love with a very light Negro man. She broke off the affair to marry a brown-skinned boy though he was lower in socio-economic status. Her reason? "I would rather not have the embarrassment of having to explain to folks that our children were *mine* — that I was not their nursemaid." Another brown-skinned girl states that though she doesn't want an "ashy black" or a "shiny black" husband, she would take such a man if he were a superior person. "But I'd have to be absolutely sure he was superior. My ideal type is a brown-skin, so that I could have pretty brown-skinned children. Also I'd like him to have good hair." Another said that she wouldn't have a black-skinned man, no matter what his qualifications: "To be frank with you, personally I don't even like black coats. And a black man? Honey, I just can't use one!"

That brown-skinned people should express such sentiments is natural. But the darker folks, too, seem to idealize brown skin-color. One very dark woman reveals this attitude when she related an unhappy love experience:

I'm off of love. Some day I hope to get married, but it will be for security. You see, I don't feel there is security in love because love has its limitations. I was very close to, and loved, a boy once, but he decided that because I was dark and he was dark it would be unfair to our children for us to get married and propagate another dark generation. So he went and married a very fair girl and they have a beautiful light-brown child. In the beginning, when he intimated the difficulties of our getting married and having children, I didn't take it too seriously. But he showed me!

Another woman who had a bitter love experience (her husband had divorced her for a light woman) rationalized the difficulty as follows:

I feel it's my fault in a way. He always wanted children, and I am so black and ugly I just didn't want any children to look like myself. So I wouldn't have any. He is so proud now that he is going to have a child of his own. I am really proud for him. He is a good man and really deserves what he wants. He kissed me good-bye twice. We both cried. Now he is gone.

Girls sometimes consider these questions before getting married. A high school girl described her dream-children:

> I would have the boy very fair. That would be more of an advantage to him in his business or profession. I would have the girl a beautiful brown-skin, very attractive, with a million-dollar personality. It isn't essential for a girl to be fair to get along, but is essential that she have a good personality.

Another girl declares: "Well, if I had children of my own I'd want a brown-skin husband. The children would be brown, and that's the way I'd like them."

The Lessening Importance of Color

Though color is an important measure of the man in Bronzeville, it is by no means the most important one. A very dark woman may find her skin-color a handicap in getting the man she wants, but it is no bar to her being accepted by the community as a brilliant, useful, and admirable woman. A Negro man does not find his opportunity to get an education or to make money limited by his black skin. Bronzeville people sense what most sociologists agree on — that, as one doctor said: "Color-distinctions among Negroes are gradually disappearing. Some older people have told me of the time when color was the thing." He added: "I feel that ability counts more now." Another man observes that "with the older group color played an important part. With the younger generation it is different. I don't think color is as important as it used to be."

Many factors have contributed to the lessening importance of skin-color as the measure of the man within Bronzeville: the extension of education, the increase of "race pride," the accumulation of money by dark people. An additional factor of extreme importance should be mentioned — the tendency of successful dark men to marry light. Most of the children will be darker than the mother and lighter than the father. Any tendency toward the growth of a light-skinned caste is continually being defeated by the rise of the darker people into the higher-status brackets. Very dark Negroes can't do much about changing their skin-color, but they can get a favored occupation, secure a higher education, or accumulate wealth. And when they do so they win prestige and respect.[10]

Job Versus "Position"

Emphasis upon skin-color differences within the Negro group was at one time associated with occupational differentiation. During slavery, the lighter-skinned Negroes were very often given preferred spots at "The Big House" or were favored with other posts away from the fields. With the passing of slavery, the free Negroes in both southern and northern cities became the nucleus for the formation of an upper class. Predominantly a mulatto group, they were at the pinnacle of Negro society — often the personal servants of wealthy and influential white people. They had a head start over the rest, and from their ranks emerged doctors, preachers, lawyers, and publicists. By the time of the First World War, however, the Negro servants to the wealthy were rapidly losing their privileged position within the Negro communities, and the professional and business men were consolidating their position at the top of the social pyramid. The Great Migration brought a mass base to the northern cities to support this top stratum. Today in Bronzeville, if we examine the occupational structure in terms of a social prestige scale, we find a small group of people holding down what the people call "positions" — professionals, proprietors, managers and officials, clerical and kindred workers — and a large mass of people who have "jobs." (Figure 1.)

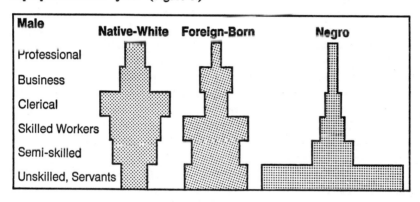

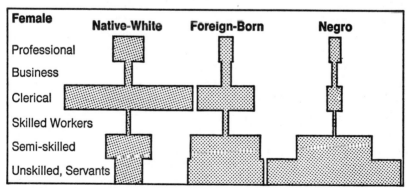

From tables in Scott, "Occupational Changes Among Negroes in Chicago: 1890–1930." The ranking of occupations is that used in Alba M. Edwards, *A Social-Economic Grouping of the Gainful Workers in the United States*, U.S. Dept. of Commerce, Bureau of the Census, 1938.

Figure 1: Comparison of the Negro and White Occupational Structure: 1930

The Professions

There are over 2,000 Negroes in Midwest Metropolis practicing medicine, law, or dentistry, teaching school, or functioning as social workers. The more successful of them have incomes ranging from $5,000 to $10,000 a year. The less successful, though their salaries are smaller, still have high status by virtue of their "position," since they exercise control over the complicated processes of the human mind and body. Classified as professionals, too, are some editors, chemists, designers, architects, engineers, and librarians. These are less often in the public eye than the members of the learned professions and are often unknown to the masses. Occasionally, however, one of them becomes highly publicized as the "first" or the "only" Negro to hold such a position and thus becomes established as a Race Hero.

Businessmen and Public Officials

Bronzeville also accords very high status to successful businessmen. This is both a reflection of general American standards and a function of the weak economic position of Negroes. Virtually excluded from the general field of commerce and industry except as laborers, and looking out as they do upon a world where the industrial magnates are men of power and prestige, Negroes feel that "The Race has a body without a head," that it is truncated and incomplete. Bronzeville admires anybody who opens up a business and employs Negro white-collar workers.

Since Negroes are conspicuously absent from the decisive sectors of the city's commercial life, the first Negro who gets a place on the Stock Exchange or in the grain pit will be a *real* "hero." The absence of Negroes from the key positions in commerce has some far-reaching repercussions. The Race Leaders who are recognized by whites tend to be politicians, social workers, and professional men rather than businessmen. There are no Negroes of great wealth to sit upon the philanthropic boards and to function on the Community Fund. This means that when an influential Negro does sit with his white "peers" he is in a very insecure position because he cannot match them in wealth or influence.

Except for a small number of political appointees and elected officials, there are fewer than a dozen Negroes in key positions of public administration or in managerial posts in industry and commerce. It is understandable, therefore, why the appointment of a department store manager in the Black Belt was a community event of great importance. It is clear, too, why the Negro community jealously guards its political power. It can put a representative on the Illinois State Commerce Commission, though no Negro could hope to be president of a corporation under that body's jurisdiction.

Large numbers of Negroes in Bronzeville take the civil service examinations whenever they are posted. Sometimes a Negro receives an appointment which makes him a "first" or an "only." Sometimes, too, the Negro passes, but does not get the job for which he qualifies. Such people, too, become Race Heroes and almost Race Martyrs — they beat the white people at their own game but didn't get the job.

Membership in the learned professions, or an important supervisory or technical position in government or industry, places a man or woman at the "top" in Bronzeville.

Clerical and Kindred Workers:

White clerical and kindred workers are commonplace in Chicago. Thousands of such people are unnoticed, taken for granted. But in Bronzeville, stenographers, bookkeepers, clerks, and typists have a fairly high status. This seemingly exaggerated appraisal of white-collar work flows directly from the fact discussed in Chapter 9, that Negroes have traditionally been shut out from these fields. This exclusion has given rise to a tremendous demand for Negro businesses that can employ more white-collar Negroes and for jobs in Black Belt stores operated by white people.

The significance of the white-collar position is illustrated by what happened when the Postal Telegraph Company after years of pressure decided to employ a colored office manager. The first girl selected was from one of Bronzeville's most prominent professional families. The event was highly publicized. The girl became a symbol of the Negro's successful struggle against discrimination.

Negro leaders complain continually of the forces that bar Negro women from the commercial life of the city and often cite this type of discrimination as a factor contributing to prostitution and rackets. During the Depression, policy employed more Negro white-collar help than all the other businesses in the Black Belt combined. The Second World War relieved this situation temporarily, but it is probable that the prestige of white-collar jobs will become even higher if colored employees are dropped during the reconversion period.

Some 16,000 Negroes have carved out a niche in the city's life by securing jobs in the postal service. In the post office one will find not only colored high school graduates, but also men with advanced college degrees seeking economic security and students studying medicine and law. In 1939, at least a half-dozen Negro postal employees were writing books! The "postal worker" is a social type in Bronzeville ranking lower socially than professionals and businessmen, but of definitely high status.[11]

During the Depression years an increasingly large number of Negroes were absorbed into the Federal and State Civil Service. It is an ironic commentary that many of these received their first contact with white-collar work on various WPA projects. One such project, at the peak of WPA employment, had over 200 colored workers receiving training on various types of office machines and in clerical procedures. So long as Negroes are denied general white-collar employment, even comparatively minor clerical positions will seem very important in Bronzeville's scheme of things.

Skilled Labor

Within the Negro community there is a sharp social break, as there is among whites, between the white-collar ("clean") workers and manual laborers. Often a single family will incorporate both manual and white-collar workers, but the latter are thought of as those who have "progressed" or who are advancing the family status. Though this is particularly true of attitudes toward women workers, it is also true of male occupations. While there are still ethnic groups that perpetuate a tradition of pride in craftsmanship, the development of mass production has cut the ground from under the prestige associated with skilled labor. In the pre-Migration days white craftsmen drew the color-line against Negroes primarily because of tradition and pride; today, with craft work on the decline, they do so primarily out of fear of Negro competition. The new skilled workers — factory employees — try to draw the line just as tightly, but with less success, owing to the operation of seniority provisions in plant regulations and union contracts.

Because Negroes have been denied an opportunity to compete freely for skilled jobs, such occupations become invested with some prestige value. Negro carpenters, bricklayers, or machinists are considered an "asset to the race." Civic leaders urge young Negroes to turn their attention from white-collar work on one hand and domestic and personal service on the other so that the gap in the Negro's occupational structure may be filled in. They have little success, however, for much of the emphasis upon skilled trades is lip service. Like their white counterparts, Negro leaders praise the "worker" but prefer white-collar work for themselves and their children.

The Alba Edwards prestige scale of occupations lists policemen and firemen as skilled workers. Bronzeville places them in a different category, rating them almost on a level with teachers and social workers. They are "officials" — symbols of authority. Among the unsophisticated they cut quite a figure. They are an ever-present evidence of the fact that Negroes in the North are "free." The traffic policeman on Bronzeville's main boulevard dresses impeccably and directs the flow of automobiles with the grace of an orchestra leader. He knows he is on display. A lifted hand — and hundreds of white men must stop at his command. A wave — and they may proceed. No policeman would get an invitation to a professional men's party, perhaps, but he has high status of a sort.

The Second World War offered an opportunity for thousands of Negroes to become skilled laborers in factories and changed the basis of popularity of this type of work from that of "race pride" to that of the "good, well-paid job." But if Negroes are displaced in great numbers in the reconversion process, skilled work will again become high-prestige work — because Negroes are shut out from it.

Semi-skilled Workers

It was during the First World War that Negroes broke the Job Ceiling at the semi-skilled level. In the succeeding years, they have come to see nothing unusual in a Negro being an operative in the steel mills, the stockyards, laundries, and numerous other industries. There is still some tendency to look down on women who work in factories, but as constantly growing numbers of Negro women have become emancipated from the more personal ties of domestic service, a shift in the evaluation of Negro female factory workers has taken place. This re-evaluation was speeded up by the Second World War. Semi-skilled jobs for both men and women are today considered nothing out of the ordinary.

Unskilled Workers vs. Servants

Although rated above servants in the Alba Edwards scale, it is probable that unskilled factory and building laborers have the lowest status in Bronzeville. Servant occupations may involve a certain amount of servility, but they are relatively clean and light compared with work in foundries and stockyards, or the digging of ditches. To call a man in Bronzeville "a ditch digger" is the height of insult. The relatively high economic status of Pullman porters and Red Caps has elevated these servant occupations above the level of unskilled labor, but domestic service and portering are very close to the bottom of the scale.

In assessing the relative status of unskilled labor and service, the age-differential is important. Older Negroes are oriented toward "service," the younger Negroes away from it. As the educational level of the Negroes rises they become more and more dissatisfied with personal service. At the same time, however, they also detest "common labor." For thousands of Negro men, however, an unskilled factory job is prized, and increasing numbers of Negro women prefer the industrial plant to the "white folks' house."

"The Relief"

During the Depression years, with about half the Negro families dependent on relief or emergency work, the whole occupational status scale was askew. In Bronzeville it was no disgrace to be on WPA, even for people on the white-collar level. The WPA set-up was made parallel with the job hierarchy in private industry: there were white-collar projects and labor projects, and the former had a wage-spread of from $65 at the bottom to nearly $100 at the top.[12] A large number of Negroes were thus able to maintain their accustomed standard of living despite the fact that they were on WPA; some were even able to improve it. In fact, for many young people in Bronzeville the WPA offered the only opportunity to learn how to operate business machines or to use white-collar training acquired in high school. By 1940, government emergency projects had disappeared, but memories of "the Relief" did not carry the implications of shame which large sections of the white population attached to such an "occupational" status.

Money to Spend

A job is an index to status. It is also, of course, a means of earning money. There is no one-to-one relationship between the prestige of a job and its money value, although there is a general relationship. In Bronzeville, however, job status and earning power are often far out of line, as they sometimes are within white society. A stenographer earns much less than a foundry worker, but enjoys a higher social status. A prize-fighter makes considerably more than a doctor, but does not have so much prestige. Pullman porters and mail carriers receive a larger and steadier income than some dentists and physicians, but are not ranked so high socially. In the long run, however, what a man has to spend becomes almost decisive as his measure.

A study of family income in Chicago, conducted in 1935–36 by the United States Department of Labor, provides the best available information on Bronzeville's purchasing power. The findings of this study indicate that, taken in the aggregate, Negroes were close to the poverty line. (See Table 1.)

Table 1: Percentage Distribution of Family Income in Chicago, 1935–36 *

Income Class (Dollars)	All Families	Native-born White	Foreign-born White	Negro
Under 500	13.7	12.0	13.1	30.9
500–999	18.4	14.7	19.6	37.0
1,000–1,999	39.8	39.7	42.0	25.9
2,000–2,999	18.2	21.1	16.9	4.3
3,000–4,999	8.0	9.7	7.3	1.1
Over 5.000	1.9	2.8	1.1	0.8
Total	100.0	100.0	100.0	100.0

* Adapted from *Family Income in Chicago, 1935–36,* United States Department of Labor, Bureau of Labor Statistics, Bulletin No. 642, Vol. I, Washington, D.C., 1939, Table 3, p. 8.

Almost 70 per cent of the Negro families in Chicago in 1935–36 had less than $1,000 a year ($83 a month) to spend. Their situation was just the reverse of the white population's — only a little over 30 per cent of the white families received incomes of less than $1,000 a year.

More than 30 per cent of the Negro families, as compared with about 13 per cent of the white, had annual incomes of less than $500.

Almost one-half of the Negro families — as compared with somewhat more than one-tenth of the white families — were on relief.
Out of every 100 colored families only five had more than $2,000 a year to spend; out of every 100 white families, more than 30 had over $2,000 a year to spend.

Of course, the relatively much larger proportion of Negro families on relief accounts to a considerable extent for the lower incomes. But in almost *half* the families in which at least one member had a job, the earnings were still less than $2,000 a year.[13]

At the very top of Bronzeville's economic pyramid is one family reputed to have inherited a fortune in Oklahoma oil property. A handful of individuals below this family probably have a few hundred thousand dollars in investments, and an annual income that runs into three figures. These are the policy kings, one prominent physician, and two small manufacturers. Far below these men, but far above the ordinary professional group, is a larger group of families with accumulated "wealth" of between $25,000 and $50,000 and a supplementary annual income of over $5,000 a year. Most of these are people who've made money through smart real-estate deals, petty manufacturing enterprises, investment in insurance companies, or earnings as artists, professionals, or athletes. Not over 30 out of Bronzeville's families could, by any objective American standards, be called "wealthy."

Underlying the small group of actually wealthy Negroes are several hundred Negro families which, even during the Depression, received incomes of from $5,000 to $15,000 a year. The men in most of these families are professionals, businessmen, or higher civil servants. *This group, middle-class by general American standards, forms the core of Bronzeville's upper class.* As we shall see in Chapter 19, this group jealously guards its social status, stressing "culture," "refinement," and "education," and erecting social barriers against the "upper shadies" — the very wealthy who have gained their wealth through "rackets." The upper class admits to its circles many whose incomes are far less than theirs, but who possess other valued attributes, such as advanced education or high standards of public decorum.

Education

A physician in Bronzeville, commenting on social status, remarked that "social position doesn't depend on the kind of work you do. There are a lot of my own fraternity brothers who 'went on the road' after they got out of school [i.e., they took jobs as Pullman porters or dining-car waiters]. And there are plenty of fellows with university degrees working in the big hotels." This remark points up a peculiarity of the Negro social-status scale in America: a heavier weighting of education than of occupation. With a very narrow occupational spread, education is used to mark off social divisions *within* the same general occupational level.

Persons who wish to circulate near the "top," whatever they may lack in money or job, must have enough education to avoid grammatical blunders, and to allow them to converse intelligently. Ignorant "breaks" and inability to cite evidence of education — formal or informal — can bar a person permanently from the top. The "learned professions" have been the traditional top occupations in the Negro community, and all of these require some education beyond the high school level. Fine distinctions are drawn among the people of the uppermost stratum — between those who attended top-flight northern universities and those who went to schools of lesser rank; between those who have earned higher degrees and those with "honorary" degrees; Ph.D.'s and Phi Beta Kappa keys are prized possessions for those who have them, and a topic of conversation among those who haven't. Such people think in terms of sending their children to the best schools they can afford. There are some 4,000 adults in Bronzeville with a complete college education, and about 6,000 who have attended college. They make up about two in every 100 individuals.

This small college-trained group rests upon a broad base of people who have never been beyond the eighth grade. (In this Bronzeville does not differ greatly from the white society where 7 out of 10 persons have not been beyond high school.) (Figure 20.) Black Metropolis is essentially a community of sixth-graders. While the adults, most of them from the South, have had very limited educational opportunity, the compulsory school laws of Midwest Metropolis are keeping an ever-increasing number of Bronzeville's young citizens in school until they are 16 years old. Of these, far fewer go on through high school than among whites, but enough do so to maintain two large high schools in the area which turned out over 9,000 students between 1930 and 1940. Over 60 per cent of these were girls.

For the bulk of Bronzeville's population, finishing high school is considered a "great step upward." High school diplomas are often ostentatiously displayed in ramshackle homes, and one interviewer's comment on a girl she met is very significant: "The daughter is very proud of being a high school graduate and feels that it reflects considerable ambition and determination upon her part." It is highly probable that for a large number of girls in Bronzeville, graduation from high school means an increased chance of avoiding domestic service and factory work. It also means a greater likelihood of "marrying up." There is a tendency for girls still in high school, and for women graduated from high school, to form cliques and social clubs that draw lines tightly against "ignorant people." The following comment by a social club secretary is not unusual: "No member is allowed to bring in anyone who does not at least have a high school education."

Education is an important measure of the man (or woman). Because it reflects earning power, and more importantly because it denotes a broadening of intellectual horizons and tastes, it becomes a natural basis for clique groupings. In general, too, securing an education is the most effective short-cut to the top of the Negro social pyramid. Money and occupation are important, but an educated man without a high-status occupation or a very large income, might be admitted to circles that a wealthy policy king or prize-fighter would find it hard to enter.

Standard of Living

Money and a job are important primarily because they offer a base upon which a "standard of living" may be erected.[14] In the final analysis, the way in which people spend their money is the most important measuring rod in American life, particularly among people *within* the same general income range. In Bronzeville, where most incomes are comparatively low, a man's style of living — what he does with his money — becomes a very important index to social status. It is through the expenditure of money that his educational level and ultimate aspirations for himself and his family find expression. Stockyards Worker A may spend his $150 a month on flashy clothes and plenty of liquor, while his wife and children live in squalor. Stockyards Worker B brings his pay check home, his wife and children are well clothed and fed, and a bank account for the children's education is piling up. Bronzeville puts A and B in quite distinct *social* classes. Difference in occupation and income sets the broad lines of status division, but standard of living marks off the social strata within the broad income groups.

This emphasis upon standard of living is apparent in the two statements quoted below from interviews with Bronzeville's professional group:

These people are just common ordinary people having no intellectual inclination whatsoever. I have known them for approximately a year, and I find they spend a large sum of money on food and don't bother so much about clothes. They are not affiliated with any club or social group. I should put them in the middle class so far as income is concerned, but socially in a class slightly lower.

Now take that house next door. Why, for three years people lived over there who were the nastiest folks I have ever seen. The building was condemned and they didn't have to pay any rent so they just lived there like pigs or dogs. The water was cut off. The man who had the garage in back used to let them come over and get water. They brought their pails. You should have seen them go in droves after the water. They reminded me of people in the South. . . . Most of them were working, but they were just a bunch of no-good Negroes.

During the Depression, the masses of the people were operating on a "subsistence budget" which allowed little surplus for savings or "culture."[15] Within the community were thousands of clients on direct relief, each visited periodically by a case-worker who gave him a small check for rent and food; for other commodities he went to a government depot. When he was sick he got free treatment at a public clinic. Others had WPA jobs netting an average of $55 a month. Obviously the standard of living for all such was rather rigidly limited, dependent as it was on a meager income plus what little could be gleaned from policy winnings or earned by occasional domestic service. Many people on relief had been used to something better during the Fat Years, but had been gradually reduced to "subsistence level." They lived in hope that prosperity would return. Thousands of people on relief and WPA were drawn back into productive employment by the industries of the Second World War. With plenty of money in their hands some concentrated on "getting ahead," while others devoted their time and money to a round of immediate gratification. The business of selecting a pattern of expenditure and saving became vital.

All during the Depression, at least a third of Bronzeville's families could be classified as "strainers" and "strivers." These were people who were determined to maintain what America generally regards as "the middle-class way of life." They were interested in a well-furnished home, adequate clothing, a car, and membership in a few organizations of their choice. Their ideal was to be what Bronzeville calls "good livers." Wartime jobs allowed them to realize some of these goals.

Those members of the business and professional group who weathered the Depression, and those with stable incomes from civil service jobs, formed the status bearers of Bronzeville. They were likely to look down somewhat on "strainers" and "strivers" who had accumulated money but didn't know how to spend it with taste. Thus one physician ridiculed the pretensions of the climbers:

A person who has little or no background usually feels that it is necessary to have a high-priced car, loud in color with flashy gadgets that will single him out. Such persons seek houses and apartments in good neighborhoods, but their furnishings are not always in good taste. Yet some of the 'strivers' are smart enough to have an interior decorator when they realize that their knowledge is limited. Now a person who has education, family connections, and background will satisfy himself with a modest and comfortable home and an inexpensive car.

Bronzeville's more conservative well-to-do people — "those who are used to something" — were particularly critical of the rapidly mobile, especially if the latter had got money through "shady" enterprises. One man who had a long criminal record, but who opened a successful business, managed to get into an exclusive apartment house. A resident with "education, background, and family connections" belabored him for his "crudeness":

"All individuals like J —— feel a need for elevating themselves socially, you know. Well, he's gone in for display in dress with his loud suits. He's dressing a bit better now. I think he must have started buying his things from some good clothing store downtown, and he must be taking its suggestions about his clothes because they are more conservative now."

Standard of living is decisive in measuring the status of a family, and standard of living is one aspect of that important characteristic — "front."

The Importance of "Front"

Over and over, people in Bronzeville told interviewers that "it's not what you do that counts, but how you do it." This dictum is applied to varied aspects of behavior — dancing, liquor-drinking, wife-beating, church-going — by those who maintain a rather stable and relatively high standard of living. There is a very sharp division, as we shall see later, between those who value "front" — who stress decorous *public* behavior — and those who don't.

Because of the stress that the "dicties" place upon correct *public* behavior they are often the target of the less sophisticated people who dub them "hypocrites." They are constantly gossiped about by people who do not value front and who exult at finding a chink in the "stuck-ups" armor. But one of the most fundamental divisions in Bronzeville is that between people who stress conventional, middle-class "American" public behavior and those who ignore it. Professional men, postal workers, clerical workers and others with "position" rail constantly at the "loud," "boisterous," "uncouth" behavior of other segments of the society. The "respectable," "educated," and "refined" believe in "front," partly because it is their accustomed way of life and partly in order to impress the white world.
The decisive measure of the man is how he acts in public.

Family, Clique, and Class

All the measures of the man that we have described are either objective traits or types of behavior. More important, however, in placing people are their social relationships. People not only ask, "What kind of person is he?" They also want to know, "What kind of family does he come from?" "Who's in his crowd?" "What kind of organizations does he belong to?" Occupation, income, education, standard of living, and public behavior ultimately find their reflection in social groupings.

Family background is not too important in Bronzeville. Three generations ago nearly all Negroes were slaves, and "getting ahead" by education and the acquisition of wealth have gone on at too fast a pace to allow any tradition of "old families" to mean much. But contemporary family *behavior* is very important in placing people.

Far more important in "placing" people than their family connections are their clique affiliations. The rough rule that "birds of a feather flock together" is used to stratify people in Bronzeville. A man takes on the reputation of his crowd. In a rapidly changing society, clique affiliations become important for social mobility also. People may change their cliques easily, and thus change their social personalities. The cliques become "selectors," and at the top of the society the small high-status cliques become the social arbiters for the community.

It has become fashionable for a broad section of Bronzeville's people to formalize their small cliques as social clubs devoted to card-playing and dancing. Between "Society" at the top and the disorganized masses at the bottom are several thousand of these social clubs. To belong to any of them a person must discipline his behavior, keep up a front, and spend his money for socially approved types of clothing, entertainment, and whatever other appurtenances the social ritual requires. These social clubs are a distinctive feature of Bronzeville's middle class.

In a very limited sense, churches, too, are ranked in a system of social prestige. Congregational and Episcopal churches are considered high-status; Holiness and Spiritualist churches low-status. Most churches, however, include people of all status levels. Neither the question "What church does he belong to?" nor the question "Does he go to church?" is important in placing a man, except at the very top and the very bottom of the social scale.

For persons "on the make" or "on the rise," getting the proper "connections" becomes extremely important. People change their status by acquiring money and education, and then changing their "set." The dynamics of social mobility in Bronzeville can only be understood by observing individuals actually shifting from clique to clique, church to church, and club to club in the struggle to get ahead. The people who are "in" control this upward mobility by setting the standards and holding the line against those who don't make the grade. They also limit the number of persons who are "accepted." At the same time the socially ambitious are able to copy the behavior of the strata above them and to bring *new* cliques, churches and clubs into existence with the desired pattern. After a time such new increments are accepted and the ambitious rise as a group.

The System of Social Classes

Everybody in Bronzeville recognizes the existence of social classes, whether called that or not. People with slight education, small incomes, and few of the social graces are always referring to the more affluent and successful as "dicties," "stuck-ups," "mucki-mucks," "high-toned folks," "tony people." The "strainers" and "strivers" are well-recognized social types, people whose lives are dominated by the drive to get ahead and who show it by conspicuous consumption and a persistent effort to be seen with the right people and in the right places. People at the top of the various pyramids that we have described are apt to characterize people below them as "low-class," "trash," "riff-raff," "shiftless." The highly sensitive professional and business classes, keenly aware of the estimate which the white world puts on Negro behavior, frequently complain that white people do not recognize the class distinctions within the Negro community.

Class-thinking is essentially a way of sizing up individuals in terms of whether they are social equals, fit for acceptance as friends, as intimate associates, and as marriage partners for one's self or one's children.[16] It differs from caste-thinking (which dominates Negro-white relations) in that the people in the upper strata expect some of the people below them to enter the upper levels of society once they have qualified. The individual measures of the man are weighed and combined in such a way as to strike a rough average of position. According to these estimates, and out of the cliques, families, and voluntary associations that arise from them, people in Bronzeville become grouped into several broad social classes.

A Negro social worker is referring to this class system when she says to an interviewer:

I think education gives social status. And of course money talks. After a person gets an education I think he should try to get money so as to be able to live at a certain standard. Of course there are different classes of people. The educated won't go with the ignorant and those with money won't go with poor people.

The Upper Class

At the top of the social pyramid is a scant 5 per cent of the population — an articulate social world of doctors, lawyers, schoolteachers, executives, successful business people, and the frugal and fortunate of other occupational groups who have climbed with difficulty and now cling precariously to a social position consonant with what money, education, and power the city and the castelike controls allow them. They are challenged at every point, however, by the same forces that condemn the vast majority of the people to poverty and restricted opportunities (Figure 2).

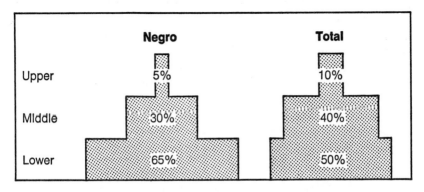

Figure 2: The Negro Class Structure. Comparison of Class Distribution of Negroes in Chicago with Total Population, Using Education, Rental and Occupation as Criteria

Carrying the responsibilities of the major Negro institutions and cooperating with sympathetic and liberal whites who give them financial and moral support, this Negro upper class becomes symbolic of racial potentialities, and, despite the often caustic criticisms leveled at them from the classes below, they go their way supplying goods and services to the Negro community; seeking to maintain and extend opportunities for themselves and their children; snatching some enjoyment from the round of bridge and dancing; seeking cultural development from the arts and sciences; and displaying all of the intraclass conflicts which a highly competitive social and economic system has made characteristic of any group in an insecure position — as this upper class certainly is. Yet they have a measure of satisfactory adjustment which makes their life pattern fruitful if measured by any of the objective standards of "success," except for certain disabilities that *all* Negroes share.

The Lower Class

The Chicago adult world is predominantly a working-class world. Over 65 per cent of the Negro adults earn their bread by manual labor in stockyard and steel mill, in factory and kitchen, where they do the essential digging, sweeping, and serving which make metropolitan life tolerable. During the Depression whether on public projects or in private industry, the bulk of the employed adult negroes, with a minimum of education and still betraying their southern origin, were toilers, working close to the soil, the animals, and the machinery that undergird Chicago's economy. Many of them also were forced to "only stand and wait" at relief stations, on street corners, in poolrooms and taverns, in policy stations and churches, for opportunities that never came and for the work which eluded both them and their white fellow-hopers.

A part of this working class constitutes the backbone of Bronzeville's "middle" *social* class, identified by its emphasis on the symbols of "respectability" and "success." The largest part of this working class is in a "lower" *social* position, however, characterized by less restraint and without a consuming drive for the symbols of higher social prestige. Desertion and illegitimacy, juvenile delinquency, and fighting and roistering are common in lower-class circles.

Not alone by choice, but tossed by the deep economic tides of the modern world, pressed and molded by a usually indifferent and occasionally unkind white world, and hounded by an often unsympathetic Law, the lower social classes in Bronzeville have their being in a world apart from both white people and other Negroes.

The Middle Class

About a third of Bronzeville is in a social position between the "uppers" and the "lowers" — an amorphous, sandwich-like middle class. Trying with difficulty to maintain respectability, they are caught between the class above into which they (or at least their children) wish to rise and the group below into which they do not wish to fall. Some of them are in white-collar pursuits; many of them just do manual labor; a few of them are secure in civil service jobs. Released somewhat from the restraints of poverty, they have not found it necessary to emphasize the extremes of religious or recreational behavior, or to tie their lives to the rhythm of the policy drawings or the very occasional relief or WPA check as has the lower class. Life to them has some stability and order; expectations for their children and for their own future can be predominantly this-worldly; and the individual psyche is given form by the church and associations whose dues they are able to pay with some regularity and from whose functions they are not barred by inadequate clothing or by lack of education, formal or informal.

The "Shadies"

But the class structure of Bronzeville is not a simple tripartite system through which individuals move by attaining the class-behavior pattern which their occupational and educational position permits and their training stimulates. Within each class there is a group, proportionately smallest in the upper class and largest in the lower class, which has secured and maintained its position by earning its income in pursuits not generally recognized by the community as "respectable." The marginal position of the Negro in the economic system and the traditional role of the Negro community as an area for exploitation and risqué recreation by the white community have brought into existence and maintained the whole complex of "protected business" — illegal enterprises winked at and preyed upon by cooperative politicians. This complex is composed of the "policy" business, prostitution, and allied pursuits, and is intimately connected with the legal but none-the-less "shady" liquor interests and cabarets. Thus a considerable proportion of each class is connected at some points with these businesses, and the more mobile individuals are able to rise even to the top where they challenge the position of the upper "respectables" who, as one student has phrased it, "find it politic to accord them some measure of social recognition." These "upper shadies," in turn, are by no means entirely scornful of the opinions of the "upper respectables." They seek to secure prestige in the eyes of this group by assuming many aspects of its behavior pattern, and by attempting to become Race Leaders even to the extent of supporting the organizations of the upper and middle classes, becoming the patrons of the arts, and entering legitimate business.

Bronzeville's upper class is oriented around a *secular* pattern of living, with emphasis on "culture" and "refinement" as well as "racial advancement." A smaller group within the upper class is church-centered, and a very small but powerful group earns its living in "shady" pursuits. As we leave the top of society, however,

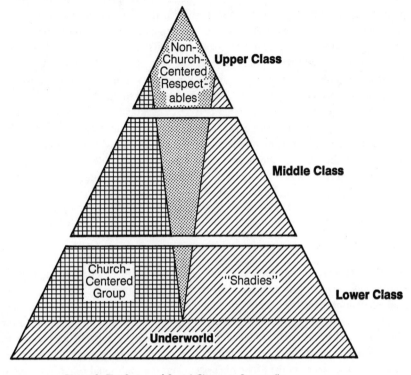

Figure 3: The System of Social Classes in Bronzeville

and move toward the bottom, the proportion of "church minded" people and of "shadies" increases, and the group of "non-church" respectables decreases. (Figure 3).

Notes

[1] Most of these color evaluations are very imprecise. What one man calls a "dark" woman another may call "light." The important differential is between *very* dark-brown women and all others.

[2] Some less exclusive restaurateurs feel that light women are "hard to get along with." One such employer states: "I have tried both real light girls and darker girls. I find that the darker girls give the best service. If you ask them to help keep the place clean they will do so. On the other hand the light girls will complain, and then they'll take their spite out on the customers. Light girls only serve the people that they know will tip. I hire only black girls and give them a decent salary so they don't have to depend upon tips."

[3] As to the charge that southern employers prefer dark servants the truth is rather complex. It does seem that there is something to the following homely explanation, however:

"The southern whites prefer dark Negroes, and the Yankees prefer the light Negroes. The southern white man says that light Negroes think they are white, that they don't use the Uncle Tom language as frequently as black negroes."

⁴ Detailed confirmation of this observation can be found in a study by W. Lloyd Warner, Buford Junker, and Walter Adams, *Color and Human Nature* (American Youth Commission, Washington, D.C., 1940), based on materials collected in Bronzeville and dealing with personality problems arising from color differentials within the Negro community.

⁵ Negroes in Bronzeville are continually charging that white people in exclusive downtown stores and restaurants treat the lighter Negroes with more consideration than the darker. This belief, whether true or false, puts an additional premium upon a light complexion.

⁶ This affirmation sometimes takes the form of repeated references to "black people" in public speeches by darker folk. It also emerges in a tendency to decry the infusion of white strains into the Negro group and to insist that a "pure black" is better than a "half-caste." It has even assumed organized expression in the form of the "Garvey movement" during the Twenties — a mass movement among Negroes with a "Back to Africa" emphasis. Garvey, a West Indian Negro, was very hostile to what he called the "traitorous mulatto leadership" among Negroes. In general, however, this aggressiveness operates on an individual level, with people refusing to accept any estimate of their color which implies that they are inferior. On the lower cultural level derogatory remarks about blackness are a fighting matter. On the upper levels various types of compensatory behavior emerge.

Many dark-skinned Negroes develop the opposite personality traits. Dark people with a "sweet disposition" can be extremely popular in Bronzeville. The myth persists, however, that most dark people are "touchy," easily offended, and oversensitive. The very persistence of such a belief reinforces whatever tendency there is for them to be sensitive about their color.

⁷ Note the popularity of a movie actress like Lena Horne among both white people and Negroes.

⁸ When Negroes disapprove of "blackness" they often mean a whole complex: dark-skin color, pronounced Negroid features, and kinky hair. Sometimes they do not mean color at all! Thus, it is common to hear a person say "She is a pretty black girl." Here the person (usually) means that the girl has Caucasoid features and hair that is not kinky. (Sometimes the term is used for a person with Negroid features *if* these are well proportioned.) In all such evaluations hair-type is crucial. Negroes do not like "kinky" hair, whatever the color of the girl's skin. A whole industry has grown up around the manufacture of "hair-straighteners." "Good hair" means straight or wavy hair. The emerging ideal type is similar to the Brazilian "moreno": brown skin, soft but not Negroid features, and "good" hair.

⁹ A statistical study of color preferences among Negro high school students in several northern cities, including Chicago, reveals that 34.5 per cent of the boys and 35.1 per cent of the girls thought black was "the worst color to be" and 28.8 per cent of the boys and 27.9 per cent of the girls thought yellow was the worst color to be. Over half the boys and girls thought that "black is ugly." About two-thirds of them preferred a "light brown" or "brown" complexion, and nearly 70 per cent thought that "the most handsome person" of the opposite sex was "brown" or "light brown." (Cf. Charles S. Johnson, *Growing Up in the Black Belt*, American Council on Education, 1941. The Cayton-Warner Research questioned over 300 high school students in Chicago at Dr. Johnson's request.) E. Franklin Frazier, in *Negro Youth at the Crossways*, American Council on Education, 1941, reports similar color preferences among young Negroes in the border states.

¹⁰ There is some evidence to indicate that the proportion of light-brown and light Negroes is still higher among the more affluent people in Bronzeville than among the rank and file. This, of course, has nothing to do with the superiority of their "white blood." It is the result of a *social* process which has, in the past, made it easier for the lighter Negroes to get ahead, and of the tendency for the more successful men to marry women lighter than themselves.

¹¹ Interview studies indicate that the post-office worker is associated in the popular mind with affluence and stability. The income is steady. Postal employees must pay their bills or lose their jobs for repeated delinquencies. Carriers wear a uniform and therefore have an official status; clerks are white-collar. Both must be literate.

[12] A few non-relief administrative employees on WPA projects in Bronzeville earned nearly $200 per month.

[13] Richard Sterner summarizes the studies which contain data on Chicago in his *The Negro's Share* (Harper, 1944). In addition to the Department of Labor study, he cites the National Health Survey, published in 1935–36 by the U.S. Public Health Service. This study revealed that while 66.9 per cent of the white families had over $1,000 a year to spend, only 31.8 per cent of the Negro families had even this much. In other words, two out of three Negro families were living on less than $85.00 a month!

[14] The term "standard of living" is used here in its popular sense to apply to the actual level of living. It is customary in some academic circles to reserve this term for the level on which a family would like to live, and to use the term "plane of living" for the actual state of affairs.

[15] In 1935, the standard emergency budget as set up by the WPA for the family of a manual laborer with two children under 16 was $973 per year. At least 40 per cent of Bronzeville's families were existing on or below this level, supported by WPA or relief. Of the families with jobs in private industry or domestic service, only a third received an income greater than the WPA minimum.

[16] See A Methodological Note, pp. 769–82, for a discussion of types of social stratification.

A Wadsworth Series: Explorations in the Black Experience

General Editors

John H. Bracey, Jr.
Northern Illinois University
August Meier
Kent State University
Elliott Rudwick
Kent State University

Robert C. Weaver, "The Villain—Racial Covenants"; Robert C. Weaver, "The Role of the Federal Government"; Herman H. Long and Charles S. Johnson, "The Role of Real Estate Organizations"; Loren Miller, "Supreme Court Covenant Decision—An Analysis"; Herbert Hill, "Demographic Change and Racial Ghettos: The Crisis of American Cities"; Roy Reed, "Resegregation: A Problem in the Urban South"

4   The Process of Ghettoization: Internal Pressures

Arnold Rose and Caroline Rose, "The Significance of Group Identification"; W. E. B. Du Bois, "The Social Evolution of the Black South"; Allan H. Spear, "The Institutional Ghetto"; Chicago Commission on Race Relations, "The Matrix of the Black Community"; E. Franklin Frazier, "The Negro's Vested Interest in Segregation"; George A. Nesbitt, "Break Up the Black Ghetto?"; Lewis G. Watts, Howard E. Freeman, Helen M. Hughes, Robert Morris, and Thomas F. Pettigrew, "Social Attractions of the Ghetto"

5   Future Prospects

Karl E. Taeuber and Alma F. Taeuber, "Is the Negro an Immigrant Group?"; H. Paul Friesema, "Black Control of Central Cities: The Hollow Prize"

Suggestions for Further Reading

Black Matriarchy: Myth or Reality?

Introduction

1   The Frazier Thesis

E. Franklin Frazier, "The Negro Family in America"; E. Franklin Frazier, "The Matriarchate"

2   The Question of African Survivals

Melville J. Herskovits, "On West African Influences"

3   The Frazier Thesis Applied

Charles S. Johnson, "The Family in the Plantation South"; Lee Rainwater, "Crucible of Identity: The Negro Lower-Class Family"; Elliot Liebow, "Fathers without Children"

4   The Moynihan Report

Daniel P. Moynihan, "The Negro Family: The Case for National Action"; Hylan Lewis and Elizabeth Herzog, "The Family: Resources for Change"

5   New Approaches

Herbert H. Hyman and John Shelton Reed, " 'Black Matriarchy' Reconsidered: Evidence from Secondary Analysis of Sample Surveys"; Virginia Heyer Young, "Family and Childhood in a Southern Negro Community"

Suggestions for Further Reading

Black Workers and Organized Labor

Introduction

Sidney H. Kessler, "The Organization of Negroes in the Knights of Labor"; Bernard Mandel, "Samuel Gompers and the Negro Workers, 1886–1914"; Paul B. Worthman, "Black Workers and Labor Unions in Birmingham, Alabama, 1897–1904"; William M. Tuttle, Jr., "Labor Conflict and Racial Violence: The Black Worker in Chicago, 1894–1919"; Sterling D. Spero and Abram L. Harris, "The Negro Longshoreman, 1870–1930"; Sterling D. Spero and Abram L. Harris, "The Negro and the IWW"; Brailsford R. Brazeal, "The Brotherhood of Sleeping Car Porters"; Horace R. Cayton and George S. Mitchell, "Blacks and Organized Labor in the Iron and Steel Industry, 1880–1939"; Herbert R. Northrup, "Blacks in the United Automobile Workers Union"; Sumner M. Rosen, "The CIO Era, 1935–1955"; William Kornhauser, "The Negro Union Official: A Study of Sponsorship and Control"; Ray Marshall, "The Negro and the AFL-CIO"

Suggestions for Further Reading

The Black Sociologists: The First Half Century

Introduction

1 Early Pioneers

W. E. B. Du Bois, "The Study of the Negro Problems"; W. E. B. Du Bois, "The Organized Life of Negroes"; George E. Haynes, "Conditions among Negroes in the Cities"

2 In the Robert E. Park Tradition

Charles S. Johnson, "Black Housing in Chicago"; E. Franklin Frazier, "The Pathology of Race Prejudice"; E. Franklin Frazier, "La Bourgeoisie Noire"; Charles S. Johnson, "The Plantation during the Depression"; Bertram W. Doyle, "The Etiquette of Race Relations—Past, Present, and Future"; E. Franklin Frazier, "The Black Matriarchate"; Charles S. Johnson, "Patterns of Negro Segregation"; E. Franklin Frazier, "The New Negro Middle Class"

3 Black Metropolis: Sociological Masterpiece

St. Clair Drake and Horace Cayton, "The Measure of the Man"

Conflict and Competition: Studies in the Recent Black Protest Movement

Introduction

1 Nonviolent Direct Action

Joseph S. Himes, "The Functions of Racial Conflict"; August Meier, "Negro Protest Movements and Organizations"; Lewis M. Killian and Charles U. Smith, "Negro Protest Leaders in a Southern Community"; Ralph H. Hines and James E. Pierce, "Negro Leadership after the Social Crisis: An Analysis of Leadership Changes in Montgomery, Alabama"; Jack L. Walker, "The Functions of Disunity: Negro Leadership in a Southern City"; Gerald A. McWorter and Robert L. Crain, "Subcommunity Gladiatorial Competition: Civil Rights Leadership as a Competitive Process"; August Meier, "On the Role of Martin Luther King"

2 By Any Means Necessary

Inge Powell Bell, "Status Discrepancy and the Radical Rejection of Nonviolence"; Donald von Eschen, Jerome Kirk, and Maurice Pinard, "The Disintegration of the Negro Non-Violent Movement"; Allen J. Matusow, "From Civil Rights to Black Power: The Case of SNCC, 1960–1966"; Joel D. Aberbach and Jack L. Walker, "The Meanings of Black Power: A Comparison of White and Black Interpretations of a Political Slogan"; David O. Sears and T. M. Tomlinson, "Riot Ideology in Los Angeles: A Study of Negro Attitudes"; Robert Blauner, "Internal Colonialism and Ghetto Revolt"; Charles V. Hamilton, "Conflict, Race, and System-Transformation in the United States"

Suggestions for Further Reading